Vying for the Iron T

Vying for the Iron Throne

Essays on Power, Gender, Death and Performance in HBO's Game of Thrones

Edited by
LINDSEY MANTOAN *and*
SARA BRADY

McFarland & Company, Inc., Publishers
Jefferson, North Carolina

ISBN (print) 978-1-4766-7426-1
ISBN (ebook) 978-1-4766-3473-9

LIBRARY OF CONGRESS CATALOGUING-IN-PUBLICATION DATA

BRITISH LIBRARY CATALOGUING DATA ARE AVAILABLE

Front cover photograph by Atypeek Design (iStock)

Printed in the United States of America

McFarland & Company, Inc., Publishers
Box 611, Jefferson, North Carolina 28640
www.mcfarlandpub.com

To my Stark family: let's never ride south.—L.M.

To all of my peasant male ancestors
who bent the knee to dragon mothers.—S.B.

Acknowledgments

As Season Seven of *Game of Thrones* was wrapping up, we were completing our first edited collection of essays (*Performance in a Militarized Culture* [Routledge, 2017]) and excited to collaborate again. It was like the Light of the Seven shone upon us when we discovered that we were both fans of *Game of Thrones*. We had this outrageous idea to try and create a book, from start to finish, between the last episode of Season Seven and the first episode of Season Eight. Layla Milholen at McFarland has been wonderful to work with and miraculously had the same timeline in mind for the book. The contributors gamely wrote faster than Drogon flies, and the exchange of ideas we experienced through the editing process was fun and thrilling. It was all very irregular, but life is irregular.

In addition to expressing our collective gratitude to Layla and the contributors here, we each have people we'd like to individually acknowledge.

From Lindsey: I would like to thank my father-in-law Dennis Grzenczyk for buying me the first four *A Song of Ice and Fire* books back in 2005. Thanks go to Noa Levanon Klein for her creative support of this project. Sara is my Master of Whispers. My love goes to my little dragons, for lighting the world on fire; my Arya, for wearing many faces; my Melisandre, for always believing; and my Jaime, for holding his oaths.

From Sara: This book would not be possible without Jon Snow's hair; Cersei's sips of wine; Tyrion's wit; Arya's courage; Sansa's patience; Samwell's smile; Ygritte's nerves; Cat's perseverance; all of the Direwolves; Dany's … everything; Brienne's heroism; Jaime's changes; Theon's bad luck; Oberyn's robe; Osha's care; Varys's voice; Sir Jorah's … love; dragon babies; Missandei's wisdom; and the Hound's humanity.

Table of Contents

Death

Performance

Introduction

Raven: On Drinking Wine and Knowing Things

LINDSEY MANTOAN *and* SARA BRADY

Called "the world's most popular show" by *Time* magazine, *Game of Thrones* has changed the landscape of serial narrative during an era hailed as the "golden age of TV" (D'Addario 2017). While an adaptation of George R.R. Martin's epic fantasy *A Song of Ice and Fire*, the television show has taken on a life of its own with original plotlines that advance past those of Martin's published books. The power and influence of *Game of Thrones* can be felt across the television landscape. With the death of protagonist Ned Stark at the end of Season One, *Game of Thrones* launched a killing spree in television: major characters die on popular shows every week now (for an excellent analysis of this trend and a demographic breakdown of who's getting killed off, see VanDerWerff [2016]). While many shows kill off major characters for pure shock value, death on *Game of Thrones* produces seismic shifts in power dynamics and resurrected bodies that continue to fight.

War in early seasons is solidly the purview of men, but by Season Six, women are literally and figuratively changing the battlefield, overthrowing the men who have dominated and controlled them and vying for the Iron Throne. For a show that's been accused of mishandling rape (see Osterndorf [2014] and Robinson [2015]), using it for titillation and voyeurism rather than condemning it, the writers seem to be playing a different game with female characters as the narrative rushes toward its conclusion. Women have gained power, sometimes through embracing masculine displays of authority, sometimes through alliances with figures who resist the common trope of the hypermasculine hero, sometimes through refiguring what power itself might look like.

And yet power always seems wrapped up in violence and death.

Characters in *Game of Thrones* use spectacular displays of death to communicate authority. Performances of violence, rituals associated with death and mourning, and state control over punishment are themes present in almost all epic narratives; *Game of Thrones* asks what happens when death is not the end? These deaths and rebirths are sometimes literal, as with Berric Dondarrion, Jon Snow, and the wights resurrected by the White Walkers, and sometimes symbolic, as with Sansa, Arya, and even Jaime, who all leave behind versions of themselves. Their performances of self evolve as they endure trauma, and for Arya in particular, performance and theatre become tools through which she gains power. Members of noble Houses also perform their alliances to their family through their word choice, attire, and even hair style.

Death, gender, power, performance. These four braid together in *Game of Thrones* to produce complex dynamics that resonate with the fantasy world of Westeros and our contemporary one. This book explores the inextricable links among power, gender, death, and performance, asking questions such as "What kinds of performances of masculinity, femininity, and sexuality do we see in this show, and how do reiterated displays of gender identity collide with power, real and imagined?" "What is the distinction between alive and not, and how does religion intersect with this question?" "How do politics and gender intersect differently north of the Wall, in Dorne, on the Iron Islands, in the rest of Westeros, and across the sea?"

Although power, gender, death, and performance form a complex tapestry of intersecting threads, we have divided this book into sections focusing on each one, with echoes of the others still present. Some essays focus on a specific character or relationship between two characters, some focus on production elements such as costume and music and how they relate to narrative, and others focus on the interplay between medieval and contemporary values in *Game of Thrones*. Interspersed among the essays are brief meditations called "Ravens"—messages on characters and themes from the show. And in the epilogue of this book, Adam Whitehead details the state of the television industry and the ways in which *Game of Thrones* has forever altered it.

This book has been a labor of love for us; it brings together our primary area of research (performance, politics, and war) with one of our favorite shows. Tyrion reminds us that "a mind needs books like a sword needs a whetstone, if it is to keep its edge" (1x2 "Kingsroad"). We put this book out into the world excited that it will become part of the broader conversations about this important work of culture and the social phenomenon it has become. *Valar morghulis*, friends. But first, we'll live.

REFERENCES

D'Addario, Daniel. 2017. "*Game of Thrones*: How They Make the World's Most Popular Show." *Time*, 10 July. Accessed 5 April 2018. http://time.com/game-of-thrones-2017/.
Osterndorff, Chris. 2014. "TV's Rape Problem Is Bigger Than *Game of Thrones*." *Salon*, 22

April. Accessed 4 April 2018. https://www.salon.com/2014/04/22/tvs_rape_problem_ is_bigger_than_game_of_thrones_partner/.

Robinson, Joanna. 2015. "*Game of Thrones* Absolutely Did *Not* Need to Go There with Sansa Stark." *Vanity Fair*, 17 May. Accessed 5 April 2018. https://www.vanityfair.com/ hollywood/2015/05/game-of-thrones-rape-sansa-stark.

VanDerWerff, Todd. 2016. "TV Is Killing Off So Many Characters That Death Is Losing Its Punch." *Vox*, 1 June. Accessed 5 April 2018. https://www.vox.com/2016/6/1/11669730/tv-deaths-character-best.

The Realm Is Dark and Full of Deities

Religion, Class and Power

ANDREW HOWE

Noted for its study of power and moral ambiguity, HBO's *Game of Thrones* also presents a nuanced portrayal of religion and the role it plays in society. The show involves five main religions/gods: the Faith of the Seven, the Lord of Light (R'hollor), the Many Faced God, the Old Gods, and the Drowned God. The first two exhibit real-world influences, and each of the religions serves a unique function in the story. The relationship portrayed between each religious order and their respective class structures reveals symbiotic relationships that eventually become parasitic, empowering either the secular or the religious leadership. For instance, throughout the first four seasons the Light of the Seven is quietly co-opted by the monarchy. The faith itself is corrupt, as evidenced by the High Septon, who in a brothel selects from prostitutes who dress up as the seven faces of God. The arrival of the High Sparrow in Season Five, however, signals a shift in tone for this religion and its relationship to Westeros. Poverty and civil war have resulted in a groundswell of support for an offshoot group, known as the Sparrows, who champion monastic vows of poverty and purity and whose fanaticism translates to violence against those they view as sinners. The inclusion of the rural sept in Season Six, however, indicates that poverty can lead to belief without militancy. Similarly rich veins for potential analysis involve R'hollor, whose priests and priestesses are assigned to "turn" nobility, but also preach to the masses.

A diversity of religions and deities exists in this fictional world. Two of these—the Old Gods and the Drowned God—are unique to Westeros. Two more—R'hollor and the Many Faced God—are largely practiced in Essos, but enjoy some purchase in Westeros. It is interesting to note that the Light of the Seven started out with the Andals in Essos but has become extirpated on that continent, now the dominant religion in Westeros. This distinction is key, indicating how migration and conversion play a role in the rise and fall of religions. Each of these five faiths possess unique qualities: the Old Gods are about nature, the Many Faced God a death cult. R'hollor is about conversion, the Faith of the Seven about appealing to class structures, again underscoring that this religion is the dominant one in Westeros, not having to worry about conversion, only the enforcement of orthodoxy. The manner in which these religions play a role in the story and in the political and social struggles that underpin the overarching narratives indicates how different societies understand the role of religious institutions: in some cases, the desire is to control the population, in others to provide a structure for civilization through contractual laws and social norms. Those in power use religion in order to control, whether they be believers such as Stannis Baratheon and the High Sparrow, or those who do not suffer from an over-abundance of belief, such as Robert Baratheon and Cersei Lannister. In Westeros at least, the faith and the crown at varying times attempt to use one another in order to further their agenda. Stannis and Melisandre are a rare example of a unified vision, although even that relationship proves unable to hold up to the weight of their mission, as Stannis breaks from her when he attacks King's Landing—nearly choking her to death and demanding to know "where is your god now" (2x10 "Valar Morghulis") following his defeat—and she later abandons him at the Battle of Winterfell.

From Melisandre's introduction in "The North Remembers" during Season Two, the political struggle for power in Westeros following Robert's death becomes increasingly intertwined with religion, not only with Stannis's conversion to R'hollor and the Greyjoy return to the "old ways," but also with the rise of the Sparrows several seasons later. At the beginning of the series, a general spirit of ecumenical openness is present, with Thoros of Myrh welcome at King Robert's court, a sept in Winterfell, a godswood in King's Landing, and other evidence of multicultural religious belief. With different factions vying for power due to Joffrey's shaky ascendancy, however, religious factionalism becomes more pronounced and of a distinctly violent species. As Andrew Jones points out, the "trend toward theocratic militarism within Westeros had been weeded out in centuries past and its return does not bode well for the world" (Jones 2012:117). Jones ignores the fact that there was some religious conservatism during the Targaryen dynasty, most notably, as we learn from both Tywin and the High Sparrow when schooling Tommen, with Baelor the Blessed. Generally, however, Jones is correct: religious fanaticism is implicated as a key part of the violence that plays out in the wake of a strong ruler's demise.

The Light of the Seven, which was brought to Essos during the Andal invasion, is a monotheistic religion that celebrates seven different facets of God. It is practiced by the vast majority of Westerosi and is at the core of rituals that have largely lost their religious connotation, including hospitality rites (setting a place for the Stranger) and marriage practices (wedding vows, the cloaking, and the bedding ceremony). There are many parallels between this religion and medieval Catholicism. Much like the crusaders and more specialized orders like the Knights Templar, the Sparrows can be identified by the markings they display, most notably a seven-pointed star in a circle. The concept of a godhead is very familiar, although with seven parts instead of a trinity. Seven is a number coded strongly in medieval Christianity, with the seven virtues and the seven deadly sins. Several of the godheads evoke figures from the very origins of Christianity: the Maid and the Smith are reminiscent of the parents of Jesus of Nazareth. Much as Jesus and, later, the Franciscan monks did, the High Sparrow walks across the land barefoot, ministering to the poor. The Great Sept of Baelor has its counterpart in St. Peter's Cathedral, and septas appear in garb similar to a nun's habit. The structure of the church is also similar, including a top down autocratic hierarchy with a High Septon elevated over all the rest and septas generally subservient due to their gender. The godhead itself is also indicative of gender inequality. The Seven is a toolbox that provides different facets of God coded for peoples from different backgrounds and at different life stages. As Ryan Wittingslow notes, the seven-part deity is really two gendered triads (one male, one female) plus an androgynous figure thrown in for good measure (Wittingslow 2015:115). Although this seems gender equitable, Valerie Frankel argues that medieval gender biases are very evident in the breakdown: whereas all three of the female gods are about life stages, only one of the male faces (the Father) is, the other two involving professions from which women, in this world, are generally excluded (Frankel 2014:163).

In the first few seasons of *Game of Thrones*, despite being the dominant religion of the land, the institutionalized presence of the Light of the Seven is almost nonexistent. Grand Maester Pycelle sits on the High Council, not the High Septon, suggesting that it is science and not religion that holds sway with the rulers of the realm. As Carolyne Larrington points out, most of the septons seem to be "ineffectual, socially conservative, timorous or drunken and criminal" (Larrington 2016:134). Joffrey's High Septon is killed during the riot in King's Landing (2x6 "The Old Gods and the New"), and Tommen's frequents brothels. After seven prostitutes, each dressed as one of the seven faces of God, parade around him, he is addressed by the brothel manager: "You have served us well, my son…. Which of the seven will you worship today?" (5x3 "High Sparrow"). It is into this world of ineffectual leadership and moral decay at the highest levels that the Sparrows flutter. In their merger of faith with militant action, Wittingslow notes that their order is akin to both the Templar and Teutonic Knights (Wittingslow 2015:114). In their extreme vows of poverty and in their travel through rural areas preaching to the poor, they are also reminiscent of the Franciscan Order. There is also an Augustinian core to the High Sparrow and his conversion story. As he tells Margaery, he believed initially that happiness involved immersion in the excesses of the flesh: "Each time I indulged, I felt myself ascending to something better." After putting on a huge feast, however, he awoken from a stupor and left, never looking back (6x4 "Book of the Stranger").

From the moment the Sparrows rise to prominence in King's Landing, they focus on punishing vice, reminiscent of Oliver Cromwell and the Roundheads in their struggle against a monarchy they saw as corrupt. Following Cersei's walk of shame, the High Sparrow indicates to Jaime Lannister that no one, whether a commoner, clergy member, or monarch, is above moral law: "We are weak, vain creatures" (6x2 "Home"). As Susan Vaught notes, the world of *Game of Thrones* is a world of moral grays: "In Westeros, as in the real world, there are few if any saints, or even adults, who do not sin at one level of severity or another" (Vaught 2012:92). The High Sparrow's view is that judgment should be carried out by God's earth-bound agents. As he tells Cersei, after the High Septon is forced to walk naked through the streets for visiting a brothel: "Hypocrisy is a boil. Lancing a boil is never pleasant" ("High Sparrow"). This is where the threat of violence begins to creep into the interactions between clergy and monarchy, and the Lannister program of exerting full autocratic power begins to crumble. As Lancel Lannister notes when talking to Cersei about his own conversion experience, the Sparrows are a two-edged sword: "I'm a different person now. I found peace in the Light of the Seven. You can too. They watch over all of us. Ready to dole out mercy. Or justice. Their world is at hand" (5x1 "The Wars to Come"). When word-fencing with Jaime, who threatens him with violence, the High Sparrow focuses upon the power that comes from a massive populace marshaled in the same direction: "Every one of us is poor, and powerless. Yet together, we can overthrow an empire" ("Home").

Cersei has no one to blame but herself in facilitating the ascendancy of the Sparrows, first of all by being careless in her treatment of the peasants, making them more receptive to a new message, but most importantly in allowing the Faith Militant to reactivate (5x4 "Sons of the Harpy"). She is able to accomplish her immediate goal of undermining the position of her enemies, most notably the Tyrells, but is a victim of blowback in that the High Sparrow is so good at galvanizing the population of King's Landing that in very short order he becomes her equal in power. The mob is a fickle beast, and the same population that, quite literally, tore the initial High Septon to pieces elevates the High Sparrow. The Sparrows put their newfound power to use, going first after vice, then the nobility (the Tyrells), and eventually the monarchy. Their initial rampage through the streets, focused upon alcohol and prostitution, is reminiscent of Joffrey's purge of Robert's illegitimate children (2x1 "The North Remembers"), both ending with violence in Littlefinger's brothel ("Sons of the Harpy"). As Lancel notes to Baelish upon the latter's return to King's Landing: "The city has changed since you were here last. We flooded the gutter with wine, smashed the false idols, and set the godless on the run" (5x6 "Unbowed, Unbent, Unbroken").

The Sparrows are equally as violent in their campaign against the nobility, which is reminiscent of the medieval Investiture Struggle between the Pope and European monarchy. Margaery is beaten and subjected to propaganda in the form of being read to from the Seven-Pointed Star, the holy book of the Light of the Seven (6x1 "The Red Woman"). Loras is essentially starved and tortured into submission, pleading guilty, renouncing his name and fortune, and allowing himself to be marked on the forehead (6x10 "The Winds of Winter"). Cersei's fate is the most surprising, as she goes from wielding a power that not even her late husband held to imprisonment and, later, a humiliating walk of shame (5x10 "Mother's Mercy"). It is interesting to note that, during her punishment, the crowd is initially quiet, her aura as a monarch enough to cloak her. However, once a few moments have passed and they have grown comfortable with her demystification in a loss of grace sanctioned by the faith, they hurl threats, vegetables, and even feces at her. As Larrington points out: "Cersei's imprisonment reveals to her how far the apparatus of terror, formerly the prerogative of the Crown, has now become an instrument of the Faith" (Larrington 2016:112). Until their destruction in "The Winds of Winter," the Sparrows demonstrate the horrible and destabilizing power that can come about from a species of religious fanaticism that appeals to the poor.

Not all depictions of the Light of the Seven in *Game of Thrones* are negative, however. Appearing in only a single episode—"The Broken Man"—Brother Ray not only serves as a guiding light for Sandor Clegane, he also illustrates the positive role that religion can play in society. His story shares several key features with that of the High Sparrow, although the divergence is notable. The latter indulged in wine and women; Brother Ray was a soldier, even going so far as to murder a man in front of his mother. Unlike the High Sparrow, Brother Ray's conversion does not lead to a drive for power and influence, but instead to ministering to a rural flock and building a sept for them to worship in. In talking about his conversion experience, he focuses upon the redemptive nature of action: "Now, I know that I can never bring that lad back. All I can do with the time I've got left is bring a little goodness into the world" (6x7 "The Broken Man"). He follows that up with advice not to rely upon the gods: "You have to answer your prayers yourself." Indeed, Ray seems almost like a deist, telling Sandor:

There's plenty pious sons of bitches who think they know the word of god. I don't. I don't even know their real name. Maybe it's the Seven, or maybe it is the Old Gods. Or maybe it's the Lord of Light. Or maybe they're all the same fucking thing. I don't know. What matters, I believe, is that there's something greater than us ["The Broken Man"].

Brother Ray believes in redemption, in community, and even in divine providence. He does not, however, try and interpret signs or use them as a means of enforcing compliance. His community is more equitable. Sure, there is a clear gendered division of labor, but altogether the rural sept community is one of mutual acceptance and respect. This is religion at its finest, a community-based notion that, unfortunately, in its singular quality in *Game of Thrones* is vulnerable to attack.

The other religion that is critical in *Game of Thrones* involves the Lord of Light. It is interesting to note that the religion itself does not have a name, focused solely upon its deity R'hollor. This god is not embodied in the same way as the Seven, although consistently referred to with male pronouns, as is the Great Other, a counter-deity who serves as a foil to R'hollor. There are plenty of similarities to Christianity, most noticeably in the duality of good/evil incorporated from two Persian belief systems that overlapped, and influenced, early Christian thinkers: Zoroastrianism and Manicheanism. As Larrington notes: "fire is central in Zoroastrianism as an element of ritual purity" (Larrington 2016:179). Melisandre's practice of burning nonbelievers at the stake, as both a punishment for their doubt and as ritual offering to R'hollor, is reminiscent of the English Reformation, when many Protestants suffered a similar fate due to their belief. Daenerys is, in many ways, a Joan of Arc figure in the narrative, although in her case it is a self-immolation that she survives (1x10 "Fire and Blood"). In prognosticating to Tyrion and Varys how Dany will become an agent of punishment—"The dragons will purify non-believers by the thousands, burning their sins and flesh away" (6x5 "The Door")—Kinvara, the high priestess of the Lord of Light, sounds uncomfortably like the High Sparrow. The tendency of those who promote R'hollor to think exclusively in black and white terms resonates with the Manichean elements of Christianity. As Larrington points out, the good/evil divide is "comparable with the beliefs of medieval Cathars and similar heretical sects, who regarded this world as irredeemably fallen and thought that salvation could only come in the next world" (Larrington 2016:177). The Cathars, who drew from Manicheanism, are further resonant with the followers of R'hollor in that women were allowed to be priests. As Wittingslow identifies, the focus upon moral agency in choosing sides is also reminiscent of Zoroastrianism (Wittingslow 2015:126). And as Jaron Schoone argues, the manner in which evil is understood by the proponents of R'hollor underscores the Augustinian notion of natural evil (e.g., long winters are caused by the Great Other), which presages moral evil committed knowingly by humans (Schoone 2012:162–64). As one of the key early Christian thinkers who set up religious identity in medieval Europe, it is no surprise that some of Augustine's ideas would be replicated in this world. Prior to his conversion, Augustine was a Manichean, and the duality present in that religious system is reflected in his Christian writings.

Whereas the Light of the Seven is fascinating for its study of institutionalized power between secular and spiritual leadership, the Lord of Light is interesting for the character studies present in the narrative. In "The North Remembers," which opens Season Two and introduces religion as a key component of the struggle for succession, a complex religious ritual gathers imagery from different parts of western culture, including the mythological (Stannis signaling his chosen status by pulling the sword from the fire, with its Arthurian implications) to Christian antiquity (the burning of the seven effigies symbolic of iconoclasm, also mirroring what the Andals did when they invaded Westeros and chopped down Weirwood trees, carving the seven pointed star on everything) to more contemporary history and the marginalization of those who do not believe. Melisandre has found true believers in not only Stannis but also his wife Selyse, who doesn't bat an eyelash when Melisandre graduates from burning effigies to burning actual people, including her brother Ser Axell Florent (4x2 "The Lion and the Rose"). Selyse's faith tolerates adultery: when Stannis has intercourse with Melisandre to further his ascendency Selyse remarks, "No act done in service to the Lord of Light can be a sin. When she told me, I wept with joy … I thank god every day for bringing Melisandre to us" (3x5 "Kissed by Fire"). Disturbingly, Selyse even approves when her daughter Shireen is burned at the stake (5x9 "Dance of Dragons"), although she does have a last-minute change of heart and hangs herself afterward (5x10 "Mother's Mercy").

Melisandre is one of the most powerful figures in *Game of Thrones*; the most powerful political figure in her religious order, the high priestess Kinvara, is also female. What might seem like a positive feminist model of religion is undermined, however, by Melisandre's use of her sexuality as a weapon, seducing and later controlling Stannis. She deploys her sexuality to keep the would-be king from asking too many questions about her prophecies and dictates. In speaking with Kinvara, Varys even brings up the self-sealing nature of prophetic infallibility: "Isn't that the point of being a fanatic? You're always right. Everything is the lord's will" ("The Door"). Kinvara also demonstrates that those working to promote the Lord of Light focus not only on the nobility (e.g., Thoros sent to Robert's court and Melisandre turning Stannis), but also in connecting with the masses. In "High Sparrow," the fire priestess preaching on the street corner in Volantis gives the exact same spiel as Melisandre does about being a slave, although in this case it is the commoners who are her audience. In Meereen, Kinvara's agents move through the city, spreading pro–Dany propaganda during her absence: "From the fire she was reborn to remake the world. Daenerys is a gift from the Lord of Light to her children. If we are steadfast in our love for the Queen and her faithful advisors, no man will ever lock us in chains again" (6x8 "No One"). The inclusion of "faithful advisors" indicates that, much like the High Sparrow, Kinvara and Melisandre have political agendas of which they are very willing to conflate with a religious message.

Melisandre is more than just manipulative, however. She is also a murderer. As Jesse Scoble argues: "it is not an image of fire but of shadow that represents Melisandre" (Scoble 2012:136). The shadow demon episode is proof positive that she is willing to go to any lengths to help Stannis secure the throne, not only because she has seen this outcome in the flames but that it will also facilitate R'hollor's spread to Westeros. It is ironic that a shadow murders Renly (2x5 "The Ghost of Harrenhal"), as the world of shadow is the terrain of the Great Other. The implication is that, in sacrificing a moral imperative for power, Melisandre is actually serving against purpose, much like the medieval Christian crusaders who raped, pillaged, and murdered in their god's name. The torments she subjects Gendry to, and most notably her murder of Shireen, indicate that Melisandre has lost herself in her attempts to secure the throne for Stannis. Perceiving Davos to be a threat, she even goads him into attacking her by telling him that his son Matthos died nobly: "Death by fire is the purest death" (3x1 "Valar Dohaeris"). She is calculating and willing to destroy the lives of others if such acts further her agenda. Conversely, Thoros of Myrh, the only other religious figure of note in the series who is an adherent of the Lord of Light, is portrayed in a more sympathetic manner. Prior to the start of the series, Thoros's backstory has him sent to the court of King Robert to convert the Westerosi monarch. Instead, he becomes something of a jester, an entertaining drunk known for lighting his sword on fire prior to battle. Speaking to Melisandre about his ability to bring Beric Dondarrion back from the dead, he discusses his conversion:

> I've always been a terrible priest. Drank too much rum. Fucked all the whores in King's Landing. It's a terrible thing to say: by the time I came to Westeros, I didn't believe in our lord. I decided that he, that all the gods were stories we told the children to make them behave…. Until the Mountain drove a lance through this one's heart. I knelt beside his cold body, and I said the old words. Not because I believe in them but … he's my friend, and he was dead. And they were the only words I knew. And for the first time in my life, the lord replied. Beric's eyes opened, and I knew the truth. Our God is the one true God, and all men must serve him ["Kissed by Fire"].

Thoros exemplifies skeptics within the clergy, but also the ability to be born again and have a renewed sense of mission. Altogether, Thoros is more benign than is Melisandre, although far from the notion of an ideal religious figure.

One final component of this religion that bears consideration is the critical role played by prophecy. In *Game of Thrones*, there are a number of prophecies, the majority of which come true (Wittingslow 2015:129), although the characters involved often misinterpret them. Aside from Melisandre, this is true of Mirri Maz Duur ("Fire and Blood"), Quaithe ("The Ghost of Harrenhal"), and Maggie the Frog (5x1 "The Wars to Come"). The series is also filled with dreams and visions that also come true, including those of Bran ("The Ghost of Harrenhal"), Dany ("Valar Morghulis"), and Jojen Reed (3x7 "The Bear and the Maiden Fair"). But how do dreams, visions, and in particular prophecies relate to religion? Melisandre is the only character listed above, aside from perhaps Mirri Maz Duur, for whom her prophecy is intricately related to her religious life. There are two problems with her prophetic vision, however: it is subject to interpretation, and because of this normative moral order is subverted. Time and again, Melisandre is wrong. As she tells Stannis following his defeat at the Battle of the Blackwater: "The Lord of Light only allows me glimpses" ("Valar Morghulis"). As Jones notes:

> One has to imagine that Melisandre is surprised at the mismatch between the victories she's seen in her flames and those she's witnessed in real life. When she does finally let her air of confidence slip, she justifies the failure of the world to match her prophecies by placing the blame not upon her perfect and infallible Lord of Light, but upon herself [2012:115].

The ability of religion to explain away any error becomes damaging when decisions are made that affect the lives of innocents. In one of her prophecies, Melisandre sees a snowy battlefield at Winterfell, with herself walking the battlements and the banners of House Bolton lowered to the ground (5x7 "The Gift"). Mistaking this prophecy as pertaining to Stannis's campaign against Ramsay Bolton, and recognizing that he doesn't have the horses or men to prevail, she burns Shireen at the stake in order to win R'hollor's favor. As it turns out, she is actually seeing the aftermath of the Battle of the Bastards, and burning Shireen at the stake does not have the effect she intended. Even if such an act were to attract R'hollor's favor, Stannis must deal with collateral damage in the desertion of an army that he needs in order to win ("Mother's Mercy"). After Stannis's death, Melisandre immediately claims that Jon is the Prince That Was Promised (6x3 "Oathbreaker"), demonstrating just how quickly a failed prophecy can find a new interpretation. She does at a later time admit to Dany, however, that prophecies are difficult to interpret (7x2 "Stormborn"), demonstrating some measure of growth.

There are other religions in *Game of Thrones*, and when considered in combination with the Faith of the Seven and the Lord of Light, they too demonstrate skepticism in relation to institutional practice. The Drowned God, the worship of whom includes a ritual akin to Christian baptism, is marshaled by the Iron Islanders in support of murder, rape, and pillage. With statues from many other religions in the House of Black and White, the religion of the Many Faced God seems ecumenical, and indeed the backstory involves the mines of Valyria and workers from numerous cultures and religious creeds. As Arya gets pulled into its orbit, however, it becomes clear that this religion is a death cult that promotes the total evacuation of the self so that the individual can become a mindless vessel (Arya is told that she must become "no one"). This cult also preys upon the poor, acquiring faces from those who, in essence, are convinced to commit suicide. And finally, the faceless men have monetized religion through a for-hire murder racket. Religion in *Game of Thrones* does not generally provide answers, and for every Selyse or Lancel there are dozens of characters who are more agnostic in their beliefs. Responding to Matthos's religious fervor, Salladhor Saan states that the one true god "is what's between a woman's legs." A short time later, Davos tells his son that "King Stannis is my god. He raised me up and blessed me with his trust" (2x2 "The Night Lands"). Some are more philosophical, however, in their rejection of the gods. In "Fire and Blood," Jaime raises a question that has bedeviled western theology for over a thousand years: "if the gods are real and they are just, then why is the world so full of injustice?" Jones notes that religions systems in *Game of Thrones* are similar to real world analogues in that all require leaps of faith, with trust placed in institutions that are flawed and focused upon the accumulation of power (Jones 2012:108).

Religious identification is largely determined by background, although Arya demonstrates the possibility of seeking out the new in her fluidity of movement, Stannis indicates the power of conversion from one frame of reference to another, and Samwell Tarly shows that occasionally physical distance from one's origin, and new relationships, can be influential. Despite the moments of division, isolation, and change, there are rare incidents during the series of shared religious identification. For instance, the red comet in "The North Remembers" is a shared experiential sign. True, it is interpreted differently by those in the Red Waste, Craster's Keep, and Dragonstone. Even in a single location, such as Winterfell, a variety of interpretations is evident. Responding to Bran, who has heard that the comet signals that Robb has won a military victory, Osha says the following: "I heard some other fools say it's Lannister red. Means the Lannisters will rule all Seven Kingdoms before long. Heard a stable boy say it's the color of blood to mark the death of your father. The stars don't fall for men. Red comet means one thing, boy. Dragons" ("The North Remembers"). Despite all of these different views, the comet is an example of how religion can, on occasion, serve to bring people together rather than divide them. Sadly, it is an incident so very rare in the portrayal of the religious life of Westeros and Essos.

REFERENCES

Frankel, Valerie. 2014. *Women in Game of Thrones: Power, Conformity, and Resistance*. Jefferson: McFarland.
Jones, Andrew. 2012. "Of Direwolves and Gods." In *Beyond the Wall*, ed. James Lowder, 107–22. Dallas: BenBella Books.
Larrington, Carolyne. 2016. *Winter Is Coming: The Medieval World of Game of Thrones*. London: I.B. Tauris.
Scoble, Jesse. 2012. "A Sword Without a Hilt: The Dangers of Magic in (and to) Westeros." In *Beyond the Wall*, ed. James Lowder, 123–40. Dallas: BenBella Books.
Schoone, Jaron. 2012. "'Why is the world so full of injustice?' Gods and the Problem of Evil." In *Game of Thrones and Philosophy: Logic Cuts Deeper than Swords*, ed. Henry Jacoby, 154–66. Hoboken: John Wiley & Sons.
Vaught, Susan. 2012. "The Brutal Cost of Redemption in Westeros: Or, What Moral Ambiguity?" In *Beyond the Wall*, ed. James Lowder, 89–106. Dallas: BenBella Books.
Wittingslow, Ryan. 2015. "'All men must serve': Religion and Free Will from the Seven to the Faceless Men." In *Mastering the Game of Thrones: Essays on George R.R. Martin's A Song of Ice and Fire*, ed. Jes Battis and Susan Johnston, 113–31. Jefferson: McFarland.

The Crack of Dorne

Mat Hardy

The Footprints of Giants

Sir Isaac Newton acknowledged that he stood upon the shoulders of giants when making his own scientific discoveries. Such debts occur in fantasy literature as well. In remarking upon the similarity to Tolkien's work in Terry Brooks's *The Sword of Shannara*, Frank Herbert observed, "Don't fault Brooks for entering the world of letters through the Tolkien door. Every writer owes a similar debt to those who have come before. Some will admit it. Tolkien's debt was equally obvious" (Herbert 1977).

The work of George R.R. Martin also follows in the path of the epic fantasy that has gone before it, though the multi-faceted plots and the sheer darkness of the story sets it apart from many predecessors. Given the strong story and the dearth of previously successful fantasy television shows, the HBO television adaptation stands out as an even more innovative and satisfying spectacle that has broken new ground in terms of audience numbers and critical appreciation of what has usually been a niche genre. Martin, like Tolkien, will assuredly be one of the giants that future authors will balance upon.

But even giants must rest their feet on something. Sometimes the particular work or mythos on which they rely is obvious and explicit, as with the saga of Percy Jackson and his Olympian heritage. Other times the basis is more generic, such as the continuous use of medieval settings and technologies in fantasy works, where no society, no matter how long-lasting, ever seems to progress beyond castles and chainmail. The works of J.R.R. Tolkien and Robert E. Howard could be seen as seminal in this regard for modern fantasy authors, with a pattern of cultural and geographic sameness becoming so firmly established that subsequent writers (and their fans and publishers) shy away from any reinterpretation (Young 2015). Even the cartography and topographic layouts of multiple fantasy worlds tend to conform to an ortho-doxy that is based upon the orientation of medieval Europe (DiTommaso 2006). Gender roles are also commonly stereotyped in fantasy, with a histor-ical reliance on male protagonists and viewpoints. Race is a further latent trope of fantasy settings; central characters are often white, or at any rate Western in their outlook, even when non-human. Going hand-in-hand with the common Eurocentric historical settings, "fantasy formed habits of White-ness early in the life of the genre-culture, and is, in the early decades of the twenty-first century, struggling to break them" (Young 2015:10).

The consequence of this reliance on white, Western characters is a dis-connection with those fantasy peoples who do not fit into this category. People and races that tend to cling to the edge of fantasy maps are usually "others": at worst mere background extras, at best, supporting actors whose differences are there to provide exoticism and a contrast to the norms of the central cast. In *Game of Thrones*, the turbulent mobs of slaves, the barbarous Dothraki, and the maimed Unsullied all serve as a colorful backdrop for the progression of Daenerys Targaryen's character development (Hardy 2017).

Such "othering" is one plank in the platform that our fantasy giants stand upon. It is likely not a conscious decision but an underlying cultural bias that has become just as entrenched in fantasy as dragons, elves, and longbows. This predisposition is not specific to the fantasy genre either, but stems from our own received wisdom about non–Western lands; a cultural heritage that has been centuries in the making. In basing our stories on what has gone before, we accept the questionable along with the worthy.

The result of this is apparent in *Game of Thrones* and its forerunning book series *A Song of Ice and Fire*. How, this essay asks, has the cultural bag-gage of two centuries shaped even a modern fantasy epic set in an imagined world? The repetition of these norms to a new audience is noteworthy. While previous discussion in this regard has tended to focus on the continent of Essos (Hardy 2015; Nae 2015), I will turn to the southern principality of Dorne as a case study. Existing as an Eastern culture on the western continent, the depiction of the Dornish follows most of the established tropes of fantasy heritage in presenting a non–Western society. A predilection for violence, betrayal, and hypersexuality is part of this typecasting and demonstrates that for all its breathtaking novelty, *Game of Thrones* is still grounded in stereo-types that are comfortable for its vast audience.

So Said Burton

In examining why fantasy realms reflect our own real world (and its biases) the pioneering work of Edward Said remains pertinent. In *Orientalism*

(1978), Said sought to explain how Western cultural hegemony had developed from a position of colonial strength. With an unshakeable assumption of the superiority of Western culture, those in the East had been assigned a set of stereotypes and an imagined interpretation that owed little to reality and more to the need for Europeans to set themselves apart as a more advanced and noble society. "Orientals" tended to be portrayed as somehow "fallen" in their behavior and childlike in their lack of mental faculty. Said offers these words from the British Controller-General of Egypt, Earl Cromer, who later wrote a kind of imperial "how-to" guide for dealing with "subject races":

> The European is a close reasoner ... his trained intelligence works like a piece of mechanism. The mind of the Oriental, on the other hand, like his picturesque streets, is devoid of symmetry. His reasoning is of the most slipshod description.... They are often incapable of drawing the most obvious conclusions from any simple premises of which they may admit the truth [The Earl of Cromer 1917:146, quoted in Said 1978].

Cromer's *magnum opus* then goes on to explain that Orientals are "devoid of energy and initiative" (148), prone to "fulsome flattery," cunning, conspiratorial, irredeemable liars, "lethargic and suspicious" (161) and generally the opposite of all that is good and upright in the Anglo-Saxon race (in Said 1978: 38–39). There was the implication that, with this heritage, the males of the Orient were not as manly as those of Europe.

According to the tenets of Orientalist thought, decency and moderation were also not characteristic of Easterners when it came to sexual behavior. All manner of appetites and depravities were ascribed to "The Turk" or "The Arab," practices to make the principled European shudder: sexual slavery, group sex, same-sex acts, bestiality, and an all-round lasciviousness and open lust. The allegation of pervasive homosexuality was another means of portraying the Easterner as less masculine and more corrupt, with men and boys depicted either as passive playthings or rapacious predators (Colligan 2003). Fuelled by sensational novels, "journalism," and Orientalist artworks that focused on naked white women being sold at slave auctions, a vicarious thrill developed and a suite of sexual fantasy tropes were established: "harems, princesses, princes, slaves, veils, dancing girls and boys.... The Orient was a place where one could look for sexual experience unobtainable in Europe ... readers and writers could have it if they wished without necessarily going to the Orient" (Said 1978:190).[1] Said is pointing out that such stereotypes and fantasies eventually spread beyond dull and pompous memoirs by Foreign Office delegates and entered the mass market. By the 1890s, European popular culture was depicting Arabs and other Easterners in the same derogatory manner as Cromer, along with a "tut-tut" or "nudge-nudge" tone regarding their sexual proclivities. And while it is highly unlikely that modern fantasy writers are channeling the Earl, they are much more likely to be propped on the shoulders of Sir Richard Francis Burton.

Burton's explorations of India, Africa, and the Middle East between the 1840s and 1870s are not nearly as significant as the literary impact he had on the West. With over 40 books to his name and an incalculable number of journalistic pieces, Burton was instrumental in building an image of the East during the very time when mass-market publishing was on the rise. Burton's writings often displayed an intense interest in the sexual cultures of the places he travelled and his translation and publication of the *Kama Sutra* in English both scandalized and titillated Victorian society. His commentaries and footnotes, even in works of fiction, were presented in a pseudo-academic style, adding a perceived scientific veracity to what were really quite spurious barrack room anecdotes included for smutty entertainment (Kabbani 1986:59–60). Earnest descriptions of Syrian boarding school lesbianism, Somali penile dimensions, and the pelvic muscle talents of Abyssinian slave women are among Burton's mountain of observations.

Burton's translation of *The Book of the Thousand Nights and a Night* (1885) left a much greater imprint on Western fantasy literature than his lewd and largely forgotten explorer's yarns. The anthological story of Scheherazade introduced Western readers to tropes such as flying carpets, magic lamps, genies, talented thieves, and treacherously cruel Eastern despots. Contrary to the sanitized Disney versions of today, Burton's omnibus included plenty of lewd sexual activity, thus cementing the connection between Easterners and depravity. (The very premise of the story is born of a female's infidelity and a man's desire to consume a nightly succession of unspoiled virgins before killing them each morning.) This collection of tales has been a major contributor to Western imagination of the East ever since, and gives rise to the sub-genre of Arabian Fantasy, which Clute and Grant (1997) describe as containing "deserts, oases, bazaars and slums, jewelled caravans and minaret topped edifices.... The cast—beggars, houris, eunuchs, caliphs, viziers, adventurers, genies ... magic carpets" (51).

Such is the influence of *The Thousand Nights* that these are the off-the-shelf ingredients that modern fantasy authors still tend to reach for when they need to depict Oriental geographies, even when they are creating totally fictional worlds. Robert Irwin (2004) notes that asking about the influence of these tales on Western literature is akin to asking about the influence of the Bible:

> science fiction, sword-and-sorcery fantasy, horror, romance, crime and thrillers. These are mass-market genres which had not been thought of when the first English versions of the *Nights* began to circulate, but in their origins all these types of the literature of entrainment surely owe something to the ancient oriental story collection [Irwin 2004:291].

More subtly, by including the checklist of Arabian fantasy stereotypes, authors make their works seem more realistic precisely because this is what the audience has been conditioned to imagine for generations. An Eastern setting that *did not* include deserts, bazaars, minarets, sexual depravity, treachery, and so on would be inconceivable as an Eastern setting. It would be something else entirely.

This then is the sturdy platform that much modern fantasy is built upon. The audience for *Game of Thrones* is testament to how entertaining and imaginative it is. Its grit and realism are also subjects for frequent praise. But in depicting non–Western cultures, this realism is more founded in received literary stereotypes than in any authenticity. This heritage is evident in the portrayal of Dorne and its people in *Game of Thrones*.

Dorne Patrol: Sex, Lies and Poison

The lands of Dorne lie at the southern end of the continent of Westeros, which is the principal setting of the series. Dorne is isolated from the rest of the continent by a standard fantasy geography of harsh desert and rugged mountains. It is culturally and ethnically dissimilar as well, with its people and lands seeming very alien to the other inhabitants of Westeros:

> The southernmost of the Seven Kingdoms is also the most inhospitable ... and the strangest, to the eyes of any man raised in the Reach or the westerlands or King's Landing. For Dorne is different, in more ways than can be told. Vast deserts of red and white sand, forbidding mountains where treacherous passes are guarded by treacherous peoples, sweltering heat, sandstorms, scorpions, fiery food, poison, castles made of mud, dates and figs and blood oranges. [Martin, Garcia, and Antonsson 2014:235.

This vision is the basis for an imagined Dornish culture that is geographically close to the more familiar medieval European fantasy world, yet distinct from it: a standard "other." Although the TV series does differ significantly from the books in certain Dorne-related plot arcs, there are fewer discrepancies to be observed in the overall setting and flavor. For example, while the parentage of the Sand Snakes and the story of Myrcella's sojourn in Dorne do not align between the book and TV versions, the descriptive backdrop of Dorne and its people are very consistent. In describing the arrival of Prince Oberyn and his Dornish court at King's Landing in *A Storm of Swords*, Martin details the apparel of the visitors: "The lords wore silk and satin robes with jeweled belts and flowing sleeves. Their armor was heavily enameled and inlaid with burnished copper, shining silver and soft red gold" (Martin 2000b:520). This accords with the group seen in the first episode of Season Four, "Two Swords." Similarly, although the mission to Dorne undertaken by Jaime and Bronn does not occur at all in the books, their encounter with a Dornish patrol sees them fighting men in burnooses and with helms wrapped in scarves, just as described in the books (520). Jaime and Bronn then adopt these costumes to disguise themselves during their clandestine mission. (Note the implicit Orientalist assumption that everyone dresses the same or that the population are so naïve that the land could be crossed and the palace infiltrated without anyone tumbling to the ruse!)

The Dornish culture is an amalgam of various Arabian fantasy clichés and real world locations. Martin has mentioned in his blog that although his influences for Dornish separatism came from cultures such as Wales and Cornwall, it is the medieval society of the Caliphate of Cordoba (now modern day Spain and Portugal) that is the principal cultural inspiration:

> South of the wall of mountains you have a hot, dry country more like Spain or Palestine than the cool green valleys of Wales, with most of the settlements along the seacoast and in few great river basins.... I suppose the closest real life equivilent [sic] to that would be the Moorish influence in parts of Spain.[2] So you could say Dorne is Wales mixed with Spain and Palestine with some entirely imaginary influences mixed in [Martin 2000a].[3]

The description that Martin provides of the Martell's palace at the Water Gardens includes marble pools, fountains, citrus groves, and fluted columns. The similarities between Dorne and the scenery of al-Andalus are easy to see, not least because locations in Seville and Cordoba were actually used for the filming. In a sense, the Dornish palace scenes are an example of an imaginary world being filmed "on location." The accents of the principal Dornish characters support this, with their intonation and enunciation being notably different from their northern neighbors.

With the palatial setting established as an Orientalist vision of Moorish Spain, there is little else to go on in the TV series regarding other elements of Dornish culture. The books provide some more details, including some standard tropes such as the Dornish enjoying heavily spiced food, hot peppers, and sauces with a dash of snake venom to add bite (Martin 2011:503). The consumption of snake meat is also noted, and in the series when Jaime and Bronn arrive on the Dornish coast, their first encounter is with a brightly colored snake, which Bronn then roasts for breakfast, although Jaime refuses to eat the flesh (5x4 "Sons of the Harpy").

That connection between serpents and Dorne is well established at almost every level. Prince Oberyn is "The Red Viper" and his formidable bastard offspring are the "Sand Snakes." The symbolism of the snake is key to the image of the Dornish and Oberyn's family in particular: fertility, sexuality, vindictiveness, treachery, and the use of poison. These elements all accord with the stereotypes of Orientalist imagining. In regard to poison, Oberyn's very nickname comes from the rumor of him at age 16 having used an envenomed blade to inflict a slow but mortal injury upon a dueling opponent, an older man who had caught his mistress and Oberyn *in flagrante delicto* (Martin 2000b:522–23). After this, Oberyn had travelled east "learning the poisoner's trade and perhaps arts darker still" (523). His use of a tainted spear in the fight against Ser Gregor Clegane doesn't bring him ultimate victory, but condemns The Mountain to a living death.

The use of poison runs in the family. Tyene Sand poisons Bronn with a dagger cut (5x7 "The Gift") and then taunts him, refusing to give him the antidote until he acknowledges her beauty. Ellaria Sand betrays Myrcella with a poisoned kiss, condemning the innocent girl to die in transit to her mother (5x10 "Mother's Mercy"). This terrible perfidy is then returned with interest by Cersei (7x3 "The Queen's Justice").[4]

A reliance on poison accords with the Orientalist belief of trickery and underhandedness being rife in non–Western cultures. It is also worth noting the connection between gender and poison in the series reflects an ancient association from Western history. This includes the strong innuendo that poison is a cowardly tool, fit only to be used by women and those males so unmanly as to be considered female. "I've heard it said that poison is a women's weapon," says Ned Stark to Grand Maester Pycelle. "Yes," agrees the elderly Maester, "women, cravens … and eunuchs" (1x4 "Cripples, Bastards, and Broken Things"). In addition to Ellaria's venomous kiss and Cersei's revenge, the main poisoning events of the series are all perpetrated by women. Lady Olenna poisons Joffrey and then commits suicide by taking poison provided by Cersei via Jaime. Arya wipes out the Frey family line with poison wine. Prior to this she had twice been given missions to poison targets in Braavos, including the job of killing Lady Crane on behalf of a rival female.[5] The only gender exceptions are the two attempts on Daenerys's life (one by a poisonous manticore hidden in a child's ball, the other by a wine merchant). However, these two assassinations are orchestrated by Varys, a eunuch.

Standing outside this gendered predilection for toxins is Prince Oberyn. His study and deployment of poison is almost passionate in nature; he even rails against the labeling of the tactic as purely feminine and argues that poison is worthy of masculinity:

> Any man who calls poison a woman's weapon is a traitor to his fellow men. A dagger, arrow, axe: these are the arms of passion. But poison is cold, calculating. Poison is the thought that wakes you in the morning, and lulls you to sleep at night. You watch your victim die a thousand times before you ever offer him that fateful taste. Is a man's hate so inferior to a woman's that we are to be denied such a weapon? [HBO 2015].

Such aberrant beliefs allow men from other parts of Westeros to impugn Dornish masculinity as substandard. Victarion Greyjoy adapts Pycelle's thoughts and muses, "Poison was for cravens, women and Dornishmen"

(Martin 2011:749).[6] Here again we see the tendency for those of non–Western background to be seen as more treacherous and less manly. It is certainly hard to imagine a traditional Western fantasy hero such as Aragorn or Conan resorting to poison to craftily dispose of a foe.

The Sand Snakes also represent a gendered exception, this time in physical violence. Whereas the series does depict females making use of violence, these women generally employ third parties to do so. Daenerys has her dragons, Cersei has her alchemists, Sansa has the Knights of the Vale. Brienne is an obvious exception, but throughout the story her *non*-femininity is emphasized; she is good at violence because she is not a "proper" woman. Arya Stark (another vociferously improper young lady) does kill at close quarters, but she is aided by supernatural forces and her assaults are often sneak attacks. Yara Greyjoy fights conventionally but is again portrayed as a character more masculine than feminine in demeanor. Ygritte is a possible exception, though her climactic use of violence in the series is stoked by a melodramatic personal vendetta. The three Sand Snakes, however, are shown as highly skilled and merciless fighters, able to match any opponent and dispense death with casual ease. Attractive, feminine, hot-blooded, and venomously treacherous, the bastard daughters of Oberyn align with many Arabian fantasy clichés.

Sexuality is central to the depiction of the Dornish in the series. Oberyn and Ellaria are the main platforms for this, with their orgiastic and bisexual brothel adventures in King's Landing. Elsewhere in Westeros, homosexuality is frowned upon as deviant, corruptive of masculinity and, by the time the Faith Militant and the High Sparrow re-emerge, an indictable offence. In discussing Loras Tyrell's "nocturnal activities," Tywin Lannister refers to this same-sex attraction as an "affliction" and a "stain upon his name" (3x6 "The Climb").

By contrast, Oberyn expounds that Dorne is superior because of its liberalness. Asked which "way" he likes his sexual encounters, he replies, "my way" (4x1 "Two Swords"). Both sexes delight him, and "when it comes to love, I don't choose sides" (4x3 "Breaker of Chains"). These Dornish "tastes" are a subject of mockery and innuendo for more northern Westerosi, who conflate bisexuality with all forms of deviancy. In an encounter in Littlefinger's brothel, two Lannister soldiers mock Oberyn and query the manager, "Why are you wasting a woman like this on a Dornishman? Bring him a shaved goat and a bottle of olive oil" (4x1). The assertion of bestiality, especially with goats or sheep, is a typical racial insult aimed at "others" and Burton's writings included lurid examples of this practice among the "debauched races" of the East.

The carnality of the Dornish is also exemplified in Oberyn. As he explains to the naked brothel manager:

Someday, if you are lucky, you will wake up and realize that you are old. That pretty arse of yours will sag, and your belly will grow soft, and your back will ache in the night, and grey hairs will sprout from your ears. No one will want you anymore. Make sure you have fucked your fill before that day [4x3].

Recognition of this hedonism is shown in Dorne's acceptance of bastard children, to the point where the Prince can attend Joffrey's wedding accompanied by his base-born lover, Ellaria. In the north, children born out of wedlock are of a lower status and their illegitimacy is forever stamped upon them by the use of regionally standardized surnames (Snow, Rivers, Storm, Flowers, and so on). Whilst still following this nominative practice, the Dornish do not accord the same stigma to such children. "Bastards are born of passion, weren't they? We don't despise them in Dorne," explains Oberyn to Cersei (4x2 "The Lion and the Rose"). Although only three appear in the series, Oberyn actually has eight illegitimate daughters from five different mothers, one of whom was a septa.

In the same way that Western men would fantasize about Eastern women and project upon them the sexual appetites that they did not want their own wives and daughters to have (Kabbani 1986:59), so too do men from other parts of Westeros daydream of Dornish women. "Dornish women are the most beautiful in the world," says Bronn as he languishes in a prison cell (5x7). Prior to this he sings a lament called "The Dornishman's Wife," which tells of a man who has a sexual encounter with a Dornish woman, only to be discovered and mortally wounded by her jealous and passionate husband. But he dies with no regrets, such is the quality of the tryst with this exotic beauty.

> Brothers, oh brothers, my days here are done,
> The Dornishman's taken my life,
> But what does it matter, for all men must die,
> And I've tasted the Dornishman's wife! [Martin 2000b:97].

Dornish history presents some further exotic contrasts with the rest of the continent. For example, whilst Cersei's unconventional rise to power is littered with corpses, had she been born into a Dornish house her path may have been simpler. This is because Dorne is the only constituent component of the Seven Kingdoms that practices *absolute* primogeniture as opposed to *male* primogeniture. That is, the oldest child will inherit lands and titles regardless of their sex. "Great ladies and famous princesses abound, and are the subject of songs and tales as much as the great knights and princes" (Martin, Garcia, and Antonsson 2014:242). Before Doran Martell became the prince of Dorne, his mother had been the ruler. By contrast, there has never been a Targaryen queen ruling in her own right or a female head of House Stark.

This custom of female inheritance is a quirk of the Dornish past. The southern provinces were unified by a refugee army arriving from the Rhoyne area of Essos, led by the formidable Princess Nymeria. In defeating a succession of petty kingdoms and city-states, Nymeria transplanted the Rhoynish culture upon Dorne. This is why it still carries those oriental characteristics despite being located on the western continent. Absolute primogeniture was a social consequence of this conquest by a powerful and redoubtable female. This system then endured because Dorne was eventually admitted to the Seven Kingdoms as an unconquered nation.[7] After many years of hostility, and finally through a mysterious capitulation by King Aegon the Conquerer, Dorne was brought into the fold of the Seven Kingdoms, not as a vassal, but as a quasi-equivalent member of a union. This is why their rulers are still allowed to style themselves as Princes and Princesses, the only use of that title in Westeros outside of the family holding the Iron Throne.

Although this sort of political detail does not come out in the TV series, it is another example of portraying the Dornish as somehow exotic or different from the norm. A further example of this differentiation from the rest of Westeros is its heraldry. In creating the rich pseudo-medieval tapestry that he has woven for his world, Martin has taken great pains to catalogue the coats of arms of even quite minor houses and knights. In the other six kingdoms the heraldic charges of the nobility follow fairly conventional European patterns and charges such as quartering, stripes, lions, stags, and so on placed upon standard "heater" type shields. However in Dorne, the coats of arms are displayed on circular shields.[8] A second heraldic difference with the Dornish arms is a trend towards gruesome images, potentially linking them with some distasteful cultural or geographic ideas. House Blackmont uses a black vulture carrying off a pink infant (Martin 2000b:518). House Manwoody has a crowned skull (518), and House Qorgyle has three black scorpions (519). Harking back to serpents and treachery, House Wyl uses a black adder biting a human foot (Garcia 2017). Given the attention to detail that is placed upon these house arms, they are not an insignificant feature for Martin, so the heraldic peculiarities in Dorne should not be considered an unintentional depiction of the culture there. In all the heraldry of Westeros, only the vicious raiders of the Iron Islands and the sadistic Boltons have a similar inclination to macabre designs.

You Know What Legacy Means?

In *A Storm of Swords*, Tyrion Lannister ponders his upcoming introduction to Prince Oberyn of Dorne, whom he has never met. "He knew the man only by reputation … but the reputation was fearsome" (Martin

2000b:522). It seems that like Tyrion, fantasy audiences and authors are guided by their own alarming beliefs and received wisdom, especially when it comes to imagining the lands and people of the periphery. The representation of the Dornish in *Game of Thrones* aligns with previous fantasy depictions of non–Western cultures. The Dornish are passionate, treacherous, violent, and sexually libertine. They live in an arid land and have a culture distinct from their more homogenous neighbors. Their palaces, in the books based upon those of Muslim Spain, are actually filmed at those locations, thus providing a seamless transition from a fantasy world to Western preconceptions of what an exotic Eastern culture looks like.

This depiction, like so many before it, is rooted in a power dynamic, but one that has nothing to do with the fantasy struggles of Lannisters or Targaryens. This power dynamic is from our own world and is embedded in those centuries when Europe looked south and east towards a group of others. At first they did so fearfully but then with a growing sense of superiority. The power imbalance of the 18th and 19th centuries saw Westerners develop a collection of beliefs and images of the Orient that has been handed down through the generations. As Tywin Lannister explains to Arya, a legacy is "what you pass down to your children, and your children's children. It's what remains of you when you're gone" (2x7 "A Man Without Honor"). For modern fantasy fans, this Orientalist legacy inherited from Burton and others is every bit as enduring and influential as the family castles and titles depicted in *Game of Thrones*.

NOTES

1. Aside from Said, many scholars have noted that, particularly in British writing, the fascination with Eastern sexual practices went hand in hand with emerging discussion on sexual identity in Europe during the late 19th century. Colette Colligan (2003:2) notes, "Burton propelled English discourse on homosexuality by focusing on the sodomitical practices of the Arabs and relying on assumptions about Arab sexuality ... these works also reveal a crucial dependence on Arab sexual difference as they explore a forbidden sexual topic." Parminder Bakshi (1990:175) describes "a tradition of nineteenth-century English homosexual literature in which the Orient represented a liberating Other, a region free of the constraints of Western sexual taboos."

2. Moor/Moorish is itself an historical term of no real specific value and an example of "manifest Orientalism." In medieval and early modern times, it was used as a catch-all "othering" label to refer to any dark-skinned peoples hailing from anywhere between the Iberian Peninsula and the Levant. Shakespeare's *Othello* is the most famed bearer of the designation, though even his exact point of origin is not specified. Outside of theatrical usage, the term is largely out of favor and can even be considered an ethnic slur.

3. It is not quite clear what historical era Martin is referring to with "Palestine" or whether he is implying the likeness is more to do with physical geography.

4. The plotline of Myrcella's death and Cersei's retribution occurs in the TV version only. The malevolence of both Ellaria and Cersei is amplified in the series, though arguably just an exaggeration of the literary characters rather than a redrawing of them.

5. In the book *A Dance with Dragons*, Arya successfully kills the crooked dockside insurance broker through the use of a poisoned coin. This differs from the TV episode "The

Dance of Dragons" (5x9), where she is distracted from selling the intended victim poisoned oysters by her catching sight of Ser Meryn Trant arriving in Braavos.

6. The character of Victarion does not appear in the TV series, with his role being taken by the piratical Euron Greyjoy.

7. The Dornish even managed to shoot down a dragon and kill the Targaryen Queen Rhaenys who was riding it. At another point the Dornish initiated peace negotiations merely as a pretense to try and assassinate King Daeron at the talks. And in a nice Orientalist triple play of treachery, poison, and exotic wildlife, the head of a kingdom occupation force was murdered by a trap involving 100 red scorpions falling from the canopy of his bed (Martin, Garcia, and Antonsson 2014:218).

8. According to Ellio Garcia, who collaborates with Martin on supplementary material to the novels, this distinction of a circular shield was the suggestion of Martin himself: "George specified that Dornish shields are depicted as round in Westeros for purposes of heraldry, so suggested we do the same" (Garcia 2016).

REFERENCES

Bakshi, Parminder Kaur. 1990. "Homosexuality and Orientalism: Edward Carpenter's Journey to the East. *Prose Studies* 13, 1:151–77. doi: 10.1080/01440359008586394.

Clute, J., and Grant, J. 1997. *The Encyclopedia of Fantasy*. New York: St. Martin's Press.

Colligan, Colette. 2003. "'A Race of Born Pederasts': Sir Richard Burton, Homosexuality, and the Arabs." *Nineteenth-Century Contexts* 25, 1:1–20. doi: 10.1080/0890549032000069131.

Cromer, The Earl of. 1917. *Modern Egypt*. Vol. 2. New York: Macmillan.

DiTommaso, Lorenzo. 2006. "The Persistence of the Familiar: The Hyborian World and the Geographies of Fantastic Literature." In *Two-Gun Bob: A Centennial Study of Robert E. Howard*, edited by B. Szumskyj, 107–19. New York: Hippocampus.

Garcia, Ellio M. 2016. The ASOIAF wiki thread. Accessed 30 December 2017. http://asoiaf. westeros.org/index.php?/topic/34958-the-asoiaf-wiki-thread/&page=72#comment-7606831.

Garcia, Ellio M. 2017. House Wyl of the Boneway. Accessed 30 December 2017. http://www. westeros.org/Citadel/Heraldry/Entry/House_Wyl/.

Hardy, Mat 2015. "Game of Tropes: The Orientalist Tradition in the Works of G.R.R. Martin." *International Journal of Arts & Sciences* 8, 1:409–20.

Hardy, Mat 2017. "The Eastern Question." In *Game of Thrones versus History: Written in Blood*, edited by Brian A. Pavlac, 97–109. Hoboken, NJ: Wiley Blackwell.

HBO. 2015. "History and Lore: Poisons." *Game of Thrones: The Complete Fourth Season*. Blu-ray DVD.

Herbert, Frank. 1977 "Some Arthur, Some Tolkien." *The New York Times Book Review*, 10 April:15, 25.

Irwin, Robert. 2004. *The Arabian Nights: A Companion*. London: Tauris Parke Paperbacks.

Kabbani, Rana. 1986. *Imperial Fictions: Europe's Myths of Orient*. London: Pandora.

Martin, George R.R. 2000a. "Historical Influences for Dorne." Accessed 10 July 2014. http://www.westeros.org/Citadel/SSM/Entry/Historical_Influences_for_Dorne.

Martin, George R.R. 2000b. *A Storm of Swords*. New York: Bantam.

Martin, George R.R. 2011. *A Dance with Dragons*. New York: Bantam.

Martin, George R.R., Ellio M. Garcia, and L. Antonsson. 2014. *The World of Ice and Fire: The Untold History of Westeros and* The Game of Thrones. London: HarperCollins.

Nae, Andrei. 2015. "Remediating Pornography in Game of Thrones: Where Sex and Memory Intertwine." *[Inter]sections* 18:17–44.

Said, Edward. (1978) 1979. *Orientalism*. New York: Vintage.

Young, Helen. 2015. *Race and Popular Fantasy Literature: Habits of Whiteness*. New York: Routledge.

Pornography,
Postwoman
and Female Nudity

AARON K.H. HO

In an interview with *The Telegraph*, actor Ian McShane, who has a cameo in an episode of Season Six of *Game of Thrones* and "was accused of giving the plot away" (spoiler alert: his character dies), dissed aggrieved viewers for caring too much for the show: "get a fucking life. It's only tits and dragons" (Farndale 2016). Perhaps McShane has unwittingly hit the nail on the head about what I argue is one of the most pivotal scenes in Season One: the rebirth of Daenerys Targaryen emerging naked ("tits") and unscathed with three dragons from the funeral pyre built for her husband, Khal Drogo. The manner in which the dragons, which rise from the ashes of Khal Drogo (and Mirri Maz Duur), are born presages the deaths and destruction they will bring to The Known World. But more generally, McShane's jibe echoes the criticism by audience and television critics that *Game of Thrones* sensationalizes violence and nudity. *GQ*, a magazine known for targeting the market of upper-middle-class men in the West, hilariously ranks and lampoons 71 nude scenes in six seasons of *Game of Thrones* according to "whether anyone really needed to be naked" (Schrodt 2017). More serious in tone, Sara David (2017) counts every instance of rape, murder, and nudity across the seven seasons as empirical evidence to argue that the mistreatment of women in the show poses a challenge to female viewers, despite the show's strong girl and women characters.

While such a statistical approach is factually accurate, it neglects to look into the details of the scenes: is nudity necessary in the particular scene or is it merely sexploitation to satisfy the voyeurism of the male gaze? In "Women, Pop Music, and Pornography," Meredith Levande (2008) observes that as mega media conglomerates profit from and even acquire adult entertainment companies, they push pornographic images to general audiences. Levande traces Time Warner's practices from pay-per-view pornography services; to the company's acquisition of Adelphia Communications, which had offered pornographic programming; to distribution of images similar to pornography; and the association of titles from Adult on Demand with pop-stars on Time Warner entertainment channels. Under Time Warner assets is HBO, which has a reputation, not unfairly, of gratifying spectators with nudity, and which distributes *Game of Thrones*. Viewers have uploaded scenes from *Game of Thrones*, such as Cersei's walk of atonement in the finale of Season Five (also commonly known as walk of shame), directly to Pornhub (*BBC* 2016). And when episodes of *Game of Thrones* premiere, viewership to Pornhub dips (Pornhub 2017).[1] Extrapolating Levande's argument that links mega media conglomerates with pornography, are the nude scenes in *Game of Thrones* presented as mere pornography, as part of Time Warner and HBO's ploy to attract viewership? There are without doubt many scenes in which nudity is gratuitous, but what is interesting to me are the scenes that necessitate nudity.

In particular, I wish to examine scenes involving Daenerys (Emilia Clarke), the most searched character on Pornhub (Nededog 2016) and most frequently naked among the main cast—so frequently naked that Clarke herself has expressed frustration about repeated questions on nudity. In an interview with *Elle* she says, "I get a lot of crap for having done nude scenes and sex scenes. That in itself is so antifeminist" (in *Elle* 2017). Although Clarke's notion of feminism may be considered simplistic, at the root of her statement is the idea that the corporeality of bare female flesh fetters itself to feminism. In reading the feminine body on screen, the French school of feminism is constructive in not only eluding the trappings of the masculine/feminine dichotomy, but also demonstrating how in a contested site like Daenerys's female body we can reach a position of postwomanhood, transcending problematic and essentialist gender roles. But ultimately, even as Daenerys's body as a written text proves to adhere to the principles of French feminism, the filming techniques upset and disrupt any semblance of female empowerment. Furthermore, contrasting Daenerys's and Cersei's nude scenes with Jon Snow's, the audience has to work against the cinematography to sexualize the man but the camerawork encourages the objectification of the females.

"I am not a feminist": Hélène Cixous and Julia Kristeva

Although they were both influenced by the 1968 upheaval in French society, neither Hélène Cixous nor Julia Kristeva adopted the term "feminist."

Still, many of their ideas illuminate the analysis of female nudity in *Game of Thrones*. Both attempt to upset the dialectics of gender, privileging neither male nor female, by not engaging in the discourse of binary. Each theorist adopts a different approach, but both believe in the ability of linguistics to shape subjectivity.

Cixous is most famous for her call to arms in "The Laugh of the Medusa" in support of *écriture feminine*, which is writing that cannot be mapped onto an empirical reality or easily conveyed in ideas (1976). Cixous uses the figure of a woman speaking for the first time in public as an embodied representation of her theory of *écriture*, describing and grounding the speaker's senses in the physicality, and in so doing, demystifying the metaphysics of ideas (1976:881). By foregrounding the physical consciousness of the female body, Cixous allows the repressed feminine a voice and, at the same, does not replicate another model of universal binary.

Like Cixous, Kristeva deals in sensory perceptions, affects, and instincts but in the realm of the preverbal. While Cixous explores the gaps between binary and everything that it cannot encompass, Kristeva (1984) delineates language into the symbolic (which is a rule-bound system connected to social order that is dependent on the chasm between the object and the subject) and the semiotic (which, like Cixous's écriture feminine, is unknown and obscure, but also pre–Oedipal, the driving force behind creativity, and associated with the *chora* meaning "space," or perhaps more accurately "womb") (1984:24). To Kristeva, meaning is formed by the interaction between the symbolic and the semiotic bound together by the thetic structure (57–59). Art can rupture the thetic structure by breaking apart traditional channels of meaning, allowing the semiotic to peep through, and in the process, reshaping one's subjectivity and forming new and manifold cultural significations. The theories of Kristeva and Cixous that allow multivalent, not dichotomous, meanings by looking into slippages of communication in texts or sites of performance provide a framework to examine the gender implications in Daenerys's nude scenes.

"I am the dragon's daughter": Daenerys as Postwoman

Nudity functions to increase power for Daenerys; whenever she is naked, she gains power. In the very first scene she appears in, she disrobes and, naked, descends into a bath, in preparation to meet Khal Drogo, her betrothed, who raises her to the position of Khaleesi (Queen), allowing her to eventually break free from her brother's physical and verbal abuses.[2] When she walks into the funereal pyre for Khal Drogo, she emerges naked with three baby dragons to the incredulity of the Khalasar members who expect her death; the dragons will eventually give her immeasurable (fire)power. She sits in a bath when Daario Naharis breaks into her chambers, offers her the severed heads of his commanders, and pledges the allegiance of the Second Sons to her. In Vaes Dothrak, she burns the Temple of the Dosh Khaleen and walks out of the burning hut naked, gaining all of the Dothraki khalasars.

While the aforementioned generalization that her female nudity brings her power is more or less true for many scenes, the birth of the three dragons complicates the assumption that Daenerys is female *and* human. In the scene leading up to the birth, George R.R. Martin's novel, *A Game of Thrones*, repeatedly foreshadows their advent through Daenerys's corporeal sensations. In her fevered delirium, she dreams that her son "opened his mouth [and] the fire poured out" (2011:752) and that "a great knife of pain ripped down her back" with "the stench of burning blood" as she sprouts wings and trans-figures into a dragon (752–53). When she recovers from her puerperal fever, "it was as if her body had been torn to pieces and remade from the scraps" (753). Not only is she physically reconfigured and reassembled, she proclaims in both the novel and the television series, "I am the dragon's daughter" (758). "She was the blood of the dragon" and "bride of dragons, mother of dragons" (804; 806). As she is a mother of dragons, her stillborn child with Khal Drogo, though grotesque, resembles a dragon more than a human with saurian scales, a tail, and leathered wings. It is clear that Daenerys has been baptized by her postpartum burning fever and reborn into something suprahuman, tran-scending human capabilities, and seen from this light, perhaps we should interpret her proclamations of being so intimately related to dragons ("daugh-ter," "bride," "mother") more literally than metaphorically, for only a dragon can birth, be born from, and marry a dragon. Daenerys's transformation to suprahuman, or at least a hybrid of a dragon/human, and the incestuous con-notations of being daughter, bride, and mother to dragons remove her from the heteronormative male/female binary that Cixous and Kristeva aim to avoid.

Although the men in her life—her brother, her partner Drogo and her son—have to perish in order for her to rule, Daenerys governs not as a woman but a postwoman, that is, her identity depends not on the dichotomy of the presence or absence of the phallus. Borrowing in part from Donna Haraway's "A Cyborg Manifesto" (1991) in which a cyborg (a person with mechanical parts, extending the human self beyond normal physical abilities, not unlike how Daenerys is reconfigured by fire) represents the "disassembled and reassembled, postmodern collective and personal self" (163), I define a post-woman as a woman who pushes the boundaries of womanhood and is not determined by her sex alone. Certainly, Daenerys adheres to some conven-tions of womanhood such as wearing dresses and sleeping with men, but she can choose to exist outside such conventions. She decides whom to sleep with, and in a battle, she is more powerful than most men, sitting on a dragon, destroying Cersei's army in the fourth episode of Season Seven, and killing White Walkers and rescuing Jon Snow in the sixth episode of the same season. Furthermore, essentialism defines women by their wombs, but Daenerys, who is said to be infertile after her stillbirth, gives birth to three dragons. The paradox that she is sterile and yet known as the Mother of Dragons implies that her biological status as a woman no longer confines her to traditionally feminine roles; she is beyond her biological body, she is a post-woman. In the novel, just before she steps into the pyre, she names three Dothraki warriors, one after another, to be her ko (lieutenants) or bloodriders: her declaration implies that she sees herself as a khal (a warlord), a position reserved for men. All three Dothraki warriors reject her in turn based on her gender—"It would shame me, to be bloodrider to a woman" (800) and "Only a man can lead a *khalasar* [tribe] or name a *ko*" (800) and "You are *khaleesi*" (801)—and yet after each rejection, she moves onto the next warrior as if she doesn't hear their objections. Daenerys no longer partakes in the male/female distinction.

The act of Daenerys bestowing titles on the three Dothraki is part of her speech to the khalasar before she walks into the pyre. Although Daenerys has been made a spectacle in front of the khalasar before (in instances such as her wedding, her brother's gold crown scene, and the eating of a horse's heart), this speech is the first time she addresses the tribe as a queen, similar to Cixous's embodied figure of a woman speaking in public for the first time; Daenerys's physicality in both the novel and the television series epitomizes Cixous's theory of écriture feminine. In the novel, the speech is followed by a scalding hot bath, drawing attention to her immunity to heat (801). In the series, her gossamer gown, not unlike the one she wears when she is first presented to Khal Drogo, implying her bridal status both to the dead Khal and the three unhatched dragons, flows with the wind (1x10 "Fire and Blood"). Later, Mirri Maz Duur's screams from the pyre also remind the audience of the heat Daenerys feels as she walks into the fire. Borrowing from Cixous, the foregrounding of Daenerys's physical response to heat demystifies the metaphysics of ideas, exposing the unreliability of the self/other binary based on the social order; instead of asking what women want, as Lacan does, instead of fantasizing that women are mysterious and unfathomable beings, the corporeality of Daenerys debunks the metaphysics of ideas and at the same time presents her with her own unique subjectivity, not having to impose a blanket generalization on all women.

Although on one level Daenerys's corporeality demystifies her womanhood, her status as the mother of dragons paradoxically establishes her as the unknown; what is she? Even though she is unknowable, Martin insists on her ordinary corporeality as Ser Jorah Mormont finds her among the ashes with a dragon suckling milk at her breast. This emphasis on the body may seem essentialist, as many critics have leveled against Cixous's theory—"There is always within her at least a little of that good mother's milk. She writes in white ink," she famously states in her manifesto (1976:881)—but Cixous's theory may be read as performative and critical since she firmly argues against essentialism. Daenerys's unknowability explores and exposes the gaps between the binary of ideas, and thus upsets the social order. Daenerys's naked body—both unknowable and substantial—is what would destabilize the false dichotomy that language is based on, according to Cixous's theory.

The obscurity and unknowability of Daenerys's body could further be read as an artistic embodiment of what Kristeva calls the semiotics. Her naked body discovered among the cinders of the pyre fulfills the requirements of the semiotics: her solution to solve her crisis by walking into the fire indicates a driving force of creativity, and the dragons bursting forth from their chora (and so soon after Daenerys's own childbirth), crying lustily, demonstrates a pre–Oedipal, preverbal aspect bearing the mother's protolinguistic embodiment. Interpreting Daenerys's body as an artistic performance of the semiotics means that the act breaks the thetic bonds between the symbolic and the semiotics, allowing the unknown to show momentarily, reconfiguring subjectivity and redefining cultural meanings. To reify the concept, Daenerys changes the way the Dothraki think of leadership and dominance, which were always masculine, and she represents a transformation of multiple subjectivity from a woman to postwoman, from a khaleesi and a princess to a queen, and from a mother of a monster to a mother of dragons.

Kristeva terms this transformation as the *sujet-en-procès* in *Revolution in Poetic Language*, which means a "subject on trial" *and* a "subject in process," playing on the homonym of the French word *procès* (1984:203). Kristeva sees subjectivity as an irreconcilable dilemma that depends on constant change and constant judgment. Since subjects are constantly changing, they cannot present themselves in stasis yet they must because they are constantly judged. The semiotics works to free the subject from this double bind of change and judgment, allowing "a venture of innovation, of creation, of opening, of renewal" (Kristeva 1996:26). Daenerys's performance of burning at the pyre as an embodied act of the semiotics frees her old subjectivity, allowing her to change, and at the same time empowers her with a renewal of life alongside her moribund tribe and with enough firepower to re-enter the race to rule the Seven Kingdoms.

While the thetic rapture actuates innovation, creation, and renewal, it can also incur psychosis unless the abject is expelled to bring about the definite severance between the object and the subject. The Mother is the prototype of the abject as the child has to separate itself from the mother to gain its own subjectivity, thus the mother is both an object of desire and an abject because of infantile reliance. In *Game of Thrones*, the most prominent mother is probably Cersei Lannister, who has much in common with Daenerys. Losing the men in their lives,[3] they both become ambitious and efficacious rulers who can be ruthless; they are both, in a trio of siblings, the only female, and the only child who gets neglected by society and family in favor of the able-bodied boys (Tyrion is an exception); they are mothers with three children/dragons; and physically they are blond and beautiful. Yet the treatment of the two women is vastly different, seen most notably in their vulnerable nude states: when Daenerys is naked, she usually gains power, but nudity degrades Cersei. In the seventh episode of Season Seven, when Daenerys sleeps with Jon Snow (who, unbeknownst to them, is her nephew) the spectator heaves a sigh of resignation, but when Cersei commits similar incestuous acts with her brother and her cousin, she is reviled. It may be fair to say that since Jon and Daenerys do not know of their relationship, they are less guilty than Cersei and Jaime. But comparing Daenerys's walk into the pyre and Cersei's naked walk of atonement in the show, we as audience are first distraught, then elated, for Daenerys's triumph, but there is a schadenfreude pleasure in watching Cersei degraded, even as viewers feel sympathy for her.[4] The similarities between the two queens could be read as the good mother/bad mother dialectics that Kristeva writes about. One of them, the bad mother or the abject—in this case, Cersei—has to be expelled or sacrificed for the audience to root for Daenerys.

Why Cersei, Not Daenerys? Film Techniques of Nude Women in Game of Thrones

Why is Cersei sacrificed in the television drama to become the abject and not Daenerys? Surely, Daenerys, who eventually becomes a postwoman and doesn't exist in Kristeva's symbolic, is more threatening to the social order of signification than Cersei? In her seminal essay "Visual Pleasure and Narrative Cinema," Laura Mulvey differentiates cinematic codes into three ways of looking: from the camera, the spectator, and the character in the film (1975). The first two ways of looking are rendered invisible so that films can achieve a mimesis of reality and that spectators, regardless of gender or sexuality, identify with the male protagonist. In the pyre scene, when the dawn breaks, signaled by the greyish lighting, the camera follows the movement of Jorah, who walks past the sleeping tribe to the pyre now in smothering cinders. He reaches the center of the pyre to find Daenerys crouched. Unlike in the novel where her long tresses are singed away, Daenerys's hair, indicating a woman's sensuality, is perfect in the show; the spectator is reminded that she is just a woman. She looks up at Jorah, who then kneels to call her, "Blood of my blood." Unlike the novel, where we more or less follow the perspective of Daenerys, the series forces us into the position of Jorah. By identifying with Jorah, who loves Daenerys, the spectator is guided to his point of view that Daenerys, despite being a postwoman, is not threatening and is worthy of adoration and veneration.

Mulvey also argues that to assuage the castration anxiety of the male unconsciousness and to make films pleasurable, tactics of voyeurism and fetishizing are employed by viewers. The first tactic, voyeurism, demystifies the female, and although I have argued via écriture feminine that Daenerys's nudity is essential to demystify the essence of femalehood, her nudity in this pyre scene serves to reduce the threat of castration when the spectator is made to identify with the male protagonist via the camerawork. If the scene were handled differently, if it were perhaps shown from the perspective of Daenerys, not Jorah, then the scene would have reinforced Cixous's theory, but as edited the cinematography works as an antinomy to écriture feminine. The second tactic transforms the female into an object of fetish, changing the physical beauty of the female into something satisfying. This tactic is also employed in the pyre scene and elsewhere to fetishize Daenerys. For instance, in the finale of the third season, after liberating a city of slaves, she walks among them. They lift her up and the camera zooms out and up from the ground in an extreme long shot, showing Daenerys, a white spot amidst a mandala of brown bodies, with cheers of *mhysa* (mother). In this scene, Daenerys is fetishized by the camera into an object, a beautiful part of a mise-en-scène, but not as a person with her own subjectivity. Likewise, in the pyre scene, Daenerys has become an object at the hands of the cinematography. John Berger famously writes that "a naked body has to be seen as an object in order to become a nude" (1972:54). That is to say that desire from the male observer (in this case, Jorah) is projected on the naked woman, making her an object. The vernation that the khalasar pays her bolsters the notion that she is an idol, an object.

Compare how Daenerys and Cersei are portrayed: Cersei has seldom been filmed as a fetishized object. Like Daenerys's transformative pyre scene, the walk of atonement is also a scene of rebirth for Cersei. Daenerys steps into fire but Cersei is scrubbed with water and her hair shorn into a boy's cut which indicates a new life. Both are naked as the day they are born.[5] But for Cersei, her rebirth in the television series is bloody and she is defeminized; her hair is shaven unlike Daenerys who retains her locks. Unlike the pyre scene which the spectator watches from Jorah's perspective, the cinematography in the walk of atonement alternates mostly between shots from the back of the rabble and those that show Cersei in medium shots. The audience identifies with the mob and revels in her debasement. Even as she is crying and hurt, the mob—and by extension the viewer—thinks that she deserves it for her transgressions; she needs to be punished and put into place.

There are, however, two notable exceptions when the camera shows Cersei's point of view during the Walk. First, two nude bodies flashing and taunting her not only establishes the rowdiness of the mob, the extras' nudity also mirrors Cersei's. Unlike Daenerys's nudity, which elevates her status and is usually depicted singularly, Cersei's nudity is compared to a "commoner"; Cersei becomes just another dirty, ignominious body, undifferentiated from the unwashed hoi polloi. The other exception occurs when she keeps her eyeline at the Red Keep. While viewers may admire her determination to reach the Red Keep, the entire scene in which Cersei lies to High Sparrow to end her imprisonment just before the Walk will remind viewers that her iron will is malicious and she will do anything to achieve her goals; if she reaches the Red Keep safely, she will bring chaos and destruction. To reinforce her malevolence to viewers, at the end of the Walk, she is gifted with the personification of violence and evil in the form of the undead and terrifying Mountain at the Red Keep. Her strong determination to reach the Red Keep becomes portentous via the camera movement. Therefore, even when spectators are placed in Cersei's position, most audience members are constantly and actively rejecting identification with her because of the mise-en-scène and narrative sequence.

The cinematography, then, is quite unlike the sympathetic portrayal of the same scene in the novel where we are placed in Cersei's perspective. Furthermore, like the third season finale scene of Daenerys as mhysa, Cersei stands out as a spot of white against brown rags in this fifth season finale. Clearly there is some sort of mirroring, but Cersei is not treated as reverently as Daenerys; Cersei is never elevated into a symbol as Daenerys is as mhysa. Cersei's emphasized corporeality in this scene offers viewers a sadistic pleasure. Like the dung, rotten food, and slops thrown at her, like the blood from the cuts she suffers during the walk, the audience is directed to treat her as the abject, something that is desirable (because of her nudity and beauty) and at the same time something filthy and disgusting to be rejected.

The Third Rebirth: Jon Snow

Spanning across episodes two and three in Season Six, Jon's rebirth resembles Daenery's and Cersei's in that they are nude and involve similar elements. Jon's body is washed and he is brought back to life by the Lord of Light, also known as the fire god. However, unlike the women's nudity, Jon's rebirth is not fetishized; it becomes mythic. The scene mirrors the Italian Renaissance artist Andrea Mantegna's famous painting, *The Lamentation of*

Christ (estimated to be completed between 1475 and 1501), which depicts the supine Jesus. Both Jon Snow and Jesus in the painting are shown lying on a table and their private parts covered with a cloth. Their skin is a patina green. Those in the room—Melisandra, Ser Davos Seaworth, and Jon's followers—may be interpreted as stand-ins for Mary Magdalene and Jesus's disciples. Previously, Jon Snow, like Jesus, is betrayed by his disciple, Olly, who stabs him at the finale of Season Five. Jon and Jesus are resurrected by a god. Even when Melisandra washes blood off Jon's body, her caressing action is de-eroticized because of the bloody stab wounds and the implication that Jon is a messiah figure. Unlike Daenerys's and Cersei's nudity, which could easily be seen as pornographic, Jon's nude scene refuses to allow viewers that privilege. It is as if men could not bear the weight of objectification.

The weight is so immense that in order to prevent objectification of men, the scene has to be disrupted and separated into two episodes. However, the scene continuing in episode three shows Jon sit up on the table, filmed from the back, revealing a bit of buttocks, and then a cut to his left profile displays a stunning full body shot as he props his left leg artfully to veil his genitals. But even here, the viewers can objectify Jon only if they ignore that he has newly risen from the dead, his body riddled with multiple stab wounds; and that they are viewing the scene from Davos's perspective. Unlike Jorah's sexual admiration for Daenerys, Davos, who seems to lack any sexual desire throughout the seven seasons, respects Jon as a loyal follower; no hint of homoeroticism exists between them. And therefore, unlike the pyre scene where Darnerys's prowess is sexualized from Jorah's point of view, Davos, as a substitute for the viewer, witnesses Jon's rebirth as a miracle and as a sign that Jon is a true leader. For viewers to perceive Jon in a sexual light, they need to read against the grain of the narrative and the perspective of the camera. Such a reading contrasts greatly from the women's nudity, where spectators are encouraged to sexualize Daenerys and Cersei.

Conclusion: The Treatment of Nude Women *in* Game of Thrones

The contrast between the treatment of nudity of the two genders in *Game of Thrones* reaches a disappointing conclusion regarding the female nudity in the show. Using Cixous's and Kristeva's theories to interpret the nude scenes of Daenerys, there exists a strong possibility that the powerful women may destabilize and expose the false dichotomy of signification in *Game of Thrones*. With her intimate relationship with dragons and her invulnerability to flames, Daenerys achieves a status as a postwoman, taking her out of the male/female dichotomy. The focus on her corporeality and her nudity is crucial to demystify her essence as a woman and at the same time her unknowable lineage—is she human or dragon?—adds to Cixous's argument of exploration of gaps between linguistic binary. This unknowability, according to Kristeva, is ultimately transformative not only to one's subjectivity but also to a culture which will generate new and myriad meanings.

Even though the body of Daenerys as a text fits into the French feminist theories, filmic strategies are employed to reduce the power and energies of powerful women in the drama. Here, I want to differentiate the novels from the television series. The two nude scenes that I have discussed at length—the pyre and the walk of atonement—are based on the novel. While the narratives of the novels and the series are similar, the treatment of women varies as I have explicated: mostly, in the novels, the scenes are told from the female character's perspective, allowing readers to sympathize with them, and Martin insists on writing about the concreteness of the body, grounding the scenes in reality or at least a semblance of reality. Martin doesn't allow the reader to elevate or fantasize about Daenerys as a mythic figure, neither does he denigrate Cersei. However, the television series works to tame powerful women. For Daenerys, her nudity, which is meant to be empowering under the French theorists' interpretation, becomes a site for the male gaze to gain control and subdue. Her beauty is fetishized so that man after man falls in love with her (and we as spectators should follow suit), and the cinematography enhances this fetishizing by often displaying her as an object, rather than the postwoman of unique subjectivity that she is. Other filmic techniques are used to reduce Cersei, another powerful woman, who becomes the abject to be expelled and rejected in the eyes of the camera. In short, the cinematography elevates Daenerys to be desired or transformed into a symbol even as it denounces Cersei, despite the many similarities between the two women: the two cinematic methods are utilized to make the powerful women less threatening to the male unconsciousness. In reductively reconstructing the women from the novels into desirable or despicable via the camera lens, not unlike the Victorian Angel/Whore dialectics, the television series has missed out on the complexities of womanhood that the novels engender.

NOTES

1. Pornhub phrases their finding ambiguously, and, I surmise, intentionally; they note the correlation between the screenings of *Game of Thrones* and the decrease of their visitors, implying but refusing to state explicitly that their visitors skip over to the TV show and even perhaps treat it as porn. Enough people seem to pick up Pornhub's implication that Emilie Clarke, who plays Daenerys, vents in an interview with *Harper's Bazaar*, "I'm starting to get really annoyed about this stuff now and people say, 'Oh, yeah, all the porn sites went down when *Game of Thrones* came back on... People fuck for pleasure—it's part of life" (Aftab 2017).

2. Clearly, in scenes of abuse and rape, Daenerys suffers physically and her ascent to power is more complicated than simply that her nudity gives her power. But it is also her body that indirectly helps her gain power.

3. Daenerys loses her father, brothers, husband, and son; and Cersei loses her father and sons. It can also be argued that her brothers abandon her.

4. However, in the novel, *A Dance with Dragons*, the narrative is told from Cersei's perspective and as readers, we sympathize with her. It is interesting but out of this article's boundaries to compare the treatment of Cersei in the novel and television series.

5. In the novel, it is clearer that it is a rebirth for Cersei as the High Holiness commands that she is shaven *everywhere* to "present yourself as the gods made you ... when you came forth from your lady mother's womb" (Martin 2013:931).

REFERENCES

Aftab, Kaleem. 2017. "Emilia Clarke in Bloom." *Harper's Bazaar*, 21 November. Accessed 30 December. http://www.harpersbazaar.com/culture/features/a13586407/emilia-clarke-interview/.

BBC. 2016. "*Game of Thrones* Is Taking Action Against Pornhub for Breach of Copyright." BBC Newsbeat, 1 June. Accessed 30 December 2017. http://www.bbc.co.uk/newsbeat/article/36417759/game-of-thrones-is-taking-action-against-pornhub-for-breach-of-copyright.

Berger, John. 1972. *Ways of Seeing*. London: BBC & Penguin.

Cixous, Hélène. 1976. "The Laugh of the Medusa." Translated by Keith Cohen and Paula Cohen. *Signs* 1, 4:875–93.

David, Sara. 2017. "Counting Every Instance of Rape, Death, and Nudity on *Game of Thrones*." *Broadly*, 7 September. Accessed 30 December 2017. https://broadly.vice.com/en_us/article/qvvx83/game-of-thrones-by-the-numbers.

Elle. 2017. "How Emilia Clarke Took Khaleesi From Alt-Medieval Virgin to Feminist Icon." *Elle*, 11 July. Accessed 30 December. http://www.elle.com/culture/celebrities/news/a46528/emilia-clarke-august-2017-elle-cover-reveal/.

Farndale, Nigel. 2016. "Ian McShane: '*Game of Thrones* Is Just Tits and Dragons." *The Telegraph*, 6 June. Accessed 30 December 2017. http://www.telegraph.co.uk/tv/2016/03/11/ian-mcshane-game-of-thrones-is-just-tits-and-dragons/.

Haraway, Donna. 1991. *Simians, Cyborgs, and Women: The Reinvention of Nature*. New York: Routledge.

Kristeva, Julia. 1984. *Revolution in Poetic Language*. Translated by Margaret Walter. New York: Columbia University Press.

Kristeva, Julia. 1996. *Julia Kristeva: Interviews*. Edited by Ross Mitchell Guberman. New York: Columbia University Press.

Levande, Meredith. 2008. "Women, Pop Music, and Pornography." *Meridians* 8, 1:293–321.

Martin, George R.R. 2011. *A Game of Thrones*. New York: Bantam.

Martin, George R.R. 2013. *A Dance with Dragons*. New York: Bantam.

Mulvey, Laura. 1975. "Visual Pleasure and Narrative Cinema." *Screen* 16, 3:6–18.

Nededog, Jethro. 2016. "*Game of Thrones* Videos Are Huge on Pornhub, and HBO Is Trying to Take Them Down." *Insider*, 1 June. Accessed 30 December 2017. http://www.thisisinsider.com/game-of-thrones-pornhub-2016-6.

Pornhub. 2017. "*Game of Thrones* Season 7 Premiere Traffic." Pornhub Insights, 18 July. Accessed 30 December 2017. https://www.pornhub.com/insights/game-of-thrones-season-7.

Schrodt, Paul. 2017. "Every *Game of Thrones* Nude Scene, Ranked by Whether Anyone Really Needed to Be Naked." *GQ*, 11 July. Accessed 30 December. https://www.gq.com/story/game-of-thrones-nude-scenes-ranked-by-relevance.

Winning the *Game of Thrones*
Conquering Westeros with Sun Tzu, Niccolò Machiavelli and John Nash

MATTEO BARBAGELLO

One of the recurring traits of a subgenre of fantasy literature, the so-called sword and sorcery, among many others, is the unavoidable victory of Good over Evil. The happy ending is usually carried out by a heroic figure or a party usually consisting of one or more warriors and helpers. Despite their endings, happy or bittersweet, Tolkien's *The Lord of the Rings* (1954–1955) trilogy and *The Hobbit* (1937) or Lewis's *The Lion, the Witch and the Wardrobe* (1950) and many other fantasy masterworks include this sort of development in their plots. As a matter of fact, the outcome of the struggle between the forces of Good and those of Evil in Tolkien or Lewis isn't decided by a relationship of causality or determined by political reasons; heroes must win, and that's all that matters.

In his *Song of Ice and Fire* books George R.R. Martin first portrays story dynamics that are potentially in line with the color-coded fantasy only to reveal that, actually, the principle ruling Westerosi politics is more rigorous and scientific. *A Song of Ice and Fire* replaces fantasy conventions with a different approach towards the overall plot and the political balance of Martin's many worlds. At the beginning of *A Game of Thrones* (1996) Martin introduces House Stark, a powerful family of the North, loyal ally of the king and safekeepers of the North for him. From the use of adjectives such as "wise," "faithful," "reliable," usually addressed to heroic figures, the reader identifies in the Starks the embodiment of all things good and, most of all, of the Seven Gods: Ned Stark is the Father, Catelyn Tully the Mother, Robb Stark the Warrior, Sansa Stark the Maiden, Arya Stark the Crone, and Bran Stark the Smith. It is no surprise that the reader can't find the Stranger among the Starks: it might be Jon Snow, the bastard, capable of bringing shame to the family because of his illegitimacy, but still it is impossible for the reader to find that missing figure at the beginning. This is due to the fact that Martin wants the reader to question the Stranger's absence, because it will be only in *A Feast for Crows* (2005) that the true identity of the Stranger will be revealed as nothing more than the infinite turning of what has been called along the centuries with the name of Divine Providence, or simply Luck.

With this in mind, it is possible to start looking at Martin's oeuvre from a different perspective.

In fact, what happens in *A Song of Ice and Fire* potentially echoes the principles described in three works coming from different backgrounds: Sun Tzu's *The Art of War*, Niccolò Machiavelli's *The Prince* (1532) and John Nash's *Non-Cooperative Games* (1951).

I will not delve much into Sun Tzu's work, but it must be noted that the rules prescribed by the Chinese military strategist have been used by conquerors of the caliber of Napoleon and Douglas MacArthur to achieve their goals both during wars and in politics. This treatise called *The Art of War*, written in the 5th century BCE, consists of 13 different chapters in which Sun Tzu illustrates the ways a ruler must follow to win battles with the least effort and preserve their outcomes. One of Sun Tzu's most famous sentence in the treatise says: "The greatest victory is that which requires no battle" (1994:35). Just from this sentence we can already consider one of Martin's characters as the embodiment of Sun Tzu's principles: Tywin Lannister, head of House Lannister and previous hand of the king.

With the priority of protecting the status of his family, Tywin Lannister started planning a war against the crown with the aim of making it collapse from the inside. That is why, after having counseled the Mad King for years, Tywin considered winning the war, which started with Robert Baratheon's Rebellion by wedding his daughter Cersei off to Robert himself, who was winning the war but had lost his betrothed Lyanna Stark. Once bonded with House Baratheon, it became easier for Tywin to control the will of the king through the figure of his daughter. Tywin's crucial move, however, comes when he secures the crown against any further rebellion with the infamous Red Wedding. As readers know, this atrocious event was made possible by the recklessness of Robb Stark to break the promise made to Walder Frey, who would have, like, Tywin, benefited from having his daughter married to the allegedly new king of the Seven Kingdoms. In breaking that promise, Robb Stark created the premise for Tywin's decision to win the war without further battles.[1]

As a matter of fact, the importance of the Red Wedding does not rely only on the presence of Robb Stark, but on his bannermen as well: by slaughtering or seizing them after having them locked up in the banquet room, Tywin managed to defeat the traitors who rebelled against the crown without having to lose more men on the battlefield. His comments to Tyrion after the event seem to echo Sun Tzu's sentence:

> TYWIN: Some battles are won with swords and spears, others with quills and ravens…
>
> TYRION: Walder Frey is many things, but a brave man?
>
> TYWIN: No. He never would have risked such an action if he didn't have certain assurances. Which he got from me. Do you disapprove?
>
> TYRION: I'm all for cheating. This is war. But to slaughter them at a wedding…
>
> TYWIN: [dryly] Explain to me why it is more noble to kill 10,000 men in battle than a dozen at dinner [3x3 "Myhsa"].

These words certainly mark the differences between a strategist and a simple soldier, as it is indeed true both Tywin and Walder Frey should have respected the hospitality laws, by which no one can be harmed under the roof of a man who offered bread and water to his guests. On the other hand, though, as Sun Tzu prescribes, "all warfare is based on deception. Hence, when we are able to attack, we must seem unable; when using our forces, we must appear inactive; when we are near, we must make the enemy believe we are far away; when far away, we must make him believe we are near" (1994:37).

The idea of seizing the moment to create an alliance with both the Freys and the Boltons and destroy the lines of House Stark is certainly more important than observing the laws prescribed by the crown who is in that moment endangered by the rebels. In a way, Robb Stark—in the context of the Red Wedding—seems closer to the delusion created by the saying "heroes must win" rather than to the cynical and certainly more rational perspective of Tywin. In fact, not only does he not consider the possibility of treason by Walder Frey who has been severely weakened in his goals by the unexpected wedding of the king in the North, but he also naively entered Frey's stronghold without any weapon, truly believing that he and his bannermen would be safe thanks to the laws of hospitality and the alliance with House Frey, re-established by Edmure Tully's wedding with another one of Frey's daughters. The only available option for Tywin Lannister then is to behave like the lion on the coat of arms of his House and go against any law to bring peace to the realm.

I have highlighted the figure of the lion which appears on the Lannister coat of arms because Machiavelli's *The Prince* moves a step forward from Sun Tzu's analysis of war and the battlefield to introduce elements related more to the personality of the ruler and the ability to consider the importance of divine providence. Like Sun Tzu's treatise, Machiavelli's works prescribe rules that the king, or more generally the ruler, has to observe in order to seize and maintain the position he has acquired. By living inside the court, Machiavelli was familiar with the concept of struggling for power and indeed still nowadays the adjective Machiavellian refers to someone who is cunning while using force at the same time. By reading Sun Tzu and Machiavelli, it is certainly possible to understand who will win and who will lose the Game of Thrones, and most of the time the identity of the real winners defies the readers' expectations. One of the key instructions in the *Prince* dictates that the ruler should never falter or allow himself to be caught off-guard for a second, both physically and mentally. If we focus our attention on the events narrated in *A Game of Thrones* and *A Clash of Kings*, it is indeed the disregard for this principle that dooms both Ned Stark and Robb Stark. As the new hand of the king and someone aware that Jon Arryn had been murdered by someone within the court, Ned Stark should have been more careful in choosing his allies both inside and outside the Red Keep. What he did, though, was trust the words of people who were known for their cunning such as Varys, Littlefinger and, why not, Grandmaester Pycelle, in order to defeat the Lannisters from the inside and defend the honor of House Baratheon and House Stark at the same time. Then, the fatal mistake: being honorable. Ned let down his guard and told Cersei Lannister what he had discovered to let her escape from the Capital before the king hanged her and the children for more than just treason. However, by not considering both the principle of deception on Cersei's part nor Machiavelli's rule of fighting every possible battle in the mind before starting one, Ned created the foundations for his future death. Had he not told Cersei but just the king, he would have had a better chance of winning the Game of Thrones. There is one more factor, though, that Machiavelli considers in his treatise: rulers must be both foxes and lions, but never sheep. The animal analogy here refers to the ability of a king to be both cunning and violent at the same time, but never too soft or cowardly.

> You must know there are two ways of contesting, the one by the law, the other by force; the first method is proper to men, the second to beasts; but because the first is frequently not sufficient, it is necessary to have recourse to the second. Therefore it is necessary for a prince to understand how to avail himself of the beast and the man.... A prince, therefore, being compelled knowingly to adopt the beast, ought to choose the fox and the lion; because the lion cannot defend himself against snares and the fox cannot defend himself against wolves. Therefore, it is necessary to be a fox to discover the snares and a lion to terrify the wolves. Those who rely simply on the lion do not understand what they are about [2015:92].

Martin's analogies arguably draw from Machiavelli in portraying Lannister = lion, Stark = wolf, Frey = fox, and Martell = snake. The different behavior of these Houses towards war and the outcome of the events narrated throughout the volumes of *A Song of Ice and Fire* align with the principles outlined by Machiavelli. Consider this excerpt in which a direct reference to Machiavelli arises:

> Tywin Lannister was as much fox as lion. If indeed he'd sent Ser Gregor to burn and pillage—and Ned did not doubt that he had—he'd taken care to see that he rode

under cover of night, without banners, in the guise of a common brigand. Should Riverrun strike back, Cersei and her father would insist that it had been the Tullys who broke the king's peace, not the Lannisters. The gods only knew what Robert would believe [Martin 1996:165].

The idea of Tywin being both a fox and a lion directly relates to his aptitude for warfare and rule of the Seven Kingdoms. It should be Joffrey Baratheon, though, behaving according to these principles. Tywin knows exactly what being a king means, and several times Martin makes the head of House Lannister utter that wearing a crown does not make someone a king. Even though Joffrey, namely the king of the Seven Kingdoms until the Purple Wedding, cannot perform his duty as king due to his unstable personality, it is Tywin's duty to rule the Seven Kingdoms in his place. Tywin is well aware that, even though House Lannister can rely on a vast army, brute force won't be enough to preserve the position of his family for centuries. Therefore, first during Robert's Rebellion and later for the Red Wedding, he allies himself with the fox, Walder Frey, to defeat the Starks, who, like wolves, are marching in pack. By destroying the alphas of that pack, the lion and the fox prevent the king from being deposed and secure a vantage point for the wars to come—as much as defeating the Martells, the snakes, with the help of the Lannister army, prevented the Freys from losing their stronghold and therefore their power in the Seven Kingdoms. One must not misunderstand, however, Machiavelli's words: a ruler must be a fox and a lion, but also compassionate; the real principle lies with the ability to change into the one or the other according to the situation and the opportunity of the moment.

In his essay "Playing the Game of Thrones: Some Lessons from Machiavelli" Marcus Schulzke considers other aspects and hidden references to Machiavelli in *A Song of Ice and Fire*. In particular, Schulzke reflects upon the importance given by Machiavelli to two different qualities: Virtù and Fortuna. Machiavelli argues that these two forces determine the outcome of power-struggles. Virtù is the skill one needs to take power and keep it, but what this skill actually consists of continually changes based on the circumstances. However, the Virtù described by Machiavelli and highlighted by Schulzke is not the same thing as virtue, since the latter refers to a person with moral qualities such as honesty, courage, loyalty, and so on. Someone showing Virtù can have all these qualities but be able to show them only when the situation requires it. On the other hand, the word Fortuna, translatable with the word luck, considers all the events which cannot be controlled or expected, regardless of their nature being potentially good or bad. Consider, for example, when Tyrion has Bronn on his side during his imprisonment within Lysa Arryn's stronghold. It is indeed just a matter of Fortuna that the sellsword decides to join the Lannister's side in order to get more money (1x6 "A Golden Crown"). Fortuna was in favor of Tyrion in that case, but this force is such an unreliable ally that Machiavelli suggests to use just Virtù to achieve our goals and be grateful for Fortuna when it is in our favor: "Fortune is a woman, and if you wish to master her, you must strike and beat her, and you will see that she allows herself to be more easily vanquished by the rash and the violent than by those who proceed more slowly and coldly" (2015:45). Machiavelli of course refers to Fortune as a woman because men are happy when Fortune agrees with them in their lives, while they are unhappy when "she" turns her back to them.

In the context of *A Song of Ice and Fire* and *Game of Thrones*, Martin seems to reinterpret Fortuna in a way that recalls a famous Italian novelist, Giovanni Verga, who changed the dynamic within Fortuna to that of a force that seems to create only bad consequences. In his famous novel, *The Malavoglia* (1881), Giovanni Verga narrates the fate of a family of fishers who have a boat called *Divine Providence*. Instead of relying on their Virtù, they leave everything to luck and, contextually, to the will of their boat: if the *Divine Providence* reaches a place where there is a bank of fishes, they will be able to make a lot of money by selling it, otherwise it will be another day without food. This attitude, however, brings them to the point of losing almost everything in their lives, including the life of some family members who decide to leave the family and move to the city, where they will face a life they are not prepared for and cannot survive.

An analysis of *A Song of Ice and Fire* illuminates how Machiavelli and Verga's conception of Fortuna talk to each other. In fact, it is only due to Fortuna that Tyrion finds Bronn as his champion for the trial, but in the long haul the chance given by Fortuna does not repay well: in fact, Bronn's testimony during Tyrion's second trial, the one that he must face for the alleged murder of King Joffrey, offers Cersei and the jury the possibility of sentencing Tyrion to death. Tyrion will of course ask for a champion, but this time Bronn will not join him, because the jury paid him enough to refuse. The same principle can be applied to Ned Stark, to whom Fortuna gives the chance of becoming hand of the king and future protector of the realm: this luck appears at first to be something important, an opportunity that will give him the possibility of freeing the court from the people dismantling it with their plots; but the turn of Fortuna and Ned's inability to use Virtù deliver him to the executioner's block.

In my view, Martin indeed gives great importance to the Machiavellian principles of Fortuna and Virtù as much as to the ability of being a fox and a lion at the same time. While considering the reasons for being both a lion and a fox, in the sixth chapter of *The Prince* Machiavelli reminds the Prince that all these principles have to be applied while playing a bigger "game" called "strategia di potere," or "strategies of power," consisting of being aware that the Prince himself won't be the only individual interested in taking the power and everything that comes with it. By warning the ruler about the danger of losing the position he has acquired and advising him on the ways to prevent this from happening and to gain even more power, Machiavelli lays the foundations for a different and certainly modern interpretation of power struggles.

Therefore, I would like to consider an additional text that relies more on economy and its theories rather than advice given to rulers. In *A Song of Ice and Fire*, in fact, there are some characters who seem to avoid the principle of Fortuna and play a game bigger than the one potentially possible by solely relying on their Virtù. These two characters are Varys and Lord Baelish, also known as Littlefinger. It seems, in fact, as if Littlefinger and Varys are aware of the rules presented in the game theory of John Nash. The name "game theory" comes from the book *Theory of Games and Economic Behavior* written in 1944 by John von Neumann and Oskar Morgenstern who tried to define in mathematical terms the way in which people behave in a situation where they could win, lose, or split something at stake. This theory can be applied to various contexts, from chess to global investments, and used to predict their potential outcomes. The essential prerequisites for applying the theory to different scenarios are as follows:

- The contestants play in order to win and maximize their winnings.
- Each contestant can make a limited number of choices.
- Each decision made by a contestant during the game has positive or negative consequences.
- The game can be cooperative if the contestants agree to take joint decisions in order to split their winnings, or non-cooperative if everyone wants to be the only winner [Durlauf and Blume 2010:29].

John Nash, in his doctoral thesis called "Non-Cooperative Games," argued that in a game with a limited number of decisions there is a point at which each contestant or player knows the strategy of the others and doesn't change strategy—instead each player will do anything to let everyone benefit from all the strategies (1950:288).

The key element in this theory is the Nash equilibrium, which focuses on the on the so-called alternative value. In fact, in a non-cooperative game all contestants will use their strategies to defeat the others and obtain the final prize. However, according to game theory, if all of them try to win by all means possible, just one of them will obtain the final prize. In fact, by the time someone reaches the payoff, the winner will have been irremediably weakened by the other contestants' strategies and the others already defeated. If one of the contestants decides not to make a play for the final prize, but to compete instead for the second or third one, the chances of winning will automatically rise and perhaps help that player win the final prize.

With these principles in mind, it is possible to glimpse in these strategies the real game played by Varys and Littlefinger in the Game of Thrones. In fact, none of the heirs to the throne survives the War of the Five Kings, as their sole aim is to conquer King's Landing and the Iron Throne in order to rule the Seven Kingdoms. On the other hand, while this war goes on, if figures like Walder Frey seem to evoke a cooperative game in which contestants ally and play the role of the double agent for the other, figures such as Littlefinger and Varys compete for "alternative values" with their manipulation of information and networks.

For example, Littlefinger possesses the ideal form of subjectivity to operate in the political world of Martin's story. Crucially, he does not desire power, but holds power in and of his position within networked conspiracies. After he has successfully orchestrated the assassination of King Joffrey, his ally and sovereign within the feudal hierarchy, he concedes that he had no motive for the murder, but presents that as its own justification, for the confusion it causes. Here, information is an amorphous substance to be modulated and deployed. Contingent to this, the schemer is no longer the early modern malcontent or the Machiavellian prince, attempting to seek revenge or to gain status, but an amorphous figure in and of himself. In Season Four, when Sansa asks Littlefinger whether he killed Joffrey, he replies:

LITTLEFINGER: Did I kill Joffrey? I've been in the Vale for weeks.
SANSA: I know it was you.
LITTLEFINGER: And who helped me with this conspiracy?
SANSA: Well, there was Ser Dontos. You used him to get me out of King's Landing, but you would never trust him to kill the king.
LITTLEFINGER:—Why not?
SANSA:—Because you're too smart to trust a drunk.
LITTLEFINGER: Then perhaps it was your husband.
SANSA: No.
LITTLEFINGER: How do you know?
SANSA: I just do.
LITTLEFINGER: You're right. He wasn't involved in Joffrey's death. But you were. Do you remember that lovely necklace Dontos gave you? I don't suppose you noticed that a stone was missing after the feast.
SANSA: The poison. I don't understand. The Lannisters gave you wealth, power. Joffrey made you the Lord of Harrenhal.
LITTLEFINGER: A man with no motive is a man no one suspects. Always keep your foes confused. If they don't know who you are or what you want, they can't know what you plan to do next [4x4 "Oathkeeper"].

Baelish, then, is not only aiming for the final prize, the Iron Throne; he also hides his strategy behind a veil of false information, such as being on his way to Harrenhal during Joffrey's wedding. The reader discovers through the eyes of Sansa that Littlefinger was actually waiting for her arrival on a ship at the harbor. In this way, by limiting and manipulating the amount of information received by the Crown, Littlefinger keeps his plans secret and at the same time gains prizes that increase his "alternative values." In particular, as specified above, Petyr Baelish first obtains Harrenhall, and then is nominated Protector of the Vale. He competes for it, he plays his strategy, and he wins, but as Nash argues, such a player might even be able to obtain the final prize. Littlefinger is definitely aiming for it. In fact, in a conversation with Sansa Stark, now disguised as Baelish's daughter Alayne, he explains why he needs her to be his daughter and why he will make her marry a minor lord of the Vale:

> "So tell me, sweetling—why is Harry the Heir?" Her eyes widened. "He is not Lady Waynwood's heir. He's Robert's heir. If Robert were to die..."
> Petyr arched an eyebrow. "When Robert dies. Our poor brave Sweetrobin is such a sickly boy, it is only a matter of time. When Robert dies, Harry the Heir becomes Lord Harrold, Defender of the Vale and Lord of the Eyrie. Jon Arryn's bannermen will never love me, nor our silly, shaking Robert, but they will love their Young Falcon.... So those are your gifts from me, my sweet Sansa ... Harry, the Eyrie, and Winterfell" [Martin 2005:605].

If the next target is Winterfell, we could assume that Baelish is planning to create a new alliance against the Iron Throne, an alliance between Winterfell, Harrenhall, the Vale, and the Iron Islands that will overcome the Lannister's armies and conquer King's Landing again.

In some ways, the dominant dynamics in *A Song of Ice and Fire* is an exaggeration and ultimately an exposition of what happens today behind the curtains of politics, such as the terrific amount of strategies within every single party to create an impeachment or to get rid of a deputy who seems to favor one party more than another.

However, perhaps Baelish won't reach the Nash equilibrium in which everyone wins, but Varys will. Varys's strategy of restoring a Targaryen dynasty to the throne with a king whom everyone loves is the safest choice for the kingdom, a choice that will create or re-establish that "equilibrium" described by Nash.

In conclusion, although in many high fantasy works the forces of Good will always overcome the forces of Evil, an analysis of *A Song of Ice and Fire* and *Game of Thrones* from the perspective of Sun Tzu, Machiavelli, and Nash reveals a different argument. What Martin does with his readers is disguise the lucky events created by Fortuna as the "natural" fate of those who perform good deeds, only to later reveal the deception by ending the lives of those characters with an unexpected turn of events and favoring others who have acted differently in the bigger scheme. In Martin's world, all characters are players, and only those who know how to fight every battle in their minds before starting one will achieve their goals but, most of all, only those who understand the principles of real politics will succeed in winning the Game of Thrones.

NOTE

1. Tywin had already lost two battles on the Kingsway against Robb Stark who had better devised his strategies.

REFERENCES

Durlauf, Steven N., and Lawrence E. Blume. 2010. *Game Theory*. Basingstoke: Palgrave Macmillan.
Machiavelli, Niccolò. 2015. *Il Principe*. Rome: Rizzoli.
Martin, George R.R. 1996. *A Game of Thrones*. New York: Bantam.
Martin, George R.R. 2005. *A Feast for Crows*. New York: Bantam.
Schulzke, Marcus. 2012. "Playing the Game of Thrones: Some Lessons from Machiavelli." In *Game of Thrones and Philosophy: Logic Cuts Deeper than Swords*, edited by Henry Owen Jacoby, 33–48. Hoboken, NJ: Wiley.
Sun-tzu. 1994. *The Art of War*. Translated by Ralph D. Sawyer with the collaboration of Mei-chün Lee Sawyer. Boulder, CO: Westview Press.

Raven: Dragons

LINDSEY MANTOAN

In 2011, George R.R. Martin explained the way Daenerys's dragons function as a weapon of war: "Dragons are the nuclear deterrent, and only [Daenerys Targaryen] has them, which in some ways makes her the most powerful person in the world" (Westmyer 2014). Dany has been by turns eager and reticent to use her dragons—and the moments when she's been most inclined to mount Drogon and light the world on fire have been deterred by counsel from Tyrion (6x9 "Battle of the Bastards") and Jon Snow (7x4 "Spoils of War"). When she *has* used her dragons to conquer territory and people, such as in her campaign against the Slave Cities, she then must confront their limitations: dragons are not useful when it comes to governing, and the devastation they wreak creates resentment and ill will among the people she now wishes to rule. Indeed, according to Timothy Westmyer, who writes for *The Bulletin*, an anti–nuclear weapons organization,

> Several fans compare Daenerys' struggle [in Meereen] to feed her people and end a homegrown insurgency to America's experience in Iraq and the Soviet Union's adventures in Afghanistan. In those theaters, nuclear weapons were ill-suited to achieving specific foreign policy goals. Daenerys ends up relying on her army to conduct counterinsurgency operations and diplomacy to reach an uneasy peace with her neighbors [Westmyer 2014].

Daenerys's hesitation to deploy her dragons once in Westeros results in disaster for her quest to capture the Iron Throne: rather than a swift campaign that ends in decisive victory, Dany instead loses battles and allies. She chafes against the leash holding her and her dragons back until she embarks on an ill-advised journey north of the wall and loses Viserion to the Night King. Michael Shurkin of the Rand Corporation describes Dany's situation thus:

Because Daenerys views herself as an emancipator and does not wish to be "queen of the ashes," she holds back, seeking victory through a more limited, proportionate use of force. So far in the show, Daenerys' idealism comes at a high price. She squanders the opportunity to win a quick and decisive victory, loses allies and finds herself having to play a much longer and more difficult game than she would have otherwise— possibly with more aggregate bloodshed by the time she's done [Shurkin 2017].

The tension between Dany and her advisors about how and when to deploy dragons is what war theorists would call the conflict between just war and political realism. Writing in 1874, Carl Clausewitz (who famously said, "War is a mere continuation of policy by other means," often misquoted as "War is politics by other means") wrote that "to introduce into the philosophy of War itself a principle of moderation would be an absurdity" (Clausewitz [1874] 2003). Essentially, Clausewitz argues that any degree of restraint in war produces higher cost in the long run—human, material, financial— because it prolongs the conflict. This notion—that the best approach to war means doing whatever it takes to end a conflict quickly—is called political realism, and it certainly has its adherents in Westeros, starting with Aerys the Conqueror and ending (at least for now) with Cersei Lannister.

The competing school of thought, just war theory, holds that war must be a last resort and proportional. Noncombatants must not be targeted and the fighters on one side must use only the minimum amount of force necessary to win. Collateral damage must likewise be kept to a minimum. Based on Tyrion and Jon's advice to Dany ("You're talking about destroying cities … I'd like to suggest an alternate approach," Tyrion says to Dany in "Battle of the Bastards" [6x9]; "If you use [dragons] to melt castles and burn cities, you're not different—you're more of the same" Jon says to Dany in "Spoils of War" [7x4]), they might be said to be just war adherents.

And yet, just war theory also requires that a party not engage in combat without a high probability of success. This tenet might seem to contradict rules of minimal force: success is more easily assured if the force exerted against an enemy is sure to outmatch their response. Shurkin elaborates, "This is why, tactically speaking, most military leaders and planners invariably seek what today's military calls 'overmatch,' meaning one fights only when success is virtually guaranteed, usually through overwhelming numbers or firepower" (2017).

Dany cannot be said to possess "overmatch" any longer, considering the Night King now has a zombie ice dragon at his command, and Cersei and Qyburn are no doubt busy crafting more scorpions to bring down any dragons that might return south with Dany. In the real world, the threat of nuclear warfare is held in check by deterrence—by both (or many) sides possessing nuclear weapons and the rationality to never use them. According to Westmyer,

Optimists who welcome nuclear weapons as a stabilizing influence insist that by their very nature, these arms cause rational leaders of stable regimes to maintain strict control over their state's arsenals and moderate their behavior—or risk retaliation. That prompts the question: What happens when nuclear weapons are in the hands of irrational leaders, less than stable countries, or non-state actors? [Westmyer 2014].

Indeed, Sophie Gilbert points out in *The Atlantic* just this challenge for Jon, Dany, and their allies: "Possessing such powerful weapons only works as a deterrent to war if your enemies are similarly appalled by the cost of using them, and Cersei in particular seems unlikely to shed tears for civilians" (2017). And while she might not have her own dragon, Cersei has demonstrated more than once her capacity to use a weapon of mass destruction— first, when she ordered the mass production of wildfire before the Battle of Blackwater (2x9 "Blackwater") and then when she lit huge parts of King's Landing on fire with it in "Winds of Winter" (6x10). Of course, the Night King likewise will show no restraint when it comes to deploying his dragon as a weapon of war. If Dany and Jon are smart, they'll put some of their people to work building their own scorpions, these ones tipped with dragonglass.

Dany, Jon, and their allies now face two irrational enemies, neither of which will be deterred by the two dragons/WMD that Dany possess. There's no hope that any of the zombies under the Night King's command will demonstrate the restraint that nuclear deterrence usually inspires (and relies on). There might be more hope in King's Landing; Cersei's use of wildfire has been indirect, with others doing the dirty work of lighting it for her. It's possible that in the human-human wars to come, Cersei will order the deployment of massive amounts of wildfire and whoever receives the order will rebel. This has happened before; her twin refused such an order from his Mad King, choosing instead to become the Kingslayer. Many fan theories propose that the past will repeat itself, with Cersei shouting, "Burn them all!" and Jaime adding "Queenslayer" to his many titles. While Cersei has vowed not to join the war between humans and White Walkers, the wildfire she possesses could sway the odds in that conflict, and war theorists in both camps might deem that battle an appropriate venue to deploy a weapon of mass destruction.

Wildfire burns at the ground level; it's dirty but effective, and it doesn't mind a bit of water, as demonstrated during the Battle of the Blackwater. Unlike the drone, the missile, the warg, or the dragon, wildfire is a chemical weapon par excellence. And it could burn right through that army of White Walkers.

And battles fought on the ground would more easily secure Tywin Lannister's stamp of approval. His approach to dragon-weapons is "dragons haven't won a war in 300 years. Armies win them all the time" (4x6 "The Laws of Gods and Men"). Now that the massive threat posed by Dany's drag-

ons has been weakened, Tywin's words are likely more salient; while the dragons battle each other in the Skies of the North, the armies on the ground will
determine who wins the zombie–human war. And, while Dany (and probably
Jon) can strategically fly dragons around the battle for King's Landing that
will likely ensue, the threat of scorpions will keep the dragons from ensuring
a quick and decisive victory. Again, the ground battle will be determinative.

Dany's dragons *were* like nuclear weapons. And the Loot Train battle of
Season Seven (7x4 "Spoils of War") demonstrated just how terrible they can
be on the battlefield. But they no longer function as deterrents or even as the
aerial weapons they once were. Irrational actors in the real world, too, are
threatening to undermine the stabilizing effect that mutually assured destruction has had on the world order since the Cold War. Some say those who
control the skies—those with airpower—win the war; but in the end life isn't
lived in the sky and battles are only and ever won or lost on the ground.

REFERENCES

Clausewitz, Carl. 1874 [2013]. *On War.* Trans. Colonel J. J. Graham. Project Gutenberg.
    Accessed 20 April 2018. http://www.gutenberg.org/files/1946/1946-h/1946-h.htm.
Gilbert, Sophie. 2017. "*Game of Thrones*: Dragons are the Nuclear Option." *The Atlantic*, 7
    August. Accessed 4 April 2018. https://www.theatlantic.com/entertainment/archive/
    2017/08/game-of-thrones-dragons-and-the-nuclear-option/536067/.
Shurkin, Michael. 2017. "*Game of Thrones*' Dragons, Nuclear Weapons, and Winning What-
    ever the Cost." *The Rand Blog*, 24 August. Accessed 6 April 2018. https://www.rand.org/
    blog/2017/08/game-of-thrones-dragons-nuclear-weapons-and-winning.html.
Westmyer, Timothy. 2014. "Game of Thrones: The Dragons and Nuclear Weapons Nexus."
    The Bulletin, 2 June. Accessed 2 April 2018. https://thebulletin.org/game-thrones-drag-
    ons-and-nuclear-weapons-nexus7217.

Raven: Sansa

LINDSEY MANTOAN

Kristin Iverson's 2014 article "The Problem with Sansa Stark: In Defense of One of the Most Hated Characters in *Game of Thrones*," which appeared in *Brooklyn Magazine*, details some of the vitriol leveled by fans at Sansa during the first three seasons ("Most people with whom I've spoken have this to say, 'She's the fucking worst. She should have died instead of her direwolf.'"), and attempts to recuperate Sansa's character. Iverson explains that fans unfairly malign Sansa for being "achingly passive," and argues that "there remains in Sansa an inherent humanity and an ability to relate to other people that few of the other, more loved characters have. This is what gives us hope for Sansa and demonstrates a resilience that is essential to survival." Survival, in Sansa's case, has meant enduring physical and emotional trauma, and part of the audience's antipathy for her, I would suggest, comes from the way audiences are often conditioned to punish victims—especially female ones.

I also want to suggest that Sansa's character does important work toward re-gendering strength and power in this medieval world, and our contemporary one. Most of the other characters in the narrative reinforce the conflation of strength with masculinity—even the female characters. Catherine Pugh writes in this book about the ways in which Yara's gender performance is masculine, Audrey Moyce explains Brienne's adherence to a chivalric code and her status as a female knight, and Carol Parrish Jamison describes Arya as a consummate performer, but one who always retains her tomboy persona. These women all possess power, but they choose a more masculine gender performance as a way to project strength. Cersei, as Rose Butler writes in her essay on costume, projects masculinity as she amasses power; once she becomes Queen of Westeros, her attire emulates her father and her dresses include military epaulettes and ornamentation. And Daenerys exchanges dresses for pants as her power grows—a move that somehow retains or even increases her sexiness. Overwhelmingly, the women with power in Westeros (and Essos) take steps to amplify their masculinity as a show of authority and strength. Sansa, however, refuses to view masculinity as necessary for power, and in so doing, she reveals the fallacy of conflating the two.

Unlike her siblings and most of the other women in positions of authority, Sansa is achingly human. She draws strength from her family and her sense of self—she does not rely on magic to protect her. Dany has dragons, Cersei has Ser Robert Strong/Gregor Clegane, Bran wargs into animals and trees, and Arya wears other people's faces. Without access to magic, Sansa relies on cleverness and emotional strength. Confronting Littlefinger after having survived Ramsay's torture (6x5 "The Door"), Sansa demonstrates that some confrontations can be won without dragon fire, wildfire, or brute strength. By forcing Littlefinger to imagine the ways in which Ramsay tortured her, Sansa flips the balance of power between them—an important move given that in our contemporary world, women who come forward about surviving rape are often further victimized by their audience. Megan Garber finds that Sansa's recitation of Ramsay's torture "is a telling moment of verbal vigilante-ism. Because Sansa has, in her current state, very little recourse for Ramsay's abuse, and no way to undo the past. But she has her words, and she will weaponize them as best she can" (Garber 2016). On its face, this scene seems focused on the past, but Sansa cleverly establishes conditions that will benefit her in the future. Through winning this confrontation with Littlefinger, Sansa ensures he will respond when she calls for his aid on the eve of the battle for Winterfell.

Sansa's resilience and her style of leadership demonstrate that one need not abandon femininity to possess and project strength, and that she need not rely on sexuality to earn allies. While the other power players in the game of thrones jockey for position, Sansa focuses on feeding and clothing her people during the coming winter (see, for example, 7x3 "The Queen's Justice" and 7x4 "Spoils of War"), moves that have positioned her as a threat to Jon's claim on the North, whether or not she has any desire to supplant him. She might not have fought the Battle of the Bastards, but she won it—and, importantly, she won it without compromising her integrity. In a *Vox* article, Aja Romano points out that "Sansa has never used her position to manipulate other characters, seek power over other characters, or enact revenge simply for revenge's sake" (Romano 2017). She promises Littlefinger nothing for his aid at the Battle of the Bastards, and that includes herself, distinguishing her from Daenerys, who cunningly uses her status as a potential wife to court allies, and Cersei, who uses a marriage promise to gain Euron Greyjoy's support.

Certainly, in the world of *Game of Thrones*, violence, masculinity, and power are tightly interwoven, and most of the women who attain some degree of power do so through aggression. Sansa unsettles these relationships. She doesn't embrace violence the way Cersei, Dany, Arya, and Brienne do, but neither does she shy away from it. Her killing style might be viewed as more feminine, since she doesn't wield the sword herself, but rather, kills indirectly through Littlefinger's army and Ramsay's dogs. Nevertheless, Sansa blurs this distinction between direct and indirect violence. At the end of Season Seven, she sentences Littlefinger to die, and Arya executes the order. Ned Stark's philosophy that the person who passes the sentence ought to swing the sword would seem to be violated here: Sansa nods, and Arya slices. And yet, Elie Mystal points out that Arya *is* the sword, and Sansa swings her (Mystal 2017). The killing is both a collaboration between the sisters and a fully embraced reunion after some truly awkward moments between Sansa and Arya (especially when Sansa finds Arya's bag of faces in 7x6 "Beyond the Wall"). In this scene, the remaining Stark children become a pack, with Sansa as their leader. She presides over the trial of Littlefinger, and watches as his blood coats the floor of Winterfell's Great Hall. She enacts justice, not excessive bloodshed, having learned strategic lessons from her mentors Littlefinger and Cersei without internalizing their lust for violence or love of power for power's sake.

As one of her earliest mentors, Cersei tells Sansa that "Tears aren't a woman's only weapon. The best one's between your legs. Learn how to use it" (2x9 "Blackwater"). And yet Sansa refuses to seduce or flirt with men as a method of manipulation. Romano finds that "Sansa manages to survive and work to regain her family's power without weaponizing her femininity" (2017). She might not promise or hint at marriage or sex, but she does deploy feminized activities that she excels at as essential political tools. In Season Six, as she and Jon prepare to leave Castle Black to court allies for their attack on the Boltons, she puts her needlepoint skills to work crafting a new dress with the direwolf sigil for herself and a wolf-pelt cloak for Jon, telling him, "I made it like the one father used to wear" (6x5 "The Door"). This significant moment demonstrates "the strength and power of her house by wearing the direwolf sigil," and also sends a message about Jon's "position as a member of House Stark: the leader" (Mina 2016). The Stark family benefits from Sansa's needlework every bit as much as it needs Arya's Needlework.

Writing just a few days before the final episode of Season Seven aired, Aja Romano suggested that "Sansa uses traditionally feminine traits of passive acceptance, appeasement, and tactics of mediation in order to stall her enemies, delay action, and divert attention from herself. In the game of thrones, Sansa plays by refusing to play, again and again" (2017). The final episode (7x7 "The Dragon and the Wolf"), however, seems to challenge this assertion; Sansa has assumed a leadership role at Winterfell, earned the loyalty of many Northern houses, and taken out a major power player in the great game. She's armed with two powerful weapons, Arya and Bran, and their alliance in Littlefinger's trial seems to foreshadow how closely the siblings will work together in the wars to come. Daenerys might give speeches about breaking the wheel of a corrupt system, but Sansa's on the ground doing the hard work of governing, meting out justice, and feeding and clothing her people.

REFERENCES

Garber, Megan. 2016. "*Game of Thrones*: Sansa Stark Will Be Heard." *The Atlantic*, 23 May. Accessed 3 March 2018. https://www.theatlantic.com/entertainment/archive/2016/05/game-of-thrones-and-the-cycle-of-violence/483920/.

Iverson, Kristin. 2014. "The Problem with Sansa Stark: In Defense of One of the Most Hated Characters in Game of Thrones." *Brooklyn Magazine*, 4 April. Accessed 3 March 2018. http://www.bkmag.com/2014/04/04/the-problem-with-sansa-stark-in-defense-of-one-of-the-most-hated-characters-in-game-of-thrones/.

Mina, Courtney. 2016. "Why Sansa Stark & Jon Snow's Direwolf Outfits Matter Even More Than You Realized." *Bustle*, 24 May. Accessed 3 March 2018. https://www.bustle.com/articles/162782-why-sansa-stark-jon-snows-direwolf-outfits-matter-even-more-than-you-realized-photos.

Mystal, Elie. 2017. Reply to Lindsey Mantoan's Facebook post. 28 August.

Romano, Aja. 2017. "Game of Thrones Season 7: What Sansa's Continued Survival Means for the Future of Westeros." *Vox*, 25 August. Accessed 3 March 2018. https://www.vox.com/culture/2017/8/25/16185986/game-of-thrones-sansa-survival-passive-strategy.

Brienne and Jaime's Queer Intimacy

AUDREY MOYCE

In his essay "The Friend," Giorgio Agamben writes that "to recognize someone as a friend means not being able to recognize him as a 'something'" (2009:31). He also notes the difficulty in discussing friendship in philosophical terms because of the etymological closeness of the two words: *philo* means "friend," after all. But perhaps this is apt, he muses, since the defining quality of friendship as he sees it is a proximity that "resists both representation and conceptualization," the way two people touching foreheads find their vision of each other blurred (2009:31). When Jaime Lannister and Brienne of Tarth first encounter one another, they are nothing but an assortment of various "somethings"—Kingslayer, captive, committer of incest; beast, freak of nature, wannabe. By the end of their journey from the Riverlands to King's Landing, however, these labels have become almost un-seeable, both in their view of each other and of themselves. Eclipsing those old labels are new ones: loyal, worthy, ethical, empathic, strong, capable. Jaime, Brienne.

Game of Thrones has thoroughly developed several unlikely partnerships over its 67 released episodes. As Inbar Shaham notes, these "odd couples" result from the showrunners' choice to develop character through relationships, to compensate for the loss of the books' point-of-view technique (Shaham 2015:49). One of the series' great achievements is its capacity to subtly render so many character pairs that are rich in their complexity—especially given the relatively short amount of time we spend with any given pair of characters. Furthermore, several of these bonds do not easily fit within the categories that define the world of the show, like family, alliance, and loyalty. Tywin Lannister and Arya Stark, Petyr Baelish and Sansa Stark, Tyrion Lannister and Varys, Daenerys Targaryen and Ser Jorah Mormont, Sam Tarly and Jon Snow, Gilly and Shireen Baratheon, Ser Davos Seaworth and Shireen,

Ser Davos and Gendry, Gendry and Arya, Daenerys and Missandei, Arya and Sandor "The Hound" Clegane, Brienne and Podrick Payne.

Many of these relationships specifically explore queer models of kinship and other modes of intimacy that contradict the strictly regimented norms of how to perform man- or womanhood in Westeros. Men act "maternally" (The Hound, Tywin), they defer to girls or women as mentors (Davos, Podrick), men find closeness with men and women with women (Tyrion/Varys, Daenerys/Missandei). But the arc of Brienne and Jaime's relationship proves a particularly rich site of queered intimacy, due to the quality and degree of closeness they achieve, and their respective performances of gender.

In "Sex in Public," Lauren Berlant and Michael Warner sketch out an aspirational vision for "queer culture building" (1998:548). Their utopia is not just a world where queer sex is safe; they desire a safe zone for "the changed possibilities of identity, intelligibility, publics, culture, and sex that appear when the heterosexual couple is no longer the referent or the privileged example of sexual culture" (548). While Brienne and Jaime would fit in a heterosexual arrangement, the course of their relationship deviates from one in shifting ways. Inbar Shaham (2015) argues that their arc adheres to the generic beginnings of a romantic comedy,[1] but Agamben's sketch of Nicomachean friendship illuminates the ways this arc does *not* fit into a typical love plot.

"Friend," Agamben writes, has etymological ties to philosophy, but it also shares a condition with philosophical terms: the word has no literal or primary meaning. It is pure connotation and "simply signif[ies] being" (2009:30). There is no reference to particularity and no set of external qualities implied. Brienne and Jaime find a bond that may or may not include romance, but as Sean T. Collins points out in his assessment of their relationship, this is beside the point: the intimacy they find is of a different and arguably deeper quality (Collins 2016). Because of the unique way they come to their friendship, and the unusual way they each perform their gender, Brienne and Jaime thus provide a "structure of understanding" that reads as incoherent under heteronormativity (Berlant and Warner 2009:548). Brienne and Jaime's relationship trajectory invents a queer space of mutual recognition in which they can each overcome shame felt at their wrongness within the privileged logic of heteronormativity.

In his essay on Martin's *A Song of Ice and Fire*, Mark Buchanan discusses Jaime and Brienne as foils to one another: Jaime is a typical chivalrous knight in appearance but not behavior, while Brienne acts the proper knight but lacks the requisite title, appearance, and gender (2014:1). He argues that Martin subverts the trope of the knight—as seen in both traditional "Tolkienesque" fantasy and medieval and post-medieval lore—to create characters who are "aware of the role of gender in their lives and how they must manipulate society to achieve their goals" (14). This holds for *Game of Thrones* as well, and then some: not only do Brienne and Jaime serve as mutual reminders of the other's failure to fit into traditional knighthood, they also pull each other into a friendship because of those failures.

First Meeting

Four touchstones of Brienne and Jaime's arc, specifically in its initial gestation in and around Season Three, sketch the closeness that springs upon them, and how it finds purchase in ways that are new to each of their personal experiences, and to the conventional mores of friendship under heteronormativity both within and beyond *Game of Thrones*. Berlant and Warner write: "Heteronormativity is more than ideology, or prejudice, or phobia against gays and lesbians; it is produced in almost every aspect of the forms and arrangements of social life" (1998:554–55). Heteronormativity in Westeros polices Jaime and Brienne's every move, and the confusing fact that they each fit certain norms and not others form a constant source of shame.

Long before they even meet, Jaime is ridden with shame. Though most obviously for his title as Kingslayer from having murdered King Aerys while serving on his Kingsguard, some of Jaime's shame also connects to the way he performs masculinity. His performance is far less physically deviant than Brienne's; he is a renowned swordsman and the youngest Kingsguard member in the history of Westeros (2x8 "Prince of Winterfell"). Even so, much is made in the books of his physical beauty, and the show often portrays his chosen status—a subordinate warrior who disavows all titles and rights to produce an heir—as dishonorable, especially in the eye of his father and master strategist Tywin Lannister. Moreover, the woman he has sacrificed so much for, who is also his twin sister, constantly dominates him in a way that would only be seen as emasculating within a heteronormative society.

Brienne, on the other hand, is the more obvious gender misperformer. She actively wants to be a knight, despite the fact that women are unable to. Our first introduction to her character is when she fights for a spot on Renly Baratheon's Kingsguard; for the duration of the fight, everyone thinks she is a man, not simply because a helmet covers her face, but because of her skill and also her large size. Brienne is masculine in a way that does not seem connected to self-fashioning—before it dawned on her that other people saw her as "beastly," she enjoyed the idea of being considered beautiful. As she relates to Podrick in Season Five, her father threw her a ball to arrange her betrothal (5x3 "High Sparrow"). When everyone competed for her affections, she was at first flattered, until she realized they were all just trying to see who could "bed the beast" first. She expresses hatred for her appearance, and seems resigned to her looks making her a wrong sort of woman, probably excluded from the opportunity for love.

That said, Brienne's non-normativity does not exclusively harm her. Subtracting the effect her masculine appearance has on other people, and the scorn she endures from it, she moves through the world and acts mostly like a man. She is the protector, not the one needing protection (such as Catelyn). She is the jailer, not the prisoner (Jaime). This makes her an outcast since she is still obviously a woman (as opposed to her actively hiding it), but it affords her an independence and removal from the rules and expectations she would otherwise have.

Lastly, it is Brienne's unique position as a woman in a "man's role" that enables her to further rebel against the rules of gender in the Westerosi world. As a woman who is not only removed from the economy of marriage, motherhood, and fruitful alliances between houses, but also exempt from the sort of bannerman etiquette that dictates the loyalties of male knights, she is free to choose to whom she declares loyalty. When Catelyn saves her from being wrongly accused of Renly's death, she says she wants to swear her loyalty to Catelyn. Catelyn protests, saying she is no battle commander, but Brienne responds, "No, but you have courage. Not battle courage perhaps but.... I don't know ... a kind of woman's courage" (2x5 "The Ghost of Harrenhal"). Her phrasing gives away her indoctrination in heteronormative ideology, yet Catelyn, a woman, is who she chooses.

And as it happens, it is this relationship that catalyzes Jaime and Brienne's meeting, their first touchstone. Because Brienne is under Lady Catelyn's orders but *not* King Robb's, they are also cast as co-conspirators. Jaime is a prisoner, but they are forced onto the same team when both are captured by a bannerman for House Stark via House Bolton: Locke. And thus, in completely inadvertent fashion, Jaime and Brienne connect. Locke catches them mid-fight—Jaime has gotten ahold of a sword and though his wrists are bound together, he attempts to kill Brienne so he might escape. This fight gives them an opportunity to fully gauge one another's skill, and seems to provide a first instance of Jaime having any respect toward Brienne. This forms a sort of net where they are caught between alliances—Jaime and Brienne are still pulled toward their opposing houses, but they are also in a newly invented web of their own wherein they are definitely against Locke. The fight further allows a visceral and mutual recognition, thus accidentally opening up a connection between them.

A Helping Hand

The second touchstone in Brienne and Jaime's arc follows shortly after their capture by Locke and his men (3x3 "Walk of Punishment"). They are both imprisoned, but while Jaime is an incredibly valuable hostage, Brienne is next to dispensable. Jaime tells her to prepare herself for rape, and a lot of it.

That night, Brienne is roughly dragged away—though she lands some punches first—and we hear her awful screams: actor Gwendoline Christie finds an especially affecting shriek that conveys the extent of the violations Brienne is about to receive off-screen. We watch Jaime listening, tied up against a tree, and despite their previous antagonism he intervenes by speaking to Locke, the commander of the group. "You know why they call Tarth the Sapphire Isle?" he asks. Tarth produces every sapphire in Westeros, he says; if they return Brienne unharmed, Selwyn Tarth will pay her weight in sapphire as ransom.

This is a lie, of course. Afterward Brienne confronts Jaime: "It's called the Sapphire Isle because of the blue of its water. You knew that. Why did you help me?" Jaime remains silent, and we are left to guess his explanation.

Maybe he recalled what he had said to Brienne earlier, and empathy seizes him: if he were a woman—perhaps a particular woman with whom he can surprisingly identify, who is also a warrior, and who values one's personal definition of honor above all else—he would rather die. Reading Aristotle's *Nicomachean Ethics*, Agamben points to the idea that a friend is an other self (*heteros autos*). "The friend is not an other I, but an otherness immanent to selfness, a becoming other of the self" (2009:34–35). In this violent moment, Jaime sees himself in Brienne and is motivated to help her; he has felt "this sensation of existing [which] is in itself sweet," and her continued existence and safety is almost as important to him as is his own (32, 33).[2]

The unfortunate consequence of his gesture, however, is that Locke cuts off his right hand. As Buchanan writes, this emasculates him not only literally in that much of his identity and masculinity depend on his abilities as a swordsman, but also symbolically—he is unable "to wield his phallic sword" (2014:11). This emasculation, however, interestingly allows Brienne to keep her masculinity, since by avoiding rape her womanhood is not targeted by Locke's men. Jaime's identification with Brienne and his accidental sacrifice of his masculinity for hers mark their first step toward intimacy, and begins signifying their relationship as queer.

Such a physical disadvantage does not suit Jaime, as it turns out; "I *was* that hand," he says to Brienne (3x4 "And Now His Watch Is Ended"). Jaime refuses to eat, expressing little desire to live. His abjection creates ample space for Brienne to provide solace, ostensibly the least she can do in repayment for Jaime's intervention, and she tries to raise Jaime's spirits. When she fails to convince him to "live for revenge" as Catelyn once convinced her, she berates him in hopes that such a tactic will at least shame him into the minimal self-pride required to want to live. "Coward," she calls him. "You have a taste, one taste, of the real world, where people have important things taken from them. And you whine, and cry, and quit. You sound like a bloody woman" (3x4). Brienne is no stranger to shame, like Jaime, and her change in tactic suggests that she is aware of shame's double edge: it represses identity expression and powerful emotions, but it can also provide motivation towards a worthwhile goal. Sure enough, Jaime begrudgingly begins to eat again. But Brienne helps Jaime the most when they reach Harrenhal, and they reach the third touchstone in their relationship.

A Cave of Their Own

In apology for their rough treatment on the road, Stark bannerman Roose Bolton promises Jaime's return to King's Landing and Brienne's to Tarth (3x5 "Kissed by Fire"). He also arranges care for Jaime's open wound where his sword hand once was, and a much-needed bath for them both.

Because of said care at the hand of former maester Qyburn, Jaime arrives at the bathhouse as Brienne seems to be finishing up. Jaime steps into the same tub as Brienne—to her obvious irritation—his reasoning being that he might pass out from the pain of his recent maiming, and he's not about to die from drowning in a tub (a tacit acknowledgment that she's convinced him to live). Brienne makes a face as he drops his towel, giving her a full view of his front as the camera displays his bare backside.

The images in this scene provide but one instance of the show's cinematographic capabilities to evoke a mood instantly, in which, as Collins argues, "the pair's single most emotionally naked scene takes place [while] they're both physically naked as well" (Collins 2016). Steam rises from the water. At the sight of Jaime's nakedness, Brienne's arms cross and knees pull into her chest as she shrinks back into herself, collapsing her neck and upper spine as her shoulders rise and jut forward, her eyebrows lowering and head slightly tilting away and to the left.

At Jaime's suggestion that Brienne is incompetent, letting him lose a hand, and that it is no wonder Renly died under her watch, she reflexively jumps up in anger, exposing her naked front to him and her backside to us. The eye contact between the two of them is gripping, as they are both thrown into a scenario that their social contract has absolutely no clause for. The shot of Brienne mirrors the previous one of Jaime. We get a pictorial representation of the intimacy they share, a bond understood by no one in their world but them. Jaime immediately apologizes and proposes a truce, but Brienne reminds him that trust is necessary for any truce.

This gives Jaime an opportunity to reveal himself, and it is almost as if the shock of Brienne's nakedness, its suddenness, or the forced vulnerability it has shaken out of her compels him to trust her with one of his deepest secrets. In a rush he reveals the circumstances under which he chose to slay the king; a situation that saved the life of not only his father, but the population of King's Landing, which Aerys II "The Mad King" wanted to burn with wildfire. The energy it takes him to relay this story causes him to faint after all, and it prompts Brienne to rush forward to catch him. She calls for help for the Kingslayer, and he corrects her: "Jaime, my name is Jaime." Of this moment, Collins argues that this is Jaime's "true self, truer even than what his sister and lover Cersei has seen" (2016).

This mutual vulnerability acts upon their relationship in many ways. Seeing each other naked thrusts sexual tension into their relationship, especially because Brienne's nakedness comes as a surprise to them both in its sudden exposure and in its undeniable evidence of her femaleness. Though it is more explicit in Martin's novels, this seems to prompt Jaime to realize a sexual attraction toward her, which due to Brienne's masculine attributes forms a failure to adhere to the "heterosexual life narrative" with normative roles for both genders (Berlant and Warner 1998:557).

When Jaime faints, it puts both their naked bodies into closer proximity than ever before. Moreover—though Brienne is duty-bound to ensure his safety—her personal concern for his well-being is evident in the way she jumps to him and cradles his head like he is her child or lover, in either case playing a feminizing role in light of the masculinity she usually performs.

In Collins' assessment, when Jaime shares such a degree of psychic pain, he convinces Brienne he is someone with whom she could be emotionally intimate. "Now that she knows he's experienced such a traumatic level of isolation and pain," Collins writes, "Brienne can be assured that he's capable of understanding hers as well" (2016). In the same way that Brienne's vulnerability in the face of rape sparked Jaime to action, his psychic pain leads her to a forced identification with him, perhaps causing her to experience her own "desubjectification at the very heart of the most intimate sensation of the self" (Agamben 2009:35). Aristotle's original logic in the *Ethics* is that this sensation proceeds from "perceiving [one's] existence as sweet"—that this sense of existing splits the self into the "I" that sees and the "I" that lives, with the former almost jumping into-dislocating and deporting its sensation toward—the "I" of the friend (2009:35). Here, however, both Brienne and Jaime sense the heteros autos in each other when the sweet sense of existing is damaged or being threatened. Only after these recognitions is the sensation of sharing the sweetness of existence with one another in friendship "render[ed] sharable" (Agamben 2009:35).

The conclusion of the bathhouse scene brings an end to any significant intimacy between Brienne and Jaime for a while, but what ensues is the fourth touchstone that cements their intimacy and makes it public.

Oathkeeper

When we next see Brienne and Jaime interact, they are thoroughly ensconced in "normal" society. The man and woman who traveled great distances together, sword-fought against one another, and risked their own safety or sense of security on behalf of each other, seem like a distant memory in light of these two clean, well-dressed, slightly awkward people. Jaime has returned to his public position as Lord Commander of the Kingsguard and private one of Cersei's lover. Brienne is a guest of ambiguous loyalties in a strange kingdom. At the ill-fated wedding of Jaime's son Joffrey to Margaery Tyrell, when Brienne presents herself to the King, Cersei treats suspicions of what transpired while Brienne was with Jaime as fact: "You love him," Cersei announces, accusingly.

Still, when Brienne and Jaime meet in the chambers of the Kingsguard, their familiarity clunkily reemerges. Jaime bestows upon Brienne a Valyrian steel sword, sending a semi-private and yet clear symbol of their bond (4x4 "Oathkeeper"). The piece is incredibly valuable, and she names it "Oathkeeper," an acknowledgment of her having truly seen and heard him during that day in the bathhouse. This sword marks the understanding they share regarding the nature of loyalty and integrity: that the way things seem because of these oaths and their implacability is often contra to the truth, and that loyalty is to be personally and individually determined in order to live a life of integrity. Oathkeeper is thus an outward symbol of their living life on terms that do not fit with the harshly enforced norms around them.

Interestingly, Brienne naming the sword is a reversal from Martin's books—Jaime chooses the name, and it is thus a symbol that he wishes to keep up his end of the bargain to Catelyn. It is not just Brienne's honor at stake; it's his as well. Moreover, for each of them, this honor is defined by personal integrity, not by duty to a specific kingdom or other external set of rules. In Susan Johnston's article on *ASoIaF*, she discusses the series' "dyscatastrophic" tendencies as an indication that chivalry in Westeros is ending, but that traces of it will still remain. Jaime, she argues, is an example of a knight who converts from the external chivalric code to a "covenantal bond to the good and not just to a person" (2012:152). While Jaime once felt duty-bound to his kingdom—and therefore immense shame at being the Kingslayer—his conversion is largely provoked by his relationship with Brienne, and his gift of Oathkeeper to her is evidence of his remaking of his self and sense of honor (150).

The television version of this event furthers this symbol of remaking and makes it mutual: Brienne will use Oathkeeper and wear the armor Jaime has also had custom-made for her,[3] despite the fact that its recognizability as Lannister armor will consistently cause her greater difficulty in her quest to protect Sansa and Arya. Furthermore, beyond the ramifications this gift has on Jaime, Brienne, and their relationship, it also serves as a symbol of their queerness. Berlant and Warner argue that heteronormative intimacy is supported "not only by overt referential discourse such as love plots and sentimentality"; it is also supported *materially*: "in marriage and family law, in the architecture of the domestic, in the zoning of work and politics" (1998:562). Property and wealth are passed down lineally and subject to strict regulation. Both Brienne and Jaime are excluded from this system, since Jaime's sons are illegitimate with another name attributed to them and Brienne does not seem likely to marry and have children. But Jaime's act of giving her a sword that was bestowed upon him by his father has helped create a small "institutional matrix for [their] counterintimacies" (Berlant and Warner 1998:562).

The last gift Jaime gives Brienne is a squire, Podrick Payne. This act makes Brienne even closer to a knight, and it marks Jaime's acknowledgment of her being worthy of such a title. Furthermore, since Brienne and Podrick will form a non-normative bond, in which Brienne trains and mentors Pod like a male knight normally would, Jaime's act marks the beginning of a queer lineage, yet another small but visible trace of their counterintimacies.

When Brienne and Jaime leave their space of shared intimacy, it has clearly changed them: Jaime has higher expectations from his other relationships or is quicker to make his needs or desires known (with Cersei, Tywin); Brienne warms up to and eventually confides in and mentors her squire, letting herself be vulnerable with him. That said, the kingdoms that they fight for and their general trajectories and goals stay the same. From their reunion at Riverrun, we know they both understand this: their intimacy comes from mutual respect for one's personal definition of loyalty and integrity (6x8 "No One"). And because of where those loyalties have landed, both of their commitments to such definitions demand they not stray from that path.

But the lingering traces of Brienne and Jaime's relationship also stay: Brienne trusts she will be received safely in Jaime's camp at Riverrun. When she tries to return Oathkeeper, Jaime tells her it will always be hers. Brienne confronts Jaime in the dragon pit at King's Landing, and—though he snarls an angry "And tell her *what*?" when Brienne demands he convince Cersei to change her mind—our last image of Season Seven is, sure enough, Jaime leaving Cersei to travel north toward Brienne.

Brienne and Jaime make a queer space of intimacy with their heavily masked feelings toward and vulnerability in front of one another. Their bond was formed by accident and almost against both their wills. Still, they create a model of intimacy for friendship or romance that runs counter to the models available within the heteronormativity of their patriarchal society. The queer world, Warner and Berlant note, is both inventive and fragile, and it wants to fight for recognition of "nonstandard intimacies" that occur everywhere, with all types of people (Berlant and Warner 1998:560). The queer project, they argue, is quite broadly "to support forms of affective, erotic, and personal living that are public in the sense of accessible, available to memory, and sustained through collective activity" (1998:562). Brienne and Jaime's model hopefully not only provides a new "queer counterpublic" for heterosexual individuals to see and take inspiration from; it could also help the process of making visible or legible the counterpublics that queer people themselves might wish to create.

NOTES

1. "They meet cute, they instantly despise each other, quarrel, become close, and build mutual respect and trust" (Shaham 2015:53).

2. To address the possibility that this was a momentary un-lapse of judgment, we need only look a couple episodes later (3x7 "The Bear and the Maiden Fair"). The moment when Jaime is released to return to King's Landing, he hears that Brienne is not to be freed because Locke is unimpressed with the ransom the non-wealthy Selwyn Tarth offered. True, Jaime was the cause of this misunderstanding, but he returns to find Brienne fighting a bear in an arena, in a dress and with nothing but a wooden sword. His coming back for her shows that the accidentally created bond between him and Brienne has changed him, has made it impossible for him to turn a blind eye when he might have before.

3. A compelling detail that Shaham offers as indication of their budding romance: "Referring to the armor, he says: 'I hope I got your measurements right.' In the next scene, we see Brienne in armor that fits her perfectly, proving Jaime's accuracy in memorizing her figure" (Shaham 2015:57).

REFERENCES

Agamben, Giorgio. 2009. *What Is an Apparatus? and Other Essays*. Stanford: Stanford University Press.

Berlant, Lauren, and Michael Warner. 1998. "Sex in Public." *Critical Inquiry* 24, 2 (Winter):547–66.

Buchanan, Mark. 2014. "A Song of Fantasy Traditions: How *A Song of Ice and Fire* Subverts Traditions of Women in Tolkienesque Fantasy." Unpublished manuscript. Accessed 10 January 2018. https://open.library.ubc.ca/cIRcle/collections/undergraduateresearch/52966/items/1.0074552.

Collins, Sean T. 2016. "Jaime and Brienne's Game of Thrones Relationship Isn't Sexual—It's Even Deeper." *Vulture*, 14 June. Accessed 6 September 2017. www.vulture.com/2016/06/jaime-brienne-relationship-isnt-sexual-on-game-of-thrones.html.

Johnston, Susan. 2012. "Grief Poignant as Joy: Dyscatastrophe and Eucatastrophe in *A Song of Ice and Fire*." *Mythlore: A Journal of J.R.R. Tolkien, C.S. Lewis, Charles Williams, and Mythopoeic Literature* 31, 1:135–56.

Shaham, Inbar. 2015. "Brienne of Tarth and Jaime Lannister: A Romantic Comedy Within HBO's *Game of Thrones*." *Mythlore* 33, 2:49–71.

A Few Broken Men
The Eunuchs and Their Names

BENJAMIN BARTU

Vigilantes and Vermin

In a medieval fantasy as critically acclaimed as HBO's *Game of Thrones* (*GoT*) (Driscoll 2016), it is no surprise that a substantial number of the show's characters are larger than life. This hyperbolism takes many different forms in the hundred plus characters of the series, but one of the most frequent examples is that of hypermasculine men. The Seven Kingdoms are rife with figures so renowned for their militance and virility they have earned cognomens such as "The Mountain," "The Viper," and "The Hound." All stand out as paragons of a particularly Westerosi manliness. Though these warriors and the names bestowed upon them help reinforce the multifaceted hierarchy of *GoT*, titles are not only given to those who evince hypermasculine characteristics. Deliberate foils to such self-assertive characters can be found in the eunuchs of *GoT*: characters whose names serve to marginalize rather than mythologize.

Theon, Varys, and Grey Worm—the three eunuchs of note—have had epithets cast against them at various times throughout the series in an attempt to make them peripheral. Theon is forced to adopt the identity of "Reek" for several seasons following his castration; Varys is frequently referred to as "The Spider"; and Grey Worm was stripped of his original name as a child after being not only castrated but also enslaved, a circumscribing of a different kind. These metonyms are constructed and encouraged by the more abrasive characters of *GoT*, who serve as perfect representatives of the harsh power structure that governs the Seven Kingdoms. Over the course of *GoT*'s seven released seasons, this effort does less to successfully silence the eunuchs of the world than it does to reveal the delicate nature of the hierarchies they cannot help but inhabit. Indeed, Ramsay Bolton renaming Theon "Reek" says far less about the former's sadistic impulses than it does about power in the world of *Thrones*. By extension, the same claim is made about our own. In both, nomenclature is afforded a very important place in making these distinctions. Theon's naming works to strip him of his former, whole self, and imparts a fragmented identity—his birth name is taken from him and a new one is imposed in its place, under a particularly cruel set of conditions.

Grey Worm and Varys similarly find themselves forced to respond to the names they are given, embracing or rejecting them for success or survival. This manipulation of identity is illustrative of just how susceptible the power structure in *Game of Thrones* is to upset. For all the attention paid to how the crown has fallen from one head to the next as the seasons have passed, equally important are the adaptations marginalized characters have made to the less easily identifiable hierarchies they inhabit. The eunuchs of *GoT* serve as a prime example for the way in which rote categorization can be worked around and overcome in the series, allowing for the subversion of tropes and a traditional hegemonic structure.

"Reek"

When audiences are first introduced to Theon Greyjoy, it is as last surviving son of Balon Greyjoy, king of the Iron Islands. But Theon is no prince. He is, instead, a product of two worlds, having been wrested from his homeland as a child and raised as a ward in Winterfell, the Northern capital of the Seven Kingdoms. We learn quickly that this is a price his father paid for a failed rebellion some years before. Well before his torture, castration, and identity fragmentation at the hands of Ramsay Bolton, his narrative is already hybrid and in between, a liminoid identity (3x7 "The Bear and the Maiden Fair").

Despite Theon's peripheral point of introduction in Season One, by Season Two he becomes a noteworthy figure in the series. This occurs when, in the War of the Five Kings, the young ward launches a successful coup of Winterfell (2x6 "The Old Gods and the New"). In capturing the homestead of the very family who removed him from his own while still a child, Theon attempts to assert his autonomy the only way he knows how. His father fought against the powers that be when he was young, his adoptive family now rides against the crown, why should he not be a usurper as well? But his reign is short-lived, and his men desert him with all due haste during House Bolton's capture of Winterfell only four episodes later (2x10 "Valar Morghulis"). This quick defeat, reflective of Balon's own, leads to Theon's castration. His ablation acts as an almost fated parallel to his father's retroactive castration following his military loss (we learn in the first season that all Balon's sons either were killed in the rebellion or pried from him as punishment for taking up arms). Cyclical elements pervade. And the losses chronicled are fashioned in kind: The father rises, his children are cut down. The son rebels as well, and any hopes he had for children are extinguished—by a bastard, no less.

That Ramsay Bolton ablates Theon's legacy speaks to a harsh feudal reality in itself: The Bolton boy, as a bastard, has no hope of inheriting his father's lands when he dies. By castrating Theon, he at once extinguishes any hope that the Greyjoy might rule the Iron Islands himself, or that his children could do the same. The castration act stands in as its own bastardization.

It is noteworthy that not until after Theon's gelding does Ramsay finish him off with the name "Reek" (3x10 "Mhysa"). Ramsay shatters Theon's selfhood and gives him a new identity that classifies him as inferior. Bolton is deliberate in his unmaking of Theon: Theon is unmanned physically first, reducing his ability to resist the new name and identity Bolton gives him.

As the intact usurper of Winterfell, Theon gets more screen time than Reek, the alternate personality Ramsay constructs out of the fragments of Theon. Varys and Grey Worm, however, are introduced to us as castrated men. They perform accordingly, displaying more stereotypical physiognomies of "eunuch": their countenances are calm, always opaque. Reek/Theon, however, consistently demonstrates a fraught manner indicative of trauma, even after he escapes the Bolton bastard's clutches (6x1 "The Red Woman"). While Varys and Grey Worm's castrations exist outside of the story's action, the audience bears witness to Theon's gelding and handling of the immediate aftershocks of trauma in real time.

The word eunuch, which comes from Greek, means "bed hold/guard" (Bond 2017), and accordingly "Reek" more than once takes on the role of voyeur to scenes of bedding or the preludes to it, consensual or no (5x6 "Unbowed, Unbent, Unbroken"; 6x7 "The Broken Man"; 7x2 "Stormborn"). When bearing witness to Ramsay's rape of Sansa Stark in particular, he becomes a different kind of bystander, enabling the act of violence itself. The scene also fomented a lot of indignation among fans of the series for the directors' choice to focus on Theon's experience of the rape rather than Sansa's (Hyman 2015, Leon 2015, Stewart 2015). The scene is an example—all too frequent in *GoT*—of female suffering being turned into a "growth moment" for a male character. Becoming physically marginalized does not stop Theon's character from contributing to the patriarchal system of advantages tied in to the narrative of *GoT*.

Theon's ablation is witnessed in his physiological state as well as other aspects of his character. His nullification becomes especially apparent when he no longer wields his weapon of choice: the bow and arrow. This iconography cannot help but be attached to the nature of Theon's phallic loss, demonstrating in a literal sense his inability to "shoot." The absence of his old weapon becomes memento mori for the perishing of his intact self.

Following his escape from the clutches of Ramsay Bolton, Theon seeks out his homeland of the Iron Islands. There he runs into his Uncle Euron Greyjoy, the hypermasculine, bloodthirsty claimant to the Salt Throne. Euron mocks his nephew, commenting on his castration and calling him "Little Theon." Though Theon may have escaped the identity of "Reek," the new title—a modification of Theon's original—seems to stick: in the final episode of Season Seven one of Theon's own crew members echoes the title at him rather than obey his command. "Run away little Theon. It's what you do best," he taunts, offering a patronizing reminder of where Theon stands in the power structure. Theon, however, ends up ultimately benefitting from his ablation in the fight when a blow to the groin glances off him. Here we see the first example of castration working in his favor, and this opens up the possibility for Theon to forge a new relationship with himself and his physicality.

From being incapable of maintaining eye contact to appearing visibly uncomfortable in settings where he might be propositioned, Theon the eunuch comes to associate sex with his own disfigurement. Given that the ablation also leads to his diminished proficiency as a warrior, Theon's previous role as the hypermasculine archer who captures Winterfell evaporates. Following his castration, Theon becomes a voyeur to sexual encounters—the rape of Sansa, his sister Yara's sexual pursuits. His newfound aversion to sexual desire is also due, in part, to the intimate nature of his torture. Ramsay's depictions were particularly disturbing for the pleasure the Bolton heir seemed to draw from harming Theon.

GoT, however, manages to subvert overused tropes in the outcome of Theon and Ramsay's narratives, by avoiding Theon taking Ramsay's life and properties in an act of vengeance. As P.E. Johnson observes in an essay on male victimage in another popular contemporary television series, AMC's *Breaking Bad*, "[many viewers] could not get enough of imagining that white, male geniuses had been put to the sword by ignoble forces—and that they would have their revenge, and that this vengeance would be high art" (Johnson 2017:25). We see a plot that at first plays with these tropes and then eschews them in the case of Theon Greyjoy's arc. First Theon is an opportunistic battle commander whose tactics allow him to capture one of the strongholds of the Seven Kingdoms without losing a single man. Then he is brought down by a sadistic villain whose evil is matched only by the White Walkers and perhaps Joffrey (Jackson 2016). The vengeance exacted against Ramsay later in the series is not visited by Theon, however, but by Sansa, who was also tormented by Ramsay (6x10 "The Winds of Winter"). Theon's part in allowing Sansa to do this is not destructive, but rather life-saving: Theon assists Sansa in escaping from Ramsay, which allows her to pursue personal justice later in the series (5x10, "Mother's Mercy"). In this way, the traditional trope of male vengeance is subverted: Survival has become the imperative for Theon, not revenge.

"The Spider"

Varys, Grey Worm, and Theon understand and act on their sexuality differently. Lord Varys stands out in particular among characters in the world of *Game of Thrones* due to the lack of clear portrayals of lust. Though both Varys and Grey Worm were ablated in their youth, only Grey Worm's storyline includes sexual and romantic longing. Lord Varys, however, seems to have little interest in such pursuits. Varys is also, notably, the only one of the three eunuchs never depicted in physical combat. He is also one of the only men in the entire series depicted as having no thirst for participating in violence himself. Even his foil character, the wily Littlefinger, makes it only as far as the seventh episode of the first season before holding a dagger to another character's throat. Just as Theon loses a fundamental part of his fighting nature when he is castrated, Varys has either lost that part of himself as well or never possessed it in the first place. His physical characteristics place him within a space that so few "intact" men get to inhabit in the world of Westeros, where he can operate without having any expectation of military performance placed on him.

But Varys is by no means depicted as a character above vengeance, as evinced by his capturing of the man who cut him, presumably for the purpose of torture—a thread that seems to run through all *GoT*'s castration narratives (3x4 "And Now His Watch Has Ended"). The relationship between physical prowess and sexuality in *Game of Thrones* is hard to deny, not least because the most sexually charged characters of the series also seem to be its greatest fighters (with the exceptions perhaps of Brienne of Tarth and Arya Stark, whose characters embrace many traits traditionally prescribed to warriors, though neither is depicted as being libidinous).

"The Spider," as he is called, is a character shrouded in mystery, perhaps more than any other in the series. Most of his important actions are accomplished off-screen. Many of the scenes Varys does get to be a part of involve him giving counsel to those in positions of power, and yet he seldom shares all the information he possesses. Though Varys's position in the King's small council commands a certain level of respect in the world of the Seven Kingdoms, the epithet most frequently used to describe him is indicative of the multiple layers of his abnormal qualities. Varys is not just inherently mysterious: His external figure also helps galvanize a common need to other him because he is a castrated man living in a hypermasculine world.

Varys's sexual identity is shaped by similar forces as Theon's and Grey Worm's. Although these sexualities are created in similar spaces, however, they serve different functions. Theon and Grey Worm experience attractions and repulsions to others' bodies even in their castrated state. Varys, however, is never depicted in the throes of physical longing or fearing intimacy. His mystical narrative propels this: ethnocentricism allows Westerosi culture to dismiss Vary's castration as a nebulously "Eastern" ritual.

And before his castration? With an unknown birthplace and a flimsy backstory, Varys's origins are a mystery. His body, clothing, and femininity all evoke this, and more. There are traces of what Rosalind Galt calls an "Oriental Catholicism marked as fetishistic, effeminate, and sinful," in his character's makeup (Galt 2009:19). Varys, as a character missing a point of origin, becomes the target of an Orientalist reductionism. Galt further claims, "The rejection of the Oriental goes hand in hand … with a prescription of masculine style" (19). Varys presents as the Hollywood-crafted cenobite; tempered, bald, and possessing incredible self-control. His costume has much to do with promoting this image, with his robes reminiscent of a friar's or those of a Buddhist monk. In his character's mysteriousness, lack of sexuality, and temporally displaced castration, several representations of *GoT*'s tendency to other can be observed (Clark 2013). However, though his demeanor may be showcased as resembling that of the reductive images we see so often on screen of monks or "monkish" characters (Lachenal 2016), the logocentrism espoused by the Master of Whispers assures *GoT*'s audience that he is a product of and adherent to Western modes of thinking.

Varys is given more agency over the terms in which his castration story is revealed than his fellow eunuchs. He doesn't speak of it until midway through the third season of the series (3x4 "And Now His Watch is Ended"). This choice to share information allows him to create his own narrative for his ablation, on his own terms, and offers a partial reclamation of the incidents which have led to him becoming the politically influential lord he is. The moment is indicative of the power of story as a tool through which one's own identity, even after being fragmented or altered by external forces, can be accessed and reassumed.

While both Grey Worm and Theon find themselves in situations where intimacy with others is a possibility that they either gravitate towards or shy away from, Varys's sexuality is as mysterious as the remainder of his character. Whereas Varys seems to have no discernible relationship with sexual desire, however, Theon and Grey Worm's discomforts and desires seem bound to their identities as warriors, past and present.

"Grey Worm"

Given Varys and Reek's limited combat skills, it is a curious sight to find Grey Worm framed as one of the most talented warriors in all of *GoT*. In fact, all Unsullied are seen more as super soldiers than mere men. They function more as a conglomerate in this way than they do as individuals at all, reminiscent in some ways of the legions of clones in the *Star Wars* film franchise, rendered equally anonymous by the armor and helmets they wear.

Despite there being some 8,000 Unsullied in the series Grey Worm serves as the face for all, creating a distinct lack of representation in what is already an overwhelmingly white show. For his part, Grey Worm exists as a mostly silent figure, speaking almost exclusively on behalf of Daenerys Targaryen. Medievalist Cord J. Whitaker provides insight into representation in modern imaginings of Europe's Middle Ages, even when inspiring works of fantasy such as *Thrones*:

> To be black is also to be other to the European Middle Ages, and this fact has had major implications for the construction of modernity and the place of race in it. It is but a short hop from imagining blackness as other in the Middle Ages to imagining it as absent in the period altogether [Whitaker 2015:5].

This skirting of a line between other and absent in an imagined past is all too pertinent in *GoT*, as can be observed through Grey Worm's interactions with the Dragon Queen. His dialogue—or lack thereof—is telling.

Though a soldier like Theon, Grey Worm never suffers from overt trauma as Theon does in several episodes (e.g., 7x2). Grey Worm's castration seems of no matter to those non-eunuchs who surround him. His status as a renowned warrior and his stoic demeanor both help him circumvent the same invective polemics that Theon and Varys receive.

Theon has been given scenes in each season since his castration that vividly document his trauma, reminding us time and again of the nature of his ablation. Varys, on the other hand, is frequently reminded of his status as a eunuch, particularly by those who might find themselves in intellectual competition with him. Characters like Littlefinger and Tyrion use Varys's status as a tactic to belittle him and gain the upper hand in their frequent verbal spats. Grey Worm, however, does not receive such treatment, though jokes are made throughout the series about the collective castration of the Unsullied, generally by the (male) warriors of Westeros. Grey Worm's militant identity does more than merely transform the kinds of ridicule that he is subjected to, however: It leads him to be sexualized in a way that Theon and Varys are not in the series.

Grey Worm's transformation takes places over the course of dozens of episodes; he gradually forges a bond with Daenerys Targaryen's translator and confidant, Missandei of Narth. Maybe Grey Worm is never given a chance to speak to the origins of his own castration, but his sex scene with Missandei (7x2) retroactively points to that trauma, working as a metacastration to fill in for the violence exacted off-screen long ago upon Grey Worm's body. As Rosalind Galt notes, "the cinematic image itself structures the same castration problem that the woman's image does ... it is the presence that always harks back to absence, the excess that covers a dangerous gap" (2009:18). In kind, the scene, which lasts longer than most intimacy in the series (about two minutes, from the point of undressing to where the scene ends), cuts out as Grey Worm begins to perform oral sex on Missandei. The rarity of a man performing oral sex on a woman in a series as phallocentric as *GoT* calls to attention in this instance the absence of Grey Worm's own genitalia. The excessive time devoted to the scene exemplifies what otherwise seems to be a resounding silence, granting a space for the eunuchs of the series and a fulfillment of desire.

Grey Worm may have a certain reluctance to revisit the topic of his castration, due to the nature of the trauma. But he stands apart as the only eunuch in *GoT* who continues to be sexualized. And the nature of the Unsullied army's castrated condition is no big secret, either. There are at least two different instances of hypermasculine characters living on another continent bringing it up over the course of the series, both in the context of making a joke: Oberyn "The Viper" Martell, for example, who in the fourth season of the series states, "[I have] seen the Unsullied firsthand; they are very impressive on the battlefield, less so in the bedroom" (4x6, "The Laws of Gods and Men"). Such comments are significant because they demonstrate both the Othering of the Unsullied through the use of deprecative humor as well as the links that exist between sex and masculine legitimacy within *GoT*'s social hierarchy.

These particular narratives seem easy enough for *Game of Thrones*: The first is that the viewership inhabits a world in which such imbalanced inheritances are quite factual already—the thought of black men suffering merely for being born is no outlandish thought to process. The second is that Grey Worm and the Unsullied legion's castrations have occurred off-screen, somewhere far away, sometime long ago.

Whereas viewers witness Theon's castration in real time, Grey Worm and the Unsullied never get to showcase their pain. The choice to include both black and white eunuchs in the show but to set the castration of all the black eunuchs (who outnumber *GoT*'s cast of white eunuchs some 4,000 to 1) at some distant past point feels as though performs a history of racism that transcends far beyond the fictitious perimeters of the world of the show.

And then there is the problematic context of the Unsullied's liberation, orchestrated by Daenerys Targaryen, a white savior. Notions from various

European branches of Christianity can be detected in the name "Unsullied," whose primary characteristics, again, are that they comprise the brunt of both the black and castrated characters in the series. Black masculinity is framed as threatening in our contemporary culture and so the only way that Dany can surround herself with an army of black men is if they pose no sexual threat to her. The Unsullied's castration is, in fact, a necessary component of their very existence.

Parallels of what happens in the Unsullied's narrative can be found in Harriet Beecher Stowe's *Uncle Tom's Cabin* (1852). In Stowe's novel, the black characters who are most central to the narrative and humanized are those who also have the lightest skin. In *Thrones*, those characters who are most vital to the plot and also happen to be black are only allowed such access if they are castrated or never had male genitalia to begin with (i.e., Missandei of Narth). James Baldwin critiques this phenomenon in Stowe's writing in his essay "Everybody's Protest Novel," from the 1985 *The Price of the Ticket*: "She could not embrace them [to Stowe: black African Americans. To Dany: The Unsullied] without purifying them of sin. She must cover their intimidating nakedness" (1985:30).

For Stowe, an embracing of black humanhood can occur only through the act of whitewashing. For Daenarys, the equivalent seems to be castration. As the case of the Unsullied demonstrates, one of the requirements for black men to exist at all in the fantasy world of *Thrones* is that they be, in some sense, incomplete.

Selves Reclaimed

Thrones has chosen to handle the narratives of Theon, Varys, and Grey Worm in a way that gives rise to a plethora of issues. But to paint the series as purely an asset for marginalization would be a fallacy. By the end of *Thrones'* seventh season we find Theon, Varys, and Grey Worm all supporting Daenerys Targaryen's cause. The trio of eunuchs may be flying the banners of the Dragon Queen, but they have each come to wield a tremendous amount of power, astounding given the challenge their very bodies pose to the normative structures of *Thrones*.

Grey Worm commands thousands of highly trained troops. Varys has continually held a seat not far from the Iron Throne since the time Aegon "the Conqueror" ruled the Seven Kingdoms. Even Theon is in command of his own small fleet of Ironborn soldiers (7x7 "The Dragon and the Wolf"), the very hypermasculine seafaring people who rejected him even when he was "whole."

While the eunuchs of *GoT* act as mediators between states of being in the show, however, they are also bearers of trauma and victims of repeated attempts at marginalization. This is noteworthy because such narratives present new promise for the marginalized of *Thrones*. The hierarchic nature of Westeros and Essos's sociopolitical structures silence many. But Grey Worm, Theon, and Varys's stories all are case studies exposing the fragile, flexible nature of power. It is due to power's mercurial nature that static structures are put in place to preserve it. We see such constructs not just in the world of *Thrones* but in our own as well, and narrative arcs such as the eunuchs of *GoT* provide perspective into how the flaws in such systems may not be as intractable as they at first appear.

REFERENCES

Baldwin, James. 1985. *The Price of the Ticket*. New York: St. Martin's Press.
Bond, Sarah. 2017. "What 'Game of Thrones' Gets Right and Wrong about Eunuchs and Masculinity." *Forbes*, 20 August. Accessed 14 January 2018. https://www.forbes.com/sites/drsarahbond/2017/08/20/what-game-of-thrones-gets-right-and-wrong-about-eunuchs-and-masculinity/#3804302fc55f.
Clark, Phenderson Djèlí. 2013. "Fantasy's 'Othering' Fetish." 18 June. Accessed 20 December 2017. https://pdjeliclark.wordpress.com/2013/06/18/fantasys-othering-fetish/.
Driscoll, Molly. 2016. "What Does the Popularity of 'Game of Thrones' Say about TV Viewers?" *The Christian Science Monitor*, 11 May. Accessed 14 January 2018. https://www.csmonitor.com/The-Culture/TV/2016/0511/What-does-the-popularity-of-Game-of-Thrones-say-about-TV-viewers.
Galt, Rosalind. 2009. "Pretty: Film Theory, Aesthetics, and the History of the Troublesome Image." *Camera Obscura* 71, 24:1–41.
Holub, Christian. 2017. "John Boyega Calls Out *Game of Thrones* for Lack of Diversity." *Entertainment Weekly*, 19 July. Accessed 2 January 2018. http://ew.com/tv/2017/07/19/john-boyega-slams-game-thrones-lack-diversity/.
Hyman, Vicki. 2015. "'Game of Thrones' Recap: Why Sansa Stark's Rape Was Doubly Troubling." 18 May. Accessed 24 April 2018. http://www.nj.com/entertainment/tv/index.ssf/2015/05/game_of_thrones_season_5_episode_6_recap_unbowed_u.html.
Johnson, Paul Elliott. 2017. "Walter White(ness) Lashes Out: *Breaking Bad* and Male Victimage." *Critical Studies in Media Communication* 34, 1:14–28.
Lachenal, Jessica. 2016. "Orientalism, Whitewashing, and Erasure: Hollywood's Historic Problem with Asian People." *The Mary Sue*, 20 April. Accessed 27 December 2017. https://www.themarysue.com/orientalism-whitewashing-hollywood-history/.
Leon, Melissa. 2015. "The Rape of Sansa Stark: 'Game of Thrones' Goes Off-Book and Enrages Its Female Fans." 19 May. Accessed 24 April 2018. https://nypost.com/2015/05/19/its-a-stark-reality-outrage-over-sansa-rape-scene-misses-the-point/.
Prokop, Andrew. 2017. "Game of Thrones Season 7 Premiere: Dragonstone and the Targaryens, Explained." *Vox*, 16 July. Accessed 14 January 2018. https://www.vox.com/2017/7/16/15974304/game-of-thrones-dragonstone-recap-daenerys-targaryen.
Stewart, Sara. 2015. "It's a Stark Reality: Outrage Over Sansa Rape Scene Misses the Point." 19 May. Accessed 24 April 2018. https://nypost.com/2015/05/19/its-a-stark-reality-outrage-over-sansa-rape-scene-misses-the-point/.
Whitaker, Cord J. 2015. "Race-ing the Dragon: the Middle Ages, Race and Trippin' into the Future." *Postmedieval: A Journal of Medieval Cultural Studies* 6:3–11.

Harder and Stronger
Yara Greyjoy and the Ironborn

CATHERINE PUGH

A fierce and headstrong pirate, Yara Greyjoy[1] (Gemma Whelan) defies the patriarchal culture of the Iron Islands that sees women as just "for breeding" (2x2 "The Night Lands"). Daughter of Balon Greyjoy, Yara is a hybrid character within the storyworld of *Game of Thrones*, neither one thing nor the other. She is a woman inhabiting various "male" roles; a young and attractive female leading men in a community where her gender robs her of all value. She is a formidable captain and a traitor in chains, potential queen and successful pirate, a daughter and surrogate son, a white knight and violent killer. Openly flaunting boundaries and binaries gives Yara the fluidity to inhabit simultaneous roles; part of her power stems from her willingness to be flexible, adapting to a changing and uncertain future. Her transgressive attitude towards gender rules underlines her liminoid status, her open bisexuality, and her connections to the sea, death, and resurrection.

At first, it may appear that Yara's only role is as a companion for Theon (and, to a lesser extent, Daenerys). Yara's story is integrated with Theon's, but this does not diminish her impact or importance. For example, Yara often dominates the scene, even when Theon is supposedly the focus. Yara's body language is particularly evocative and she uses it to control those around her. In early episodes (2x2 "The Night Lands"; 2x3 "What Is Dead May Never Die"; 2x5 "The Ghost of Harrenhal"), Yara arrives on screen behind Theon. The way these entrances are shot could have made her appear passive to the audience—after all, Yara initially appears in soft focus, in the background, and/or is positioned as smaller/lower. Despite Theon remaining the subject, the gaze is often drawn to Yara. This is partly because of her open and confident body language (standing straight, chin and head up, chest open and shoulders back), but also because of the way she is framed. During the exchange between Balon and Theon in "The Night Lands," for example, Yara remains in shot, moving from background to foreground, soft and hard focus as the camera switches between the other two characters.

As the series continues, Yara's confidence also allows her to stand her ground when in a submissive role. By Season Six, Yara and Theon have sailed across the seas to align with Daenerys in exchange for her supporting Yara's claim to the Salt Throne of the Iron Islands. After their uncle Euron kills their father and takes the throne, Yara and Theon are forced to go on the run. With no safe home to go back to, and knowing that Euron's fleet is pursuing them, Yara finds herself in a desperate situation and must appeal to Daenerys for help. Yet, when she and Theon are granted an audience, Yara manages to both challenge and flirt with Daenerys. Yara speaks bluntly, shooting back that, "You and I have that in common" when Daenerys points out that her father was a "terrible king" (6x9 "Battle of the Bastards"). Discussing Daenerys and Yara's meeting in "Battle of the Bastards," Gemma Whelan states that they are

> matching each other, we're testing each other's mettle with our very sparse dialogue there, and we get the idea, we get the cut of each other's jib quickly, and we like the size of each other—what we have to say, what we both stand for, is appealing. Not necessarily in a sexual way, but in the way that power is attractive, and it's something we both want to achieve, and we can do it together [in Vineyard 2017].

Unlike her jaded father Balon or self-serving uncle Euron, Yara has the vision, determination, and willingness to fight, not only to survive, but to challenge the confines of tradition. This includes giving up the old ways that have made the Ironborn who they are. Daenerys insists on "no more reaving, roving, raiding, or raping" ("Battle of the Bastards"), to which Yara reluctantly agrees. This is not to say that Yara has been—or will be—successful in leading the Ironborn. Many abandon her, choosing Euron as their King. Yet the fact that a woman has been allowed to enter the Kingsmoot to decide the new leader of the Iron Islands at all is significant and some men still choose to follow her (6x5 "The Door").

Moving away from tradition is a recurring theme in later seasons of *Game of Thrones* as power and agency gradually shift from men—kings, military leaders, fathers, brothers, and husbands—towards female characters. This is particularly evident from Season Six onwards as female empowerment becomes more overt, moving away (for the most part) from sexual manipulation and the woman's worth as a commodity to other forms of power such as imperial (Cersei), military (Daenerys), combat (Arya), agency (Sansa), fortitude, leadership, and revenge. At the beginning of the series, fathers ruled their children; by the end of Season Five most of those fathers are dead. The authoritarian old ways are no longer effective, signified by the supposedly impenetrable Wall crashing down (7x7 "The Dragon and the Wolf"). Traditional Westerosi institutions such as patriarchy and symbols of strength such as the Wall or Casterly Rock cannot protect people from dragons or armies of the undead. Power dynamics shifting towards women may imply a more nurturing, cooperative outlook: defend rather than attack. But this is not the case. Whether their attacks succeed or fail, women consistently show a determination to fight and/or go into battle, sometimes more so than male characters (for example, Sansa/Jon, Cersei/Jaime, Daenerys/Tyrion, Arya/Jaqen H'ghar). Paula Nicolson argues that, "women's lives, circumscribed by gender roles and power relations, means that women bring different sets of experiences to their work. Patriarchal cultures tend to overlook the strengths women's life experiences potentially bring to business and personal life" (Nicolson 1996:87). The experiences that women bring to leadership in *Game of Thrones* involve rape, subjugation, humiliation, and unbearable loss. They know what it is to be invaded. Perhaps this is why they naturally emerge as leaders when the world itself comes under threat.

However, the traditionally feminine cooperative model has its place in this new world. Yara is one of three powerful women aligned with Daenerys, the others being Olenna Tyrell and Ellaria Sand. Together, they represent the four classical elements: fire (Daenerys, the Dragon Queen, the Unburnt); water (Yara, the would-be queen of the sea-faring Iron Islands); air (hot-tempered Ellaria, who hails from the arid desert and mountains of Dorne), and earth (Olenna, whose home, The Reach, with its motto "Growing Strong," is extremely fertile, known for its bountiful harvests). They create a powerful symbol of strength and spirituality, recalling the various religious and mythological beliefs in Westeros that emphasize the importance of nature. However, the power of nature can no longer be relied on because the rules of nature no longer apply, symbolized by the sudden and brutal dissolution of the alliance between the four women (7x3 "The Queen's Justice").

Like Yara, Daenerys has a habit of combining masculine and feminine traits as a leader (being both the merciful "Mother" and the brutal authoritarian who burns people alive), utilizing both "feminine" cooperation and "masculine" domination to successfully achieve power. Daenerys accepts and chooses Olenna, Ellaria, and Yara because they each represent a part of what makes her so powerful (6x10 "The Winds of Winter"). Olenna—the Queen of Thorns—is experienced, sharp and wise representing the clever and deceptive decisions that have made Daenerys a cunning and cogent leader. Passionate and merciless Ellaria characterizes Daenerys's impulsive and theatrical side, whereas fighter Yara echoes Daenerys's steely determination and warrior mentality. Therefore, it is perhaps inevitable that, going into the final season of *Game of Thrones*, Daenerys's female allies are killed or captured. For an effective narrative arc and hero's journey, she needs to be weakened before returning stronger. Daenerys already has a history of this, rising unburnt like a phoenix from some very literal flames before destroying her enemies. After all, what is dead may never die.

In *Game of Thrones*, tough and physically strong women are presented with masculine characteristics. Juxtaposing gender and class expectations, women such as Brienne, Arya, and Yara (who was raised as a princess) tend to be highborn (but not always, such as the Waif or Ygritte) and are sometimes mocked for their unfeminine traits. These women are warriors who regularly best their male counterparts and embody similar body language and speech patterns. They speak tough and act tougher, yet although they fight their way through the world, it is with a certain finesse.[2] As Hilary Neroni writes, violence is coded masculine, therefore, the introduction of violent women into a narrative "call[s] into question our conceptions of masculinity and femininity, and reveal the limits of, or failure of, ideology" (Neroni 2005:ix). She continues, "we want to preserve our society against the threat of the violent woman, but on the other hand, her threat excites us because it involves overturning the ideological structures (most especially those involving gender) that regulate our experiences" (Neroni 2005:ix). Yara's piracy, her willingness to fight and kill, all challenge the patriarchal ideology of Westeros. Violence is her first response, telling Theon, "Fuck justice, we'll get revenge" (6x7 "The Broken Man"). Yet she has the foresight to run from Euron after losing to him in the Kingsmoot ("The Door"), to gather allies and return to fight for the Iron Islands from a position of strength. To survive, she must utilize "female" cunning as well as violence, just as both she and Arya have used trickery and manipulation in the past.

Yara's skills at deception using supposedly submissive body language are particularly evident during her early encounters with Theon. Whelan notes that Yara sees Theon as a "threat because he's come from the Starks, he's seen them as his family for the past nine years, and obviously she sees herself as the heir now."[3] In order to test him, she pretends to be a commoner. Theon instantly begins to flirt with her, despite her warning him that, "You don't know what I'm like" ("The Night Lands"). After approaching him from behind, forcing him to turn to address her, she slyly begins to walk backwards. From Theon's point of view, she is backing away in a submissive gesture, whereas in fact she is drawing him to her, forcing him to go where she wants. In the next scene, they ride on horseback, Theon complaining that he should take the reins because "I'm a better rider than you." He slides his hands under her clothes, which she tolerates with a wry smile. Theon believes that he has the power in the exchange because he is invading her space. However, not only does Yara have information that he does not, but he is only touching her because she is allowing it. While he is distracted and unguarded, she is gathering as much useful information as she can about his intentions and attitude. Theon believes he is impressing her by bragging about being a future king (including "ordering" her to sleep with him), but her body language gives her away. Holding herself erect and unyielding on the horse, and refusing to look at him aside from one or two key moments, she again draws him to her by distancing herself. Although Yara controls the power in this scene, her reaction to Theon's invasive, incestual groping is still strange and disturbing. It suggests that she places little value on her own body, which begs the question of how much value she puts on the body of women in general. Has she been so desensitized to the lack of agency the Ironborn give to women that she has completely introjected their attitude? Part of this depends on whether Balon truly molded her into a surrogate son or whether she (consciously or unconsciously) "performed" that role as she performs the role of commoner for Theon. As well as feeding into the negative stereotype of the promiscuous bisexual discussed in more detail later, Yara's dismissive attitude to her brother's intimate touch suggests that she either has an unhealthy disconnection between bodies and identity, that she places an unorthodox value on her own body, or that she has the fortitude to compartmentalize Theon's actions and focus solely on her objective.

Yara actively avoids gender expectations, at least partly because she has been brought up amongst men and molded by Balon into a surrogate son. It is not made clear how much, if any, influence Yara herself had in this. Nevertheless, she has been conditioned to avoid "feminine" traits. Nicolson argues that "women are socialised into motherhood within the traditional feminine role" (Nicolson 1996:80). Yara is raised to be competitive, tough, and fierce rather than nurturing and kind. The way she treats Theon may be hard, but it is the only way she knows. Furthermore, "on the unconscious level, girls identify with their own mothers and women in general, and thus mothering has become incorporated into expectations and beliefs about women's 'styles' and work-related roles" (Nicolson 1996:81). There are quite literally no women available for Yara to identify with and therefore no one to socialize her into the traditional role of Ironborn women except her father, who treats her as a son.

Yara and Balon use femininity as an insult to mock Theon's Otherness. Upon seeing him for the first time in nine years, Balon asks, "Was it Ned Stark's pleasure to make you his daughter? I'll not have my son dressed as a whore" ("The Night Lands"). When Theon complains about Balon trusting female Yara's military ability over his, Yara quips back, "You're the one in skirts" ("The Night Lands"), offering him *The Sea Bitch* for a ship because "she'd be perfect for you" ("What Is Dead May Never Die"). The gender dynamic of the Greyjoy family has been altered, with Yara taking the place of the eldest son. Balon attempts to remold Theon as a daughter, possibly as a side-effect of projecting his disappointment and anger onto Theon, or perhaps as a more calculated effort to distance himself from a child he now sees as alien. On the misogynistic Iron Islands, a "feminine" boy is useless but a "masculine" girl can be an asset. Nicolson discusses "evidence from studies of developmental psychology that boys are more likely to be punished if they exhibit 'feminine' behaviour, while little attention is given the girls' transgression of this type…. There appears to be more anxiety about the possibility of a boy being a 'sissy' than of girls behaving like 'tomboys'" (Nicolson 1996:76). The gender politics of the family become further complicated after Theon's castration (becoming the ultimate "feminized" son that his father fears), but even prior to this Balon assigns his son the role of submissive, weak daughter.

Yara's attitude to women can therefore appear erratic: on the one hand she believes women should be able to become queens and on the other she and her followers indulge in a visit to a brothel (6x7 "The Broken Man"). Although women in Westeros (as well as other places visited across the series) are generally seen as inferior, the Ironborn are particularly misogynistic. At the time of writing, Yara is the only female Ironborn who has appeared on screen; women are irrelevant to the Ironborn way of life and therefore invisible, used only for sex and childbearing. The women of the Iron Islands are not seen as desirable; Ironborn men capture "salt wives" in order to satiate their needs. Yara's thoughts on this appear to be mixed; while she believes that "anything with a cock is easy to fool" ("The Night Lands") and asks Daenerys for help in murdering "an uncle or two who don't think a woman's fit to rule" ("Battle of the Bastards"), she nonetheless defends the Ironborn way of life, which includes the capture and rape of women. Yara's ambition and pride complicate the culture of misogyny that she has been indoctrinated into; if she truly believes, as she has been conditioned to, that women are inferior then why does she constantly strive for her own independence and success as well as respecting Daenerys as a leader?

It can be argued that Yara's visit to the brothel in "The Broken Man" is at least partly performative, not that her actions are fake or her desires unfulfilled, but that they are, to some extent, for the benefit of her audience both on and off screen. The scene offers titillation as well as practicality—the hypersexed Ironborn sate their desires before a long sea voyage. As discussed later in more detail, bisexuality has an element of spectacle about it, with bisexuals "watched" in order to determine their supposed "true" orientation. This is not to suggest that Yara's behavior is feigned, but that she is aware of being visible. However, it is notable that Yara's presence in the brothel is accepted by her men without comment, taking part as a customer rather than a prostitute (it is extremely rare in the show to see female customers and/or male prostitutes). Yara enjoys sex and is not coy about her desires, smacking a prostitute on the behind and biting/kissing her, but with an element of play and pleasure rather than humiliation. She is not aggressive about getting what she wants, preferring to charm, tease, and seduce rather than demand or force.

In contrast, Theon and the other Ironborn men hurt and degrade both their paid and unpaid lovers ("The Night Lands"). Femininity is equated with weakness and must be dismissed and defiled, yet the whole Ironborn way of life revolves around the traditionally feminine ocean. Perhaps, therefore, it is no surprise that these pirates of Pyke have such a tempestuous relationship with femininity. Laura Sook Duncombe suggests that men find the sea both threatening and seductive:

> For man, the sea and things associated with it are feminine, ripe for male subjugation or, at the very least, male adventure. The feminine sea is an exclusively male domain, where men can prove their bravery or seek their fortune. Adding women to this equation dilutes the established gender binary and threatens the near-sacred relationship between sailor and the sea [Duncombe 2017:xi].

Pirate women, such as Yara,[4] inevitably "interfere with man's storied and complex relationship with the sea itself" (Duncombe 2017:xi). Duncombe argues that the maternal, amniotic nature of water rests uneasily alongside "buxom figureheads" (xi) and undiscovered "virgin" islands that are "'conquered' by colonizing men" (xi). Sophie Kingshill and Jennifer Westwood further discuss the contradictory disposition of the sea, noting the transgressive nature of coasts and shores. They write that "legends flourish in these borders between land and sea. All things supernatural favour the territory linking one state with another—twilight between day and dark, doorways and gates between in and out, bridges, dreams between sleep and waking" (Kingshill and Westwood 2012:xi–xii).[5]

Yara's complex relationship to femininity also emerges here: as a bisexual woman who has been conditioned into masculine tropes, does she still see the sea as something simultaneously fearsome and nurturing, something to be conquered? She certainly views the water as something powerful that is to be respected, gathering strength and security from being on the waves. One of the meanings of the name "Yara" is "water lady," connected with Brazilian mythology and accentuated by the dark blue and grey palettes of her clothing. Notably, one of the few times that she appears genuinely shaken is during Euron's attack, when she looks around at the burning ships (7x2 "Stormborn"). Not only has her hard-earned sense of control been taken away from her, but a place where she feels safe and nurtured has been invaded.

Yara identifies with the ocean and draws aspects of herself from it. In "The Prince of Winterfell" (2x8), she asks Theon to come home by telling him, "Don't die so far from the sea." Although the subtext is already clear, she is not only asking him to come back, but to return to her in an early indicator of her love for him.[6] To Yara, the sea is home. It is also a site of resurrection for the Iron Islanders, needed for their ritual of rebirth. To die far from the sea is to die a very different, more final, kind of death. Furthermore, the sea is traditionally connected with death and burial, being used in many and varied myths of the afterlife as well as reflecting the unpredictable dangers of a life on the ocean. As a seapeople who follow the Drowned God, the Iron-born have a closer relationship to death and resurrection than many in Westeros. Death is not seen so much as an ending than as a transgressive state from which rebirth is possible.

Yara's open sexuality raises questions about the nature of queerness in *Game of Thrones*: is it presented as provocative or progressive (even if it is noted as fact and therefore not remarkable, this is still progressive, particularly in a show where homosexuality can equal death)? Yara implies her bisexuality; she teases Daenerys, "I'm up for anything really" ("Battle of the Bastards") and when Ellaria asks, "A boy in every port?" Yara replies, "A boy. A girl. Depends on the port" (7x2 "Stormborn"). "That's her ethos," says Whelan. "I don't think she swings any way in particular, other than the way she feels at the time. She's just open-minded, which fits the character perfectly" (in Vineyard 2016).

LGBTQ portrayals in the fantasy genres are particularly complex. On the one hand, fantasy, horror, and science fiction are all genres that encourage ideological challenges and the active transgression of boundaries. Christopher Pullen notes the influence of writer/director Russell T. Davies (*Doctor Who*; *Torchwood*), arguing that "his direct access to mainstream and domestic audiences which may accept subtle, and possibly evocative, transformations in identity ideals … paves a more accessible way to understanding" (Pullen 2009:163). As an equally mainstream program, does *Game of Thrones* offer the same "integration between gay and straight identities" (Pullen 2009:163) or are portrayals of the LGBTQ community only intended to shock, titillate and amuse? Can it do both? Pullen suggests that the key to progressive queerness on screen lies in "constructing accommodating pathways," not ignoring issues of the past and present, but focusing on "creating media dramas which frame gay identities within wider perspectives" (Pullen 2009:163). However, Pullen, along with Pamela Demory, also cautions that while "universalizing romance narratives may offer new possibilities for 'queer love,' they are at the same time embedded within heteronormative conventions that seem, for some, to disavow meaningful queer sexuality" (Demory and Pullen 2013:4).

Highlighting Yara's identity as a hybrid, bisexuality or pansexuality are particularly liminoid identity positions. However, these nonbinary statuses can cause a great deal of sociological anxiety. Bisexuals are stereotyped as promiscuous and nonmonogamous by both society and the media. Therefore, bisexuality is often presented as a temporary behavioral state rather than an identity, an ideology that "arises out of the Western dualistic conception of sexuality, in which heterosexuality and homosexuality are constructed as the two basic forms for sexuality" (Rust 1996:127). This conception means that a bisexual individual can only exist in a liminoid state because, "within this view, bisexuality can be conceptualized only as a hybrid form of sexuality, in which heterosexuality is mixed with homosexuality. The bisexual person is, therefore, not holistically bisexual but dualistically half heterosexual and half homosexual" (Rust 1996:127). Furthermore, bisexuality is "perceived as temporary or transitional" (Rust 1996:128), with the individual continually being watched for their "true" orientation. Therefore, despite his or her ability to "pass" as hetero or homosexual, bisexuality also increases the visibility of his or her sexuality; simultaneously invisible and extremely visible, an element of performance is somewhat expected.

Fulfilling the "stereotype of the promiscuous, commitment-phobic bisexual" (San Filippo 2013), Yara's sexuality, just like her gender, disrupts the patriarchal, heteronormative culture of Westeros. Characters such as Loras Tyrell and Renly Baratheon have to hide their homosexuality (at least officially) for fear of shame and persecution, to the point where Loras is imprisoned and tortured. However, San Filippo suggests that "it is now overwhelmingly the *bisexual* rather than the homosexual impulse that threatens heteronormativity's armature" (12). Dornish characters Oberyn Martell and Ellaria Sand, who are both openly bisexual, shock the citizens of Westeros with their behavior, although it is perfectly acceptable in their home country. Similarly, Yara feels no need to repress or hide her desires, reflecting the wanton, deviant and free-spirited bisexual that is so prominent in fiction; a shameless figure that threatens immorality and danger.

There are parallels between bisexuality and the piracy that is so much a part of Yara's identity. Both are related to themes of accumulation and criminality. For example, San Filippo suggests that "bisexuality becomes inextricably joined with the capitalist appetite for accumulation, whereby the latter as a socially sanctioned form of rapacity becomes tainted with the 'pathology' associated with bisexuality and vice versa" (2013:99–100). Just as pirates collect treasure, dangerous bisexuals threaten to amass as many unsuspecting new recruits as possible. However, whereas pirates kidnap and rape their victims, bisexuality is portrayed as "ensnaring and imitative—given the opportunity, any impressionable individual would fall into it—whose result is the loss of love and cohesive identity" (San Filippo 2013:99). The supposed deviancy of bisexuality (as well as its threat to monogamy) is particularly echoed in the conflicting figure of the female pirate. Whereas "women pirates live outside the laws of nature" (Duncombe 2017:xi), bisexual women and the lure of "bisexual opportunism" is a "potent enough a force to render an individual's 'real' emotional and sexual constitution opaque and even non-existent" (San Filippo 2013:99).

Bisexuality is simultaneously progressive, offering freedom, flexibility, and the disruption of ideologies, and provocative, bringing with it a performative element that includes promiscuity and titillation. Bisexuality gives Yara power over the men of the Iron Islands, transitioning her from the object status of Ironborn women to the subject—she becomes the conqueror rather than the conquered. Her sexuality is used to both disturb the traditional order and tantalize the audience, with both positive and negative aspects.

Yara's status as a transgressive, hybrid character allows her to disrupt the oppressive ideology of the Iron Islands, attempting to move them forward into a powerful and progressive future. Her piracy; connection to the sea, travel, and death; and her refusal to conform to traditional gender roles or fully commit to alternative gender roles amalgamate to allow her to say and do what others will not. As an in-between being, she is able to navigate the binary world of Westeros more freely, inhabiting different roles as needed. However, despite her transgressive nature—or more likely because of it—Yara has developed a core stability in her identity that gives her muscle in the unstable and unfair world of Westeros. Duncombe writes, "All pirate women have at least one thing in common: the desire to be masters of their own fates, whatever the cost" (xiv), noting, "The heart of piracy is freedom—freedom from society, freedom from law, and freedom from conscience" (ix). Yara's power lies in this freedom, creating a formidable force. After all, Yara is a quick-witted, bisexual pirate captain from an island full of misogynistic men who saves her brother, cuts throats with a hatchet, fights for a Dragon Queen, and kisses royal assassins. She knows who she is.

NOTES

1. In the novels, Yara is called Asha but this was changed for the television adaptation in order to avoid confusion with the wildling Osha. For the purposes of this work, I will be focusing exclusively on the television series.

2. Coincidentally, "Yara" is an anagram of "Arya" and there are similarities between them such as body language, costume, warrior status, capability for deception and issues of identity (particularly regarding gendered upbringing) that are unfortunately beyond the scope of this work.

3. Gemma Whelan, "Character Profiles: Theon," *Game of Thrones: Season Two DVD*.

4. Although not written about here, there are distinct parallels between Yara Greyjoy and the 16th-century Irish pirate queen Gráinne Ní Mháille, anglicized to Grace O'Malley, including an infamous meeting with Queen Elizabeth I, details of which can be found in Duncombe's 2017 book.

5. Although a full analysis of Yara's costume is beyond the scope of this work, her clothing reflects her status as an in-between being. Her trousers, long-sleeved tunic and boots suggest a more practical and masculine appearance. However, the clothes are fitted to accentuate her figure, the boots have an element of fetish to them and her lace-up tunic is decorated with beads that sparkle in the light. She is at once a warrior and sexualized. Several times throughout the series, she enhances her outfit with an armored breast-plate, underlining the

masculine and feminine aspect of her clothes. She wears blue and grey, fitting colors for a sea-loving Ironborn, but also associated with Daenerys, and therefore power and leadership.

6. Particularly when juxtaposed against her story of wanting to kill Theon as a baby until he smiled at her.

REFERENCES

Demory, Pamela, and Christopher Pullen, eds. 2013. *Queer Love in Film and Television: Critical Essays*. New York: Palgrave Macmillan.

Duncombe, Laura Sook. 2017. *Pirate Women: The Princesses, Prostitutes, and Privateers Who Ruled the Seven Seas*. Chicago: Chicago Review Press.

Kingshill, Sophie, and Jennifer Westwood. 2012. *The Fabled Coast: Legends and Traditions From Around the Shores of Britain and Ireland*. London: Random House.

Neroni, Hilary. 2005. *The Violent Woman: Femininity, Narrative, and Violence in Contemporary American Cinema*. Albany: State University of New York Press.

Nicolson, Paula. 1996. *Gender, Power and Organisation: A Psychological Perspective*. London: Routledge.

Pullen, Christopher. 2009. *Gay Identity, New Storytelling and the Media*. Basingstoke: Palgrave Macmillan.

Rust, Paula. C. 1996. "Monogamy and Polyamory: Relationship Issues for Bisexuals." In *Bisexuality: The Psychology and Politics of an Invisible Minority*, edited by Beth A. Firestein, 127–31. Thousand Oaks, CA: Sage.

San Filippo, Maria. 2013. *The B Word: Bisexuality in Contemporary Film and Television*. Bloomington: Indiana University Press.

Vineyard, J. 2016. "*Game of Thrones'* Gemma Whelan on Yara's Sexuality and Freezing on Set." *Vulture*, July 2016. Accessed 14 January 2018. http://www.vulture.com/2016/07/gemma-whelan-yara-sexuality-game-of-thrones.html.

Raven: Cersei Lannister,
First of Her Name

LINDSEY MANTOAN

In episode four of *Game of Thrones*'s Season Six, Daenerys Targaryen stands in a temple before a gathering of Dothraki Khals threatening to rape her ("Book of the Stranger"). As the widow of Khal Drogo, Daenerys was meant to go to the sole city of the Dothraki: Vaes Dothrak. There she was to spend the rest of her days with the other widows of dead Khals. While the male leaders debate what to do with her, she tells them: "You are small men. None of you are fit to lead the Dothraki. But I am. So I will." She sets the temple on fire, burning not only the specific men who threatened her, but also the structures and symbols of male dominance and patriarchal rule that had governed the Dothraki. Daenerys emerges naked, and the remaining Dothraki bow before her.

And so a woman who has been sold, raped, and victimized claims governance over an entire population.

Six episodes later, across the narrow sea, a group of religious fanatics gather in the Sept of Baelor to put Cersei Lannister on trial. After detaining her, then forcing her to march through the entire city naked, the High Sparrow intends to put Cersei through humiliating testimony about her sexual sins and then kill her. Instead, Cersei drinks wine and watches from the Red Keep while the Sept erupts in wildfire, destroying the misogynist religious sect and her political rivals. Cersei claims the Iron Throne for herself, through no law or right, and no one in Westeros contests her claim based on her gender (6x10 "Winds of Winter").

And so a woman who has been sold, raped, and victimized claims governance over an entire population.

The titles that accompany the Iron Throne include "Protector of the Realm," and yet in both pseudo-medieval Westeros and contemporary societies, women are framed as needing protection, and men as needing to protect women. The phrase "Protector of the Realm" seems to be the equivalent of the U.S. "Commander in Chief"—meaning, it has military connotations. "Protector of the Realm" genders the Iron Throne as much as the generations of male rule: women in fictional and real societies are not meant to be battle commanders. They are to be defended, not to make decisions about national defense. It is therefore essential that Cersei and Daenerys demonstrate their willingness to use force against their enemies before they can put forward viable claims to the Iron Throne.

And yet, both of these gestures of violence—burning Vaes Dothrak and the Sept—are the opposite of protection. They do not serve as defense of the realm, but as personal defense on the part of threatened women. These events of spectacular violence wipe away all past incidents in which Cersei and Daenerys either needed protection or failed to protect, such as both women's inability to save their (human) children from violence and death. These acts of destruction symbolically reclaim autonomy for women who have been objectified, demonstrating for the populace that these women do not need (male) protection.

Indeed, the title "Protector of the Realm" has been evacuated of any meaning by the men who have held it. When Robert was Protector of the Realm, he hit his wife and put the crown in such debt as to threaten its economic security. Aerys the Mad King burned his subjects alive. Joffrey was a sadist who tortured women, and Tommen elevated religious fanatics and issued the decree banning trial by combat, essentially putting a death sentence on his mother. All these rulers live by the code that Cersei explains to Littlefinger in Season One: "Power is power" (2x1 "The North Remembers").

Viewers and critics tend to draw sharp lines between Daenerys and Cersei, labeling the former as a white savior or benevolent "breaker of chains" and the latter as an evil villain. And yet both queens engage in realpolitik tactics, robbing enemies of power while boosting their own. Dany has been worshipped, literally, by the brown slaves she has emancipated, and their deification of this white savior figure has seeped into the fandom, which generally lavishes Dany with praise and affection. Cersei, on the other hand, is reviled and taunted, in both Westeros and our contemporary world. Laura Hudson explains that fans view Cersei as "one of the most deplorable villains on the show" (2017). But Hudson persuasively dismantles the problems with hating on Cersei. After contrasting fan responses to Arya baking a man's sons into a pie and feeding them to him, Tyrion strangling his former lover Shae, Jon betraying Ygritte, and Dany crucifying 150 former slave owners, to Cersei blowing up the Sept of Baelor, Hudson compares Jaime and Cersei's trajectories:

Both begin as beautiful, arrogant children of privilege who commit terrible acts and later suffer horrific trauma—for Jaime, the loss of his hand, and for Cersei, her Walk of Atonement. These traumas are tailored to rob them of masculine and feminine notions of value, respectively: The great swordsman Jaime loses his sword hand after being captured in battle, while the great beauty Cersei is shorn of her hair and forced to walk naked through the street for her sexual "crimes" [Hudson 2017].

Cersei responds to her cruel walk of atonement by detaching and growing more paranoid, "an understandable response to sexual trauma from someone who has experienced a lifetime of it" (Hudson 2017). It's surprising how little sympathy fans have had for Cersei, and I wonder how this response might be different had the episode aired after the #metoo moment (it's also worth considering to what extent *Game of Thrones*—along with so many other triggers—helped bring on #metoo).

Instead of recognizing the trauma Cersei has endured as inextricably linked to her drive for power, fans find Cersei's grasping as off-putting—because ambition remains outside the realm of acceptable female behavior. But viewed another way, Cersei's thirst for power has always been wrapped up in her quest for autonomy and the ability to make decisions about her own body. First sold by her father to Robert, who raped her, then stripped of her children through outside forces, then forced to walk naked while men leered at her, Cersei is proof that no matter how proximate to power, if a woman is not *in charge*, her body still belongs to others.

Cersei reclaims her body by taking the Iron Throne and also through her style choices after the walk of atonement, which are "imposing and militaristic, suggesting Cersei is battle-ready" (Bain 2017). In this volume Rose Butler explains how Cersei's attire reflects her increasing isolation and detachment from everyone around her. Writing in *Vanity Fair*, Joanna Robinson explains the significance of Cersei maintaining her pixie cut after her walk of atonement:

In our modern world, short hair doesn't necessarily *have* to equal masculinity, nor does a masculine aesthetic necessarily equal power. But in Cersei's world—where she spent a good part of her life being treated as little more than a prize to be won or a famous beauty to be emulated—this haircut choice is an extreme and decisive one [Robinson 2017].

For all the invective thrown at Cersei by fans, I'd like to see a study broken down by gender of who might actually sympathize with her. I know I do. She has been betrayed by every male member of her family, often many times over, and yet she's still fighting. For herself, now. Cersei might not be the Protector of the Realm for long. And given her disinterest in joining the fight against the White Walkers, she's clearly not invested in protecting the realm at all. But now that she has attained the pinnacle of power, she seems to have finally achieved a measure of autonomy over her own body. If (when?) she is overthrown, many fans will rejoice. But I will mourn a survivor who pointed out her unequal treatment time and time again, before finally burning the system down.

REFERENCES

Bain, Marc. 2017. "The Costumes in *Game of Thrones* Have Their Own Hidden Layer of Storytelling." QZ, 29 July. Accessed 4 April 2018. https://qz.com/1040011/the-costumes-in-game-of-thrones-have-their-own-hidden-layer-of-storytelling/.
Hudson, Laura. 2017. "In Defense of Cersei Lannister." *Vulture*, 14 July. Accessed 4 April 2018. http://www.vulture.com/2017/07/cersei-lannister-a-defense-game-of-thrones.html.
Robinson, Joanna. 2017. "*Game of Thrones*: Why Is Cersei's Hair Still So Short?" *Vanity Fair*, 2 August. Accessed 4 April 2018. https://www.vanityfair.com/hollywood/2017/08/game-of-thrones-why-is-cerseis-hair-still-short.

The "Most Shocking" Death
Adaptation, Femininity and Victimhood in the Human Sacrifice of Shireen Baratheon

RACHEL M.E. WOLFE

If you want to start a lively debate with friends, ask them which death on *Game of Thrones* they found the most shocking. Doubtless you'll hear a variety of answers, ranging from the Mountain's crushing of Oberyn Martell's skull (4x8 "The Mountain and the Viper"), to any of the deaths at the notorious Red Wedding (3x9 "The Rains of Castamere"), to the classic decapitation of Ned Stark that first introduced the series' willingness to kill off heroic characters (1x9 "Baelor"). Yet for a time, just after the airing of "The Dance of Dragons" (5x9) on 7 June 2015, there seemed to be critical consensus across the internet. Fans, news outlets, and even the show creators seemed to agree: Shireen Baratheon's burning at the stake with the knowing consent of her own parents was the worst, most shocking, and most horrible death *Game of Thrones* had ever put onscreen.

But what precisely was it that caused such intense shock? This death occurred toward the end of Season Five, when the show's willingness to kill characters under the most horrible of circumstances had already become apparent. We already knew that good and honorable characters could die; the show had proven that with the beheading of Ned Stark. Family members had killed one another on *Game of Thrones* before; Tyrion shot and killed his own father with a crossbow in Season Four (4x10 "The Children"). The manner of death surely could not be the issue; characters had been burned alive routinely since Daenerys burned Mirri Maz Duur back in Season One (1x10 "Fire and Blood"). Even children had already been killed; the farm boys that Theon Greyjoy murdered in place of Bran and Rickon Stark in Season

Two were even younger than Shireen (2x7 "A Man Without Honor"). So what could possibly have made Shireen's death, after so many others, the one that critics and fans alike, around the globe, labeled with superlatives: "the most upsetting" (Robinson 2015); "the most gut wrenching scene in the whole show" (Tower of the Hand 2017:comment 2); "una de las más lloradas por los fans de *Game of Thrones*" [one of the most wept by fans of *Game of Thrones*] (*La Prensa* 2017, my translation); "the most difficult to watch" (Vincent 2016); "a murder so disturbing and stomach twisting, it's arguably one of the most horrifying sequences yet" (Hibberd 2015)?

Obviously, there are many possible explanations that might be offered for the unusually high shock value of this death. Perhaps it was the consolidation of all these previously depicted elements into a single death compounding the amount of shock that each generated individually. Perhaps contemporary audiences find filicide somehow more shocking than patricide in the hierarchy of kin-murder. Perhaps human sacrifice in religious contexts has become so alien to the modern world that we are shocked simply by being reminded of its existence. All of these may be contributing factors, but they do not tell the whole story. I am interested in seeking further explanations within the narrative codes at work in *Game of Thrones*, particularly because the human sacrifice of Shireen Baratheon was not only not new to the show in any of its component elements, but also not new as a story. It is, in fact, a direct adaptation of a 2,500-year-old myth. I argue that audiences read Shireen Baratheon's death as so particularly horrifying because it walks the line between the unexpected and the familiar, mixing storytelling codes that have been deeply embedded in Western culture for centuries in ways that break longstanding rules about gender, innocence, and goodness. Despite a widespread rhetoric around the episode that characterizes it as novel, Shireen Baratheon's death is a beat-for-beat adaptation of the Iphigenia in Aulis myth, a commonly retold narrative dating back to the classical period. Shireen's death offers a narrative that carefully combines the choicest bits from existing ancient classical and early modern neoclassical adaptations of the Iphigenia in Aulis myth in order to maximize shock value for an audience that has largely forgotten this story, even as it clings to a set of narrative codes inherited from the neoclassical adaptations of 400 years ago.

In ancient Greek mythology, the young Iphigenia was sacrificed by her father Agamemnon, a military commander and king, to the goddess Artemis in order to rectify adverse weather conditions that kept his army from progressing toward the city he intended to attack. Many different versions of this myth exist in both surviving and lost ancient texts,[1] but several salient factors seem to be common across most variations, including the one that appeared in *Game of Thrones*. First, Iphigenia (in this case, Shireen) is always a young girl on the verge of womanhood. As we shall see, this age and gender combination has always been central to the way she is characterized and the way in which her death is read. Second, her father (Agamemnon/Stannis) is always *en route* with an army to a city that he wishes to attack (Troy/Winterfell) when his progress is delayed by adverse weather conditions (in the Greek versions, either an adverse wind or a complete becalming which prevents his fleet sailing from Aulis to Troy; in *Game of Thrones*, a snowstorm that inhibits progress on foot). Third, at this juncture, the king consults a priest from a foreign land traveling in his company (Calchas the Trojan defector in the Greek; Melisandre of Asshai in *Game of Thrones*) and is informed that the only way to lift the weather condition is by sacrificing his daughter to a powerful god (Artemis/R'hllor). Beyond these basic facts, variants appear, but the divergences are limited and tend to fall into predictable major camps. Whether the king initially fights this pronouncement, for example, varies across versions, but ultimately he always accepts the necessity of the sacrifice, sends for his daughter, and sacrifices her. In some versions, her mother (Clytemnestra/Selyse) is present and fights for her; in others she is not. Finally, in about half the versions, Iphigenia is killed; in others, she is saved by some miraculous device. Most commonly, the god in question whisks her away by magic and replaces her with a deer.[2]

Of the surviving adaptations of this myth, two in particular have been so famous and influential that they are worth examining as we look at how the Iphigenia in Aulis myth was adapted for *Game of Thrones*. The first surviving full dramatic treatment of this myth was by Euripides, one of the three famous tragedians from the Golden Age of Athens whose plays have come down to us intact from the fifth century BCE (see Garland 2004). In his Ἰφιγένεια ἡ ἐν Αὐλίδι [*Iphigenia in Aulis*], Agamemnon struggles over the decision of whether or not to sacrifice his daughter, sending numerous missives both asking her to come to Aulis and telling her to go away again (most of which he sends by means of a loyal family servant who tries to save the girl and has a clear counterpart in Davos Seaworth) (Euripides 2002b). Ultimately, she arrives in Aulis with her mother, Clytemnestra, and Agamemnon decides that once she is present there can be no stopping the sacrifice because the army would become so incensed that soldiers would kill their whole family in retribution (a situation with close parallels in "The Dance of Dragons," as several characters assert that everyone will starve to death if R'hllor does not receive a sacrifice of king's blood and melt the snow [5x9]). Clytemnestra disagrees and tries everything in her power to avert the sacrifice, but ultimately must acquiesce when—in a scene that would dominate debate about this play for centuries[3]—Iphigenia herself decides that she wants to be sacrificed and goes willingly to the altar. In this version, Iphigenia is saved by Artemis via the famed deer substitution. This ending is known not to have been written by Euripides himself and there is speculation that, like many other ancient Greek versions of the myth, this play may originally have ended with the death of Iphigenia (see Kovacs 2002).

The Euripides version has served as the basis of innumerable adaptations since (for a partial list, see Gliksohn 1985). A few adaptations became particularly famous in their own right, adding new elements into the story as it circulated in Western narratives. Most notable among these is the French neoclassical adaptation *Iphigénie* by Jean Racine, widely recognized in both his own time and ours as the neoclassical playwright par excellence. Neoclassicism, an artistic and theatrical movement that began as a part of the European Renaissance, may be broadly defined as the practice of imitating classical (ancient Greek and Roman) artworks during the early modern period. These acts of imitation came with significant changes to suit the resulting artworks to the new time and culture in which they were made (see Wolfe 2016). Consequentially, new patterns and artistic codes emerged which crystalized neoclassicism into a recognizable form different from the classical models it professed to imitate. Within the realm of theatre, no neoclassical playwright was more popular or highly regarded than Racine, whose finely crafted adaptations of ancient plays professed a strict fidelity to ancient models despite their many unacknowledged nods to contemporary taste (see Wolfe 2016). His version of the Iphigenia in Aulis myth, written in 1674 (roughly two thousand years after his Greek predecessor), became so famous throughout Europe that later adaptations virtually always worked off of *Iphigénie* rather than *Iphigenia in Aulis* as their primary source text and were judged in contemporary criticism by their relative fidelity to Racine (see Wolfe 2016). Racine's version made a number of changes to Euripides's core story, but the change that most concerns us here has to do with the characterization of Iphigenia. In the preface to his tragedy, Racine describes his heroine as "une personne … vertueuse & … aimable" [a virtuous and loveable person] (Racine 1768b, my translation). Yet she is this way because Racine specifically rewrote her to be so. This shift was largely achieved through making the new French Iphigenia more feminine by comparison with her Greek counterpart, imbuing her with the early modern feminine virtues of kindness, obedience, forgiveness, and Christian charity (attributes which, as we shall see below, the Greek Iphigenia lacked). In the dénouement, Racine saves his virtuous and loveable Iphigenia, not through a deer substitution, but tellingly by having a guilty and villainous character die in her stead (Racine 1768a). In enacting this unique substitution, Racine was following one of the cardinal principles of neoclassical playwrighting: that in the end, the virtuous must be rewarded and the vicious punished (see La Mesnardière 1639). It is unacceptable within neoclassical sensibilities to murder the virtuous and loveable, especially the young female virtuous and loveable.

This cardinal principle of neoclassicism has passed into the cultural consciousness of the West even as the Iphigenia in Aulis myth itself has largely become the purview of the ivory tower. This particular episode in Greek myth is no longer widely known in the popular culture. It may be a common truism that everyone knows Greek tragedy, but it is probably more accurate to say that everyone knows *of* Greek tragedy. When it comes to familiarity with specific Greek plays, or even with particular elements of Greek mythic cycles, it is clear that many old narratives of longstanding popularity have become the purview of specialists. Euripides's *Iphigenia in Aulis*, although it enjoyed a high degree of popularity during the European Renaissance and into the neoclassical movement, has faded into relative obscurity in the 21st century, despite its established place in the theatrical canon. Even within my own discipline, theatre, which makes knowledge of Greek tragedy a require-ment for most curricula, graduating students are far more likely to have read Sophocles's Οἰδίπους Τύραννος [*Oedipus Tyrannus*] (Sophocles 1994a) (a favorite of both Aristotle and Freud), his Ἀντιγόνη [*Antigone*] (Sophocles 1994b) (whose message of civil disobedience has made it a prime candidate for modern revival), or Euripides's Βάκχαι [*The Bacchae*] (Euripides 2002a) (which stars the Greek god of theatre) than they are to have read *Iphigenia in Aulis*, which rarely appears in anthologies of theatre history.[4] Thus, while the strong links between Shireen's sacrifice and this myth are unmistakable to anyone who has extensively studied Greek mythology, the plays of Euripi-des and/or Racine, or even the operas of Gluck ([1842] 2014), knowledge of this supposedly "canonical" story seems to be so narrowly held in the popular consciousness that one article published in *The Atlantic* made the astonishing and largely uncontested claim that

> in the annals of popular storytelling, Shireen's death has few precedents. Society basi-cally only allows depictions of filicide when either parent or child has been invaded by evil spirit or illness. Even Darth Vader didn't have the will to kill Luke, and even the God of the Old Testament didn't make Abraham go through with the sacrifice of Isaac. So in the *Thrones* tradition of torching old tropes, it's radical to have a charac-ter as generally sympathetic as Stannis kill his goodhearted daughter essentially in the name of political ambition [Kornhaber, Orr, and Sullivan 2015, n.p.].

Given that this story is a direct adaptation of the several-thousand-year-old Iphigenia in Aulis myth, calling this death "radical" is a stretch. Two days after the episode aired, Amanda Marcotte wrote an article for *Slate* entitled "Don't Be So Shocked by the Deaths on *Game of Thrones*: The Show Is a Clas-sical Tragedy." This review explicitly details the links between Shireen's sac-rifice and Euripides's *Iphigenia in Aulis* (Marcotte 2015). Yet this analysis gained little traction in the general discourse surrounding the episode. In another *Atlantic* article Spencer Kornhaber downplayed the importance of Marcotte's claim, saying: "As Amanda Marcotte summarized in an insightful post at *Slate*, 'Every beat of the Greek myth is the same as Stannis's story.' But one needn't turn to mythology to find instances of people behaving like Stannis" (Kornhaber 2015). Kornhaber's article goes on to discuss instances of human sacrifice in history without ever returning to Shireen's adaptational significance. Moreover, this cursory treatment appears to be the only instance in which another commentator paid Marcotte or the Iphigenia in Aulis myth any attention. By and large, discussion of "The Dance of Dragons" after it aired clung tenaciously to the idea that Shireen's sacrifice was unprecedented, despite the clear and publicly articulated evidence that it was not.

I attribute commentators' widespread insistence on "novelty" to the shock value generated by the sacrifice of Shireen. There must be a reason for a thing to be shocking, especially in a show that has set the bar for shock value as high as *Game of Thrones* already had. Since only the unexpected is capable of generating shock (as that which is ordinary might disgust or draw condemnation, but cannot shock), novelty is the easiest go-to explanation. But since Shireen's sacrifice was not new, what was the unexpected element that generated shock in such massive quantities across such a wide swath of audience reactions?

I believe the unexpected element in *Game of Thrones* treatment of this old myth is its use of a particularly neoclassical type of gendered characterization of Shireen combined with the use of classical Greek storytelling codes about victimhood which allow for the innocent to be sacrificed. This results in a jarring contradiction: the expected *neo*classical ending where the virtuous escape harm and are saved is jettisoned in favor of a *classical* ending in which the death is real and virtue is irrelevant. The rule that the virtuous must be rewarded and the wicked punished at the end of every story was rarely broken in neoclassicism. While the virtuous *could* be victimized (and indeed made the most sympathetic victims), their victimhood had to be temporary and reversible, subject to daring last-minute rescues. This rule may have had its start in the 17th century, but it has since been incorporated into multiple influential storytelling forms, becoming a central principle of stage melodrama in the 19th century (see Hays and Nikolopoulou 1996). From that platform, the rule strongly influenced the narrative codes of the Hollywood films which emerged out of that tradition (see Kelleter 2007 and Barefoot 2016). Modern audiences, familiar with these inherited storytelling codes via this lineage, were set up to expect some kind of eleventh-hour miracle by the characterization of Shireen as virtuous and loveable à la Racine, a characterization that presents a particularly gendered version of (feminine) innocence germane to the modern period but wholly alien to the ancient Greek context in which the Iphigenia story originated.

A quick comparison of Iphigenia/Shireen's famous acceptance speech across our three main adaptations (classical, neoclassical, and contemporary) will illustrate this point. The salient characteristic of Iphigenia/Shireen that creates such strong expectations around her in all three versions is her identity as a young girl. In ancient Greece, this identity had a certain cultural coding that has not continued into the present day. In fact, it has been almost completely inverted. The ancient Greeks perceived young, unmarried females as wild, quasi-masculine, and "untamed" (see Pomeroy 1975). The prevalent cultural narrative was that women, whose proper place was in the domestic sphere, had to be "broken" or "tamed" like wild animals in order to become domesticated and adopt their proper place in the social order. The institution of marriage was the device of this "taming" process, so females between birth and marriage were rarely characterized in Greek storytelling as exhibiting traits associated with domesticity or traditional femininity. Instead, young girls in the Greek tradition are associated with wild animals[5] and with masculine pursuits such as hunting and war.[6] Iphigenia in her Greek incarnation reflected these expectations. Declaring her willingness to die, Euripides's Iphigenia expresses a desire for glory and martial honor which explicitly codes her as masculine:

οἷα δ᾽ εἰσῆλθέν μ᾽, ἄκουσον, μῆτερ, ἐννοουμένην· κατθανεῖν μέν μοι δέδοκται· τοῦτο δ᾽ αὐτὸ βούλομαι εὐκλεῶς πρᾶξαι, παρεῖσά γ᾽ ἐκποδὼν τὸ δυσγενές. δεῦρο δὴ σκέψαι μεθ᾽ ἡμῶν, μῆτερ, ὡς καλῶς λέγω· εἰς ἔμ᾽ Ἑλλὰς ἡ μεγίστη πᾶσα νῦν ἀποβλέπει, κἀν ἐμοὶ πορθμός τε ναῶν καὶ Φρυγῶν κατασκαφαί, τάς γε μελλούσας γυναῖκας μή τι δρῶσι βάρβαροι μηκέθ᾽ ἁρπάζειν ἐᾶν τὰς ὀλβίας ἐξ Ἑλλάδος, τὸν Ἑλένης τείσαντας ὄλεθρον, ἣν ἀνήρπασεν Πάρις. ταῦτα πάντα κατθανοῦσα ῥύσομαι, καί μου κλέος, Ἑλλάδ᾽ ὡς ἠλευθέρωσα, μακάριον γενήσεται…. θύετ᾽, ἐκπορθεῖτε Τροίαν· ταῦτα γὰρ μνημεῖά μου διὰ μακροῦ καὶ παῖδες οὗτοι καὶ γάμοι καὶ δόξ᾽ ἐμή.

[Hear, mother, such things as came to me while ruminating: since it is given to me to die; I want to do this with renown, having indeed moved out of my way that which is low-minded. Consider that I speak well here between us, mother; toward me all of Greece the majestic now turns its gaze, and in my ferry [in my care] both the ships and the sacking of the Phrygians, that the barbarians may no longer think to do some great thing by stealing women from prosperous Greece, having paid with ruin for Helen, whom Paris carried off. All of these things I will draw to myself in dying, and my renown, in having set Greece free, will become blessed…. Sacrifice, pillage Troy; for these things will long be my monument and these my children, my marriages, and my glory] [Euripides 2002b: lines 1374–99, my translation].

Ancient Greeks dictated that women should keep indoors and not be exposed to public view, while specifically mandating their male citizens' participation in both public forums and war. In such a context, all of the triumphant desires expressed by Iphigenia in this speech are coded "masculine": her visibility before "all of Greece," her personal power over the fate of the army, her bloodlust for the sacking of Troy, her desire for "glory" and "renown," and her willingness to die in the cause of war (see Zeitlin 1996). The final line of this speech constitutes a public rejection of the traditionally feminine goals of marriage and children in favor of a monument to her martial victory, a quintessentially masculine goal. The Greek Iphigenia's associations with masculinity set her up to be a stand-in for the young soldiers who die when any army marches off to war, a symbolic coding which, in the Greek context, is perfectly in line with her identity as a young girl.

Contrast this Greek view with the neoclassical context of early modern France. By the early modern period, unmarried females had lost their associations with masculinity and wildness (see Bernau 2007). Under the Marian tradition of Catholic France, young, virginal females had become associated with goodness, purity, innocence, and femininity (see Lux-Sterritt and Mangion 2011). Far from being wild, they were considered naturally docile and more "civilized" than males (see Knott and Taylor 2005). The idea that a young girl might be martial or masculine in her thinking was so absurd in early modern France that improper characterization of this sort was specifically forbidden by the treatises of influential French dramatic critics like Jules La Mesnardière (1639). It is because of her identity as a young girl of noble birth that Racine declares his Iphigenia to be "virtuous and loveable." To present her otherwise would be to break with the gendered and classist associations prescribed by his society. Being female, she must be feminine. Being young (read: virginal) she must be pure and innocent. Being a princess, she must behave with nobility and virtue. All of these good traits make her loveable. Therefore, as the loveable and virtuous must be rewarded, she cannot be murdered. The sheer extent of Racine's changes to bring her character into line with his own society's expectations can be seen in the altered speech he gives her about the sacrifice. Because early modern France also practiced the gendered separation of spheres, like the Greeks assigning domestic care work to the feminine sphere and war to the masculine, Racine's version of the play swaps the original, masculinized speech for a new one in which Iphigenia still professes her willingness to die, but this time out of filial duty rather than a desire for military honor. Speaking to Agamemnon for the first time since learning about the sacrifice, Iphigenia begins with the following lines:

> Mon père!
> Cessez de vous troubler; vous n'êtes point trahi.
> Quand vous commanderez, vous serez obéi.
> Ma vie est votre bien. Vous voulez le reprendre.
> Vos ordres, sans détour, pouvoient se faire entendre.
> D'un oeil aussi content, d'un coeur aussi soumis
> Que j'acceptais l'époux que vous m'aviez promis,
> Je saurai, s'il le faut, victime obéissante,
> Tendre au fer de Calchas une tête innocente,
> Et, respectant le coup par vous-même ordonné,
> Vous rendre tout le sang que vous m'avez donné.

[My father!
Cease troubling yourself; you are not betrayed.
When you command, you will be obeyed.
My life is your property. You wish to take it back.
Your orders, without delay, could make themselves understood.
With an eye as pleased, with a heart as submissive
As when I accepted the spouse that you had promised me,
I will be capable, if it is necessary, obedient victim,
Of tendering to the sword of Calchas an innocent head,
And, respecting the blow ordered by you yourself,
Of rendering you all the blood which you have given me]
[Racine 1768a:145–46, my translation].

For the French Iphigenia, war, glory, and honor are matters of total indifference and barely worth a mention. This speech frames her willingness instead as relating to the debt of life she owes to her father, and thus is driven by the markedly feminine virtue of domestic obedience to the male head-of-household. In this way, the "public" concerns of the masculinized Greek Iphigenia are replaced by properly feminine "domestic" concerns of home and family, reflecting the gendered separation of the spheres common to both cultures while simultaneously masking their different portrayals of young females' gendered identities.

Shireen Baratheon is Racine's Iphigenia reborn. Like the French Iphigenia, Shireen is feminine, charitable, and loveable. She spends much of her onscreen time teaching illiterate characters like Davos Seaworth and Gilly to read with patience and without hope of a personal reward (see 3x5 "Kissed by Fire," 3x10 "Mhysa," and 5x2 "The House of Black and White"). Despite the disfiguring disease she has suffered and the neglectful treatment of her parents, she shows kindness to all, a deep loyalty to her family, and an undaunted sense of wonder and imagination. Shireen might accurately be described in modern parlance as "a saint." She seems to have no personal ambitions, acting almost exclusively out of a desire to help others. Her commitment to doing right by all she meets, even if they have wronged her, puts her squarely in line with Racine's presentation of the character as a font of forgiveness and Christian charity, though the religious associations of this characterization are lost in the transition from Catholic France to Westeros. Despite George R.R. Martin's famous preference for "gray" characters who are neither purely good nor purely evil, this principle is not expressed through Shireen. Her goodness is so complete that it is the main quality commented on by entertainment writers and fans. For example, the day after "The Dance of Dragons" aired, BuzzFeed ran an article simply entitled "Shireen Baratheon is a Beautiful Precious Baby. So Good. So Pure," which opened with the line "Shireen Baratheon was the sweetest child this world has ever known" (Nedd 2015). Other articles similarly have characterized Shireen as all goodness and light: "Even after death, Shireen's goodnatured efforts are living on through others" (Hedash 2017). Like both of her predecessors (but most specifically like the French Iphigenia) Shireen has a scene in which she volunteers herself for the sacrifice, albeit unknowingly. While the show foregoes a long speech by Shireen, her profession of willingness perfectly echoes the French Iphigenia's emphasis on filial duty. Listening to a vague speech about choice and duty given by her father, Stannis, Shireen cuts off his rumination by initiating the following exchange:

> SHIREEN: It's all right, father.
> STANNIS: You don't even know what I'm talking about.
> SHIREEN: It doesn't matter. I want to help you. Is there any way I can help?
> STANNIS: Yes there is.
> SHIREEN: Good. I want to. I'm the princess Shireen of House Baratheon, and I am your daughter.
> STANNIS: Forgive me [5x9 "The Dance of Dragons"].

Granted, Shireen changes her mind when it is made clear to her what her "help" will entail. But the fact that she offers her assistance without question for the simple reason of being his daughter is a clear indication that *Game of Thrones* is working with the neoclassical characters and codes that exemplified Racine's treatment of this story. Emphasizing her own identity as a princess, a term loaded with gendered and class significance in both the neoclassical context and our own, Shireen demonstrates her purity and innocence with an offer that springs from unambiguous altruism. Out of a sense of filial duty and the sheer goodness of her heart, Shireen Baratheon puts herself, literally and figuratively, at her father's disposal.

This characterization of Shireen as feminine, virtuous, and loveable in the neoclassical sense sets her apart from the other young girls in the series, and sets up different expectations for her treatment and fate under the narrative rules we have inherited from the neoclassical tradition. The two other main young girls in *Game of Thrones*, Arya and Sansa Stark, both break with the strict neoclassical codes that characterize Shireen, and thus open themselves up to other narrative possibilities. Arya is scrappy and masculinized, a "tomboy" whose ambiguous gender presentation sets her up to participate in violent male pursuits like war, assassination, and espionage (see 1x8 "The Pointy End" for the first of these). Sansa, on the other hand, may be the perfect picture of femininity with her gowns, her sewing, and her dreams of chivalry, but she is certainly not characterized as the soul of goodness and charity, frequently getting into fights with her sister, lying to promote her own self-interest, and making casually hurtful comments to her father and septa (see, for example, 1x3 "Lord Snow"). Perhaps more importantly, both Arya and Sansa Stark exhibit ambition: they have dreams and hopes, fears and desires. They are, in short, complex characters of the kind favored by a post–Freudian emphasis on psychological realism, not ingénue symbols of purity and goodness like Shireen and her neoclassical predecessor. In consequence, neither of these characters fits perfectly with the image of passive and innocent feminine virtue put forward by the neoclassical tradition. Therefore, the fact that they are put in harm's way breaks no inherited storytelling codes. They exist within the world of psychological realism. Anything that might happen to an individual in reality is fair game to happen to them.

By contrast, Shireen is characterized by an entirely different, neoclassical storytelling code governing the treatment the young, good, and pure female. This code forbids her victimhood from being anything other than a temporary and reversible state. The 21st-century audience, subtly trained to recognize the neoclassical code by its frequent inclusion in contemporary mainstream entertainment, anticipates a neoclassical ending for such a character: this virtuous and loveable little girl must be saved by some mechanism. The ending to her story, in which she is burned in sacrifice and dies, breaks this rule. It is this particular combination that generates sure-fire shock in modern audiences: using neoclassical gendered codes to create a character who is young, innocent, and feminine, yet subjecting her to a classical death. This demilitarized version of Iphigenia cannot stand in symbolically for the soldiers, so her death cannot be read as metaphorical and poetic as it is in the Greek context. As a symbol of innocence, goodness, and purity who is burned at the stake rather than rescued, she cannot be understood within neoclassical codes that reward the virtuous and punish the wicked. As a clear ingénue who is purely good and exhibits no character flaws, she cannot be understood within the less restricted codes of psychological realism that govern more complex characters. Shireen shocks us as a neoclassical character in a classical story: the disconnect between her characterization and her function in the plot renders her unintelligible within any one of the many inherited traditions we normally use to make sense of stories. What is unusual about the human sacrifice of Shireen Baratheon is not that it hasn't been done before, but rather that two versions of it, each with their own internal coherence, are combined to shake both of their structures and render this young girl's death utterly incoherent.

So, what makes Shireen Baratheon's death "the most shocking" on *Game of Thrones*? No single element, but an unexpected combination of expected elements. In spite of the collective amnesia that caused commentators to label her death as "unprecedented" despite its many precedents both inside and outside of *Game of Thrones*, this very old story with its very old narrative of the human sacrifice of a young girl can still shock. The trick, in this case, is to use known codes relating to gender, virtue, and innocence and then subvert them, combining new and old storytelling tropes in unexpected ways.

It is in some ways a testament to the power of *Game of Thrones* that after five seasons, the constant shattering of expectations, and innumerable deaths, the human sacrifice of a young girl—if characterized properly—can still shock us.

NOTES

1. These various texts include the post–Homeric epic *The Cypria*, Hesiod's *Catalogues of Women*, at least one song by the lyric poet Stesichorus of Himera, Pindar's eleventh Pythian ode, Aeschylus's *Oresteia* trilogy, several plays by Euripides, Sophocles's *Electra*, the *Fabulae* of Hyginus, and several lost plays by Roman playwrights, including Naevius and Quintus Ennius. See my own previous work for a complete catalogue of these texts, whether and how they have survived, and Iphigenia's appearances in them (Wolfe 2016).

2. This version of the myth has a close Biblical parallel in the story of Abraham and Isaac, in which a ram was substituted for the child rather than a deer. In both cases, the salient point is that the god in question directly substitutes animal sacrifice for the human sacrifice that was asked (see Genesis 22:1–19).

3. This debate began with Aristotle, who famously criticized Iphigenia's change of heart in his Περὶ ποιητικῆς [*Poetics*] and has continued to the present day, the most recent article on the subject that I have been able to find dating from last year. See Aristotle (1995) and Bacalexi (2016).

4. It does not, for example, appear in the widely used *Norton Anthology of Drama* (Gainor, Garner, and Puchner 2018), nor in the rival *Wadsworth Anthology of Drama* (Worthen 2011), nor was *Iphigenia in Aulis* selected as a case study in the newer and more experimental *Theatre Histories: An Introduction* (McConachie et al. 2016).

5. In one particular ritual practiced at the temple of Artemis at Brauron, for example, young girls were referred to ritualistically as ἄρκτοι (bears). On this ritual, see Platnauer (1938).

6. As Pomeroy (1975) has pointed out, the ancient Greek goddesses who were sworn virgins largely governed traditionally masculine pursuits, including Artemis as the goddess of hunting and Athena as the goddess of justice and warfare. See Pomeroy (1975:8).

REFERENCES

Aristotle. 1995. *Poetics*. Translated by Stephen Halliwell. In *Aristotle: Poetics, Longinus: On the Sublime, Demetrius: On Style*, edited by Stephen Halliwell, 27–141. Cambridge: Harvard University Press.

Bacalexi, Dina. 2016. "Personal, Paternal, Patriotic: The Threefold Sacrifice of Iphigenia in Euripides' *Iphigenia in Aulis*." *Humanitas* 68:51–76.

Barefoot, Guy. 2016. *Gaslight Melodrama: From Victorian London to 1940s Hollywood*. London: Bloomsbury.

Bernau, Anke. 2007. *Virgins: A Cultural History*. London: Granta.

Euripides. 2002a. *Bacchae*. Translated by David Kovacs. In *Euripides VI: Bacchae, Iphigenia at Aulis, Rhesus*, edited by David Kovacs, 12–156. Cambridge: Harvard University Press.

Euripides. 2002b. *Iphigenia at Aulis*. Translated by David Kovacs. In *Euripides VI: Bacchae, Iphigenia at Aulis, Rhesus*, edited by David Kovacs, 157–343. Cambridge: Harvard University Press.

Gainor, J. Ellen, Stanton B. Garner, and Martin Puchner, eds. 2018. *The Norton Anthology of Drama, 3rd Edition*. New York: W.W. Norton.

Garland, Robert. 2004. *Surviving Greek Tragedy*. London: Duckworth.

Gliksohn, Jean-Michel. 1985. *Iphigénie de la Grèce antique à l'Europe des Lumières*. Paris: Presses Universitaires de France.

Gluck, Christoph Willibald, and François-Louis Gand le Bland Du Roullet [1842]2014. *Iphigénie en Aulide*. San Bernardino, CA: ULAN Press.

Hays, Michael, and Anastasia Nikolopoulou. 1996. *Melodrama: The Cultural Emergence of a Genre*. New York: St. Martin's Press.

Hedash, Kara. 2017. "We Should Have Shireen It Coming: Youngest Baratheon Teased Jon Snow's True Identity Back in 'Game of Thrones' Season 3." *Movie Pilot*, 20 October. Accessed 21 December. https://moviepilot.com/p/shireen-baratheon-hinted-jon-snow-identity-aegon/4391679.

Hibberd, James. 2015. "'*Game of Thrones*' Showrunner on That Very Disturbing Death Scene." *Entertainment Weekly*, 7 June. Accessed 20 December 2017. http://www.ew.com/article/2015/06/07/game-thrones-Shireen/.

Kelleter, Frank. 2007. *Melodrama! The Mode of Excess from Early America to Hollywood*. Heidelberg: Winter.

Knott, Sarah, and Barbara Taylor, eds. 2005. *Women, Gender, and Enlightenment*. Basingstoke: Palgrave Macmillan.

Kornhaber, Spencer. 2015. "The Most Disturbing Thing About *Game of Thrones*' Most Disturbing Scene: It's Not Far-Fetched in the World of the Show or the World We Live In." *The Atlantic*, 11 June. Accessed 20 December 2017. https://www.theatlantic.com/entertainment/archive/2015/06/game-of-thrones-shireen-human-sacrifice-history/395573/.

Kornhaber, Spencer, Christopher Orr, and Amy Sullivan. 2015. "The Most Horrifying *Game of Thrones* Death Yet: Our Roundtable Discusses 'The Dance of Dragons,' the Ninth Episode of the Fifth Season." *The Atlantic*, 8 June. Accessed 20 December 2017. https://www.theatlantic.com/entertainment/archive/2015/06/the-most-horrifying-game-of-thrones-death-yet/395159/?preview=69ZPPEgPMV95Tfv5JCwNRXX1UmA.

Kovacs, David. 2002. "Introduction to *Iphigenia at Aulis*." In *Euripides VI: Bacchae, Iphigenia at Aulis, Rhesus*, edited by David Kovacs, 157–64. Cambridge: Harvard University Press.

La Mesnardière, Jules. 1639. *La Poëtique*. Paris: Antoine de Sommaville.

La Prensa. 2017. "Game of Thrones: *Shireen Baratheon y la pista sobre Jon Snow que nadie había notado antes*." 23 October. Accessed 20 December. https://laprensa.peru.com/espectaculos/noticia-game-of-thrones-shireen-baratheon-jon-snow-aegon-targaryen-davos-75692.

Lux-Sterritt, Laurence, and Carmen M. Mangion, eds. 2011. *Gender, Catholicism and Spirituality: Women and the Roman Catholic Church in Britain and Europe, 1200–1900*. Basingstoke: Palgrave Macmillan.

Marcotte, Amanda. 2015. "Don't Be So Shocked by the Deaths on *Game of Thrones*: The Show Is a Classical Tragedy." *Slate*, 9 June. Accessed 20 December 2017. http://www.slate.com/blogs/browbeat/2015/06/09/game_of_thrones_is_a_classical_tragedy_don_t_be_so_shocked_my_the_deaths.html.

McConachie, Bruce A., Tobin Nellhaus, Carol Fisher Sorgenfrei, and Tamara Underiner. 2016. *Theatre Histories: An Introduction*. London: Routledge.

Nedd, Alexis. 2015. "Shireen Baratheon Is a Beautiful Precious Baby. So Good. So Pure." *BuzzFeed*, 8 June. Accessed 21 December 2017. https://www.buzzfeed.com/alexisnedd/beautiful-cinnamon-roll-princess-too-good-for-this-planetos?utm_term=.huEbl3XJR#.ndEoa1qKJ.

Platnauer, M. 1938. "Introduction." In *Iphigenia in Tauris*, edited by M. Platnauer. v–xix. Oxford: Oxford University Press.

Pomeroy, Sarah B. 1975. *Goddesses, Whores, Wives, and Slaves: Women in Classical Antiquity*. New York: Schocken Books.

Racine, Jean. 1768a. *Iphigénie*. In *Oeuvres de Jean Racine*, edited by M. Luneau De Boisjermain, 32–204. Paris: L'Imprimerie de Louis Cellot.

Racine, Jean. 1768b. "Préface de l'auteur à *Iphigénie*." In *Oeuvres de Jean Racine*, edited by M. Luneau De Boisjermain, 23–31. Paris: L'Imprimerie de Louis Cellot.

Robinson, Joanna. 2015. "How Tonight's *Game of Thrones* Signaled a Brutal Departure from the Books." *Vanity Fair*, 10 June. Accessed 20 December 2017. https://www.vanityfair.com/hollywood/2015/06/stannis-burns-shireen-game-of-thrones-dance-of-dragons.

Sophocles. 1994a. *Oedipus Tyrannus*. Translated by Hugh Lloyd-Jones. In *Sophocles I: Ajax, Electra, Oedipus Tyrannus*, edited by Hugh Lloyd-Jones, 323–496. Cambridge: Harvard University Press.

Sophocles. 1994b. *Antigone*. Translated by Hugh Lloyd-Jones. In *Sophocles II: Antigone, The*

Women of Trachis, Philoctetes Oedipus at Colonus, edited by Hugh Lloyd-Jones, 1–128. Cambridge: Harvard University Press.

Tower of the Hand. 2017. "Shireen Baratheon May Never Die." 16 October. Accessed 20 December. https://towerofthehand.com/blog/2017/10/16-shireen-baratheon-may-never-die/index.html.

Venuti, Lawrence. 2013. *Translation Changes Everything: Theory and Practice.* London: Routledge.

Vincent, Alice. 2016. "*Game of Thrones*: George R.R. Martin Always Intended for Shireen to Meet Her Controversial End." *The Telegraph,* 14 March. Accessed 20 December 2017. http://www.telegraph.co.uk/tv/2016/03/14/game-of-thrones-george-rr-martin-always-intended-for-shireen-to0/.

Wolfe, Rachel Margaret Eller. 2016. *Iphigenia in Adaptation: Neoclassicism, Gender, and Culture on the Public Stages of France and England, 1674–1779.* ProQuest Dissertations and Theses. Accessed 21 December 2017. https://search.proquest.com/docview/1788355660.

Worthen, W.B. 2011. *Wadsworth Anthology of Drama, 6th Edition.* Boston: Cengage Learning.

Zeitlin, Froma I. 1996. *Playing the Other: Gender and Society in Classical Greek Literature.* Chicago: University of Chicago Press.

"Kill the boy,
and let the man be born"
Youth, Death and Manhood

DAN WARD

One of the most prominent recurring themes in *A Song of Ice and Fire* is the disavowal of hegemonic folk tales about heroic knights, charming princes, and beautiful princesses. Looking at the emergence of the literary fairytale in 18th-century Europe, Jack Zipes has identified the centrality within this lore of discourses "about mores, values, and manners," which would be circulated "so that children and adults would become civilized according to the social code of the time" (2006:3). This is most viscerally illustrated in George R.R. Martin's work through Sansa Stark's tragic arc, as the character most heavily invested in such romantic myths from childhood. As Petyr Baelish explains to her, "life is not a song, sweetling" (Martin 1996:473), and what she subsequently endures persuades her that "there are no heroes ... in life, the monsters win" (746). The traumas Sansa experiences point to a wider critique of the lasting consequences of indoctrination via patriarchal myth. The symbolic death of the idealistic girl that the young Sansa was ultimately allows her to develop into one of the series' survivors, an increasingly resourceful and resilient young woman. Both *A Song of Ice and Fire* and its television adaptation incorporate elements of high fantasy, political intrigue, and the medieval historical epic, and this hybrid framework challenges many of the familiar tropes of these constituent genres.

Though gender studies of Martin's work have tended to focus predominantly on women, the young men of *A Song of Ice and Fire* are no less interpolated by myths of nobility, tradition, honor and bravery than girls like Sansa are by songs which sweeten a cruel patriarchy. The primary influences shaping discourses of masculinity and maturity within the text are both familial—that is to say lessons passed down by parents—and cultural. Raewyn Connell observes that, throughout time, "hegemonic masculinity is naturalised in the form of the hero and presented through forms that revolve around heroes: sagas, ballads, westerns, thrillers" (1985:186). The songs and legends that are so central to Westerosi culture are an important element of this process, as too are official history, rituals, and codes. In Westeros, many of these concepts are interconnected: the heroes of songs are often great knights and kings of bygone days, and cultural traditions often have some kind of cautionary legend attached to them.

Jon Snow offers a perfect study for analysis, not least because he is ostensibly the figure within Martin's saga that comes closest to the archetype of the hegemonic male hero. It is first necessary, though, to frame this analysis within the context of some of Snow's peers, and how their exposure to masculine roles and expectations come to inform their eventual fate. Death plays an integral role in the narrative—the Braavosi mantra of "valar morghulis" ("all men must die") serves as a recurring reminder of the fatalistic ethos underpinning the story. In order to understand the articulation of these cultural issues within the text, it is vital to also examine the role of death in the narrative, and Jon Snow's particular relationship to it.

"Our ways are the old ways"

On numerous occasions, the importance of songs as teaching tools to both children and adults within Westerosi culture is made clear. As Daenerys recalls, "in the songs, the white knights of the Kingsguard were ever noble, valiant and true" (Martin 1996:391). Although Daenerys is herself long dispossessed of such illusions, there is no doubt that notions of chivalry and honor are integral to the images of normative masculinity that children of both sexes grow up with in Westeros. Charles Hackney suggests that the presentation of these concepts in Martin's work is "a clash between high idealism and grim reality" (Hackney 2015:132), and this is particularly notable in the example of the Stark men. Though Ned Stark is not a knight, Hackney identifies him as a character who lives "by a code of honor" (133–34), and this is illustrated in the opening episode of the series when he executes a deserter from the Night's Watch in front of his sons (1x1 "Winter Is Coming"). The scene is framed clearly as a didactic example for the Stark children, with Jon pointedly warning Bran not to look away. The themes of justice, duty, and history loom large in the lesson. As the condemned man awaits his face, Ned undertakes the formalities of the task, solemnly underscoring the responsibilities of his entrusted position: "I, Eddard of House Stark, Lord of Winterfell and Warden of the North … in the name of Robert of House Baratheon, King of the Andals and the First Men." When the deed is done, he approaches Bran to ensure that he has understood the reason for the act; though Ned is more concerned that Bran absorbs the importance of duty and personal responsibility, Bran's response demonstrates that he has also understood the weight of history and tradition on the Stark men: "our ways are the old ways."

The codes of honor and tradition with which the Starks are raised are a clear example of the hegemonic myths which are brutally debunked within Martin's unforgiving universe.[1] Ned's devotion to these notions render him fatally vulnerable to the ruthlessness of the Lannisters, and similar tendencies can be observed in his eldest son. Robb places too much trust in the loyalty of his bannerman, Roose Bolton, and in Walder Frey's observation of ancient codes such as guest rite, the consequences of this naivety unfolding disastrously at the Red Wedding (3x9 "The Rains of Castamere"). The stunting rigidity of such an apparently noble ethos is also apparent in Robb's decision to execute Lord Rickard Karstark for the murder of the Lannister hostages. Robb's insistence on upholding the lessons taught to him by his father on blind justice and the belief that "he who passes the sentence should swing the sword" (1x1) deprive him of the cold pragmatism necessary to see the importance of Karstark's bannermen to his own army, and to bend accordingly. Perhaps ironically, the connection between passing the sentence and swinging the sword is a lesson on taking responsibility for one's actions, and the consequences of those actions. While Robb may be willing to accept responsibility, his devotion to these codes renders him too myopic to objectively assess their consequences. Ultimately, this leaves his war effort woefully short of manpower, and leaves him to make increasingly desperate and devastating decisions.

An alternative argument is that it is not too much respect for codes of honor that dooms Robb, but too little. Breaking his arrangement with Walder Frey out of love for Talisa is the kind of quixotic act that does not resonate with the steadfast devotion to duty which characterized his father, and is ostensibly the seed that incites Frey's brutal act of revenge at the Red Wedding. While Frey clearly holds a grudge against Robb for the perceived personal slight, however, he is ultimately an opportunist. Just as his original agreement to join Robb's rebellion is motivated above all by the promise of an advantageous political union (the marriage of one of his daughters to the King in the North) rather than any sense of personal loyalty to the Starks, the chance to punish the Starks for their "betrayal" is a secondary incentive beyond the greater rewards offered as part of his new alliance with the Lannisters and Boltons. Walder Frey is not an honorable man, and his festering enmity towards Robb Stark is rooted in insult to personal vanity and thwarted ambition rather than any deeply felt sense of duty. He does, however, take advantage of the Starks' trust in these codes, using their belief in guest right to persuade them to let down their guard in his castle by feeding them bread and salt. At least where this particular microcosm is concerned, we can again chart the lineage of such faith in the lore the Stark children are raised on: the most famous tale concerning guest rite is the legend of the Rat Cook, cursed by the Gods because he "slew a guest beneath his roof" (Martin 2000:631). Robb is condemned by his trust in the old ways, and unable to adapt to the harsh nihilism of the new world.

"And who are you, the proud lord said, that I must bow so low?"

The Lannister conception of masculinity places far more emphasis on power than honor. Jaime Lannister exemplifies the apparent impossibility of a life in pursuit of such ideals: the archetypal valiant, handsome knight, beginning life with "a belief in glory and honor" (Carroll in Young 2015:62), but now living in infamy as the "Kingslayer" due to his inability to reconcile his chivalric duties with the competing drives of family loyalty and self-preservation in the wake of the Mad King's rampage. The importance of songs in communicating meaning within this universe is once more relevant here; the Lannister song "The Rains of Castamere" encapsulates several of these issues. The woeful lament of a rebellious vassal who rose up against Tytos Lannister, only to be mercilessly destroyed (along with his House) by his son, Tywin, the song underscores the importance of hierarchy to House Lannister. This hierarchy must be ruthlessly maintained through fear, and terrible displays of power against those who would challenge it. The song is used as a perennial reminder of the consequences that await any recalcitrant elements within the realm, as well as to remind future generations of Lannisters what is necessary to preserve their privilege. Mike Donaldson describes hegemonic masculinity as "hierarchically differentiated ... centrally connected with the institutions of male dominance" (1993:646). In Westeros, hegemonic masculinity intersects with the social hierarchies of the feudal system, and is reinforced through the subordination of others. There is no doubt that these principles have been internalized by Joffrey Baratheon during his upbringing, and are exacerbated when he comes to the throne. He repeatedly attempts to reaffirm his position by having those he considers inferior beaten, abused, or murdered, the philosophy crudely elucidated when he tells Tyrion Lannister "everyone is mine to torment" (3x10 "Mhysa"). He refers to his hulking bodyguard Sandor Clegane condescendingly as "my dog," a reminder that far more physically powerful men are still subordinated by the structural power that comes with the Lannister name and the throne.

Joffrey wields power as a blunt instrument, and the forms his performance of masculinity take are so crude and gratuitous as to ultimately reinforce his weakness and immaturity. Tywin, his grandfather, grows weary of Joffrey's grotesque parodies of strength, telling him pointedly that "any man who must say 'I am the king' is no true king" (3x10). Tywin is frustrated by Joffrey's refusal to accept counsel, ostensibly spoiled irredeemably by his mother's indulgence and Robert Baratheon's resentful disinterest, though in reality his ugly, unchecked sadism might be read as the manifestation of the familiar Lannister power principle of domination through terror, stripped of all civilizing facades and taken to its logical ends. The situation is quite different when it comes to Joffrey's brother, and this difference is illustrated when Tywin counsels Tommen in the Sept of Baelor after Joffrey's inevitable murder (4x3 "Breaker of Chains"). Though Tywin's lecture focuses on the qualities of a good king, the subtext is rooted in the broader context of coming of age as a man: the need for wisdom, to procreate, and, most pointedly of all, to accept counsel. The importance of received history and how it is relayed and utilized to mold future generations is again resonant here. Tywin relates the stories of various esteemed kings of Westeros, noting that the qualities they were most famed for—holiness, justice, strength—were ultimately not sufficient to prolong the lives of these kings or the prosperity of their kingdom. The way in which Tywin shapes his historical discourse constitutes these men as cautionary tales, examples for the younger Tommen to learn from, but not to emulate.

The scene is significant not so much for Tywin's words as for its design, and the power dynamics which play out within. Joffrey's corpse lies prone in the center of the sept, the most recent cautionary tale in Tywin's inventory of doomed kings, with Tommen and his grieving mother standing by. Cersei's apparent powerlessness at this stage of the series is emphasized when her father brusquely ignores her protestations at the timing of Tommen's "lesson," and this is entirely calculated on Tywin's part; it marks the symbolic point where responsibility for Tommen's upbringing is wrested from Cersei's grip. "Your brother was not a wise king—your brother was not a good king. If he had been, perhaps he'd still be alive," the elder Lannister pointedly tells Tommen, as the shot lingers on Cersei's tear-filled eyes. The implications are clear here: that Tywin blames her for Joffrey's maladjustment, and that he will not allow her the chance to redeem herself with Tommen. As if to make manifest this separation, Tywin turns his back on Cersei and physically leads Tommen away from his mother and brother as he explains to him the need to find a wife (the wife who, from this point on, will exercise a far greater influence over Tommen than Cersei ever will).

While Cersei is spiteful and manipulative, it is hard not to feel at least some sympathy for her in this scene. Though the worst aspects of her character were undoubtedly passed on to Joffrey through her tutelage, there is also no doubt that she is fiercely protective of her children and deeply affected by Joffrey's death. Joffrey's cruel, spoiled nature stems as much from Cersei and Robert's adversarial, dysfunctional relationship and the resentful distance maintained by the latter during his upbringing. That this is the result of a doomed political union conceived by Tywin himself seems to matter little to him as he takes stewardship of Tommen away from Cersei, just as he prepares the boy to enter into another political marriage. What is also significant here is that the history Tywin imparts to influence Tommen is an exclusively male history: it is one curated by men (maesters), with men as its central figures, and relayed by a family patriarch to convey particular "truths." Underscoring the power play in which Tywin attempts to marginalize Cersei and position himself as mentor to Tommen, we can see here the ways in which the dominant Westerosi discourse of history is constructed in a Foucauldian sense to "constitute" and reinforce particular "knowledge" around gender and power (Foucault 1979:27). Even despite Tywin's untimely death, Tommen seems to internalize the lessons on accepting counsel, to the extent that he eventually surrenders his independence almost completely to another older, male authority figure, the High Sparrow. While his brother's sadistic, sociopathic narcissism proved his own undoing, the very different Tommen also ultimately fails to mature, becoming so dependent on the approval and guidance of surrogate mentors that he finds himself incapable of going on when they are violently taken from him.

The Prince That Was Promised

The examples explored so far depict young men who come to embody a range of hegemonic traits which are integral to normative masculinity in the feudal patriarchy of Westeros: honor, tradition, dominance, piety. All are ultimately doomed to die young, and, given Martin's propensity to subvert the norms of the genres he draws on, perhaps this is to be expected. However, Jon Snow also embodies this hegemonic template, at least to a degree. Writing about depictions of the medieval hero in historical cinematic epics, Ilan Mitchell-Smith (2011:3) suggests that a typical male protagonist is defined and celebrated "by the violence he commits," and Jon Snow is certainly depicted as proficient in combat. He is also courageous, shows sufficient leadership qualities to be chosen as Lord Commander by his Night's Watch peers, and, at least in the series, is classically attractive and (by Ygritte's testimony) sexually proficient, connoting the "sexual validation" that Donaldson associates with "culturally idealised" hegemonic masculinity (1993:645). As much as Martin ostensibly sets out to challenge traditional representations of gender within the genres his work is influenced by, it is arguable that he ultimately reaffirms them through positioning a male character who embodies so many of these traits at the center of this heroic narrative.

It is necessary, though, to qualify these claims. Though his physical strength is visually signified through his ripped torso, Jon is lean rather than thickly muscled, and significantly smaller than many of his peers; Jaime Lannister, archetype of the courtly knight in the series, looms noticeably taller than him on their first meeting, using his superior size and strength to intimidate as he pulls Jon in on a less than friendly handshake (1x1). Regarding Snow's attractiveness, it is worth noting that this is often framed within the series not as evidence of his rugged masculinity, but rather as a means of feminizing him. Specifically, his appearance is most often described by other characters as "pretty." Ygritte calls him "a pretty lad" (2x7 "A Man Without Honor"), Orell decries her for thinking that "pretty" will make her happy (3x7 "The Bear and the Maiden Fair"), and Craster tells Snow that he is "prettier than half my daughters" (2x1 "The North Remembers"). It is notable that this is a description that recurs specifically in Jon's encounters with wildlings, and which in none of these instances seems meant as a compliment. Rather, it is a way of reaffirming that Jon and other Westerosi men lack the hardness of those beyond the Wall. Thus, it is a discourse which positions Jon's masculinity as subordinate within this world, even when coming from Ygritte (it is worth noting here that it does not seem incongruent for Ygritte to insinuate herself within these hierarchical discourses, the culture of the "free folk" seeming somewhat more egalitarian and devoid of the more pronounced performance of gender roles that we often see in normative Westerosi society). This sort of framing extends even to the extratextual life of the series, with Kit Harington complaining that being objectified with words like "hunk" in popular criticism is "demeaning ... in the same way as it is for women ... when an actor is seen only for her physical beauty" (PageSix.com 2015). Again, physical attractiveness is framed here not as a hegemonic trait of the male hero, but rather an acutely feminizing one.

There are signs from an early age that Jon resists typical Westerosi conceptions of gender and power. It is Jon who encourages Arya's rejection of the passive subjectivity she is indoctrinated into by gifting her with Needle, her first sword, as a leaving present, even in contravention of Ned's initial wishes. When he jokingly tells her to "stick 'em with the pointy end" (1x2 "The Kingsroad"), the symbolism in the implied appropriation of patriarchal authority is obvious, and foreshadows the kind of subversive power Arya will eventually wield within the series. This tendency becomes even more pronounced in Jon as a result of his tumultuous relationship with Ygritte, during which he is forced to recognize her as a potentially lethal physical threat to him as much as a lover. As previously argued, the wildling culture is more egalitarian and gender-blind than that of Westeros, exemplified not just by

Ygritte but by other spearwives like Osha, whose resourcefulness is such that Maester Luwin identifies her as "the only one" who can protect Bran and Rickon (2x2 "Valar Morghulis"). The impact of Jon's time amongst this culture cannot be understated: "Aye, I talk like a wildling. I ate with the wildlings, I climbed the wall with the wildlings, I laid with a wildling girl," he angrily responds when Janos Slynt questions his description of the free folk (4x1 "Two Swords"). While it would be wrong to describe the society that exists north of the Wall as uncultured, the untamed landscape does seem to lend itself to a way of life which lacks much of the systemic indoctrination inherent in "civilized" society, and this undoubtedly plays its part in shaping Jon's character.

It would be too simplistic however, to conclude that Snow's uniqueness resides in his feminine or feminist qualities, or indeed that these qualities exist without ambiguity in the character. Much of Jon's narrative arc is, after all, a very homosocial one, from his voluntary immersion in the fraternal culture of the Night's Watch, up to his ultimately disastrous foray north of the Wall with Beric, Jorah, and the rest of the exclusively male raiding party (7x6 "Beyond the Wall"). For all his encouragement of Arya's rebellious side, he also struggles to trust Sansa's judgment or potential leadership skills after their reunion. If Jon is not an unproblematically feminist character, though, I would argue that he is a nonhegemonic character, in spite of ostensible appearances. Despite his lofty secret lineage, he is raised as a bastard, loved by most of his family but clearly demarcated as Other—like his direwolf, "the runt of the litter." From an essentialist perspective, Jon is not nearly as bound by the chains of symbolic history as his peers, since he is effectively an orphan (both biological parents dying before he is able to know them). His time at the Wall also surely plays a part in his perception of normative Westerosi values and the nature of "knowledge" in Westeros. Spending a large portion of his formative years as part of a very masculine homosocial order might typically be expected to bind Jon to the prevailing hegemony of Westeros, but the reality is very different. He is swiftly disillusioned of his notions about the Night's Watch as a noble vocation of warriors and heroes, finding instead a motley collection of rapists, thieves, and disgraced nobles whom he must now count as his "brothers." This serves as a valuable lesson on the veracity of heroic myths in Westeros, and how these myths are constituted in service of power. The men of the Watch exist geographically and metaphorically at the margins of Westeros, and Jon's experience as part of this culture is another means by which he is distinguished from his significant peers within the text.

Where young men like Tommen defer to guidance from established authority figures, damning them to reconstitute the burdensome history and structures they represent, Jon's closest confidant and advisor is Samwell Tarly. Though highborn, Sam is disowned and regarded with contempt by his warrior father, who sees him as all the things he is not. Sam is "peaceable rather than violent, conciliatory rather than dominating"—the kind of character traits which Raewyn Connell and James Messerschmidt identify as typically subordinated within hegemonic formations of masculinity (2005:67). This subordination often takes the form of "abuse" (Connell 1995:79), verbal and physical, and Sam suffers both, threatened physically and taunted with names like "piggy" by other Night's Watch recruits. Jon steps in to defend him, and Sam eventually serves as a stand-in maester at Castle Black. A case can also be made that Snow is not quite so bound by codes of honor as the hegemonic archetype of the hero might typically connote, particularly as embodied in Robb or Ned. He willingly breaks his vows to the Night's Watch through his relationship with Ygritte, and, where Robb's deference to tradition and established codes loses him a large part of his army with the execution of Karstark, Jon is pragmatic enough to cast aside generations of conflict with the free folk in order to recruit soldiers for his battles to come.

Killing the Boy

In spite of the key differences I have underlined, Jon Snow does ultimately meet the same fate as these exemplars of flawed Westerosi masculinity. When read allegorically in light of the ultimately fatal flaws these characters carry with them from childhood, death works to constitute a definitive break with aspects of the old order. Death also has another function within the text, however: one concerning renewal. The insistence that "only death can pay for life" is a recurring theme within the narrative, so death is articulated as a highly ambiguous concept, one which also has productive power. That Jon is resurrected after his death sets him apart from the other characters explored in this essay. The motif of "killing the boy" in order to "let the man be born" is an integral part of Jon's arc, beset with connotations of maturation as a hardening process. Aside from the violence inherent within the language, the implication is that the transition to manhood is not a process of evolution, but a clear break with childhood and all that goes with it. Snow is first confronted with the entreaty by Aemon Targaryen, maester at Castle Black, upon his initiation as Lord Commander (5x5 "Kill the Boy"). Aemon tells him this is necessary because "winter is almost upon us," and the sense of implicit pain in the allegorical act as both inevitable and necessary recalls the broader Stark family ethos, the familiar mantra "Winter is coming" not so much a grim forecast as a call to vigilance and preparedness. Although it is configured in the narrative as a symbolic act which Aemon urges Jon to perform himself, it can also be read in the light of Jon's murder as something which Martin sees as necessary for his final evolution as a character, and to fully dispel the conventions he seeks to subvert through the character. Catherine Johnson argues that the ways in which fantasy texts engage their audiences invite them to question "not the fantastic aspects themselves, but the normative conventions of the everyday" (Johnson 2005:7), and the use of resurrection in this case can be seen to perform a similar function.

After Jon's death and resurrection, he is more able to make a definitive break with the norms of the past. Where "killing the boy" in the other examples highlighted in this essay constituted finality, an end to the ideological crutches that came to dominate the characters (and the culture surrounding them), in Jon's case it is an allegorical means of freeing him from the same constraints. Where previously he showed pragmatism where the wildlings were concerned, his attempts to balance this with appeasement of the traditions of the Night's Watch ultimately see him killed. His murder (5x10 "For the Watch") unfolds as a symbolic attempt to reassert the standards of the old order. After being lured from his quarters to a post marked with the word "traitor," a procession of men line up to drive a dagger into him. Each one of Jon's assassins repeats the words "for the Watch" as they deal their blow, the mantra intended to underline the consequences for anyone who would attempt to change the old ways. After the "boy" in him has been exorcised, he condemns his betrayers to die with it, telling Edd after the executions that "my watch is ended"—a clear statement that any allegiance he held to the ways of the past is no more (6x3 "Oathbreaker").

The younger Jon demonstrated a willingness to test the boundaries of Westerosi gender norms, scorning the prescriptive subjectivity expected of women and recognizing the warrior spirit in Arya and Ygritte; however, he still spends much of his life in service to custodians of the old ways, such as Stannis. After his resurrection, he is able to fully break with these norms. It is significant that, while Jon is murdered by men in defense of the traditions of an exclusively male order, he is brought back from death by a woman, Melisandre (6x2 "Home"). Jon's "rebirth" is not instantaneous (each onlooker having left the room after the apparent failure of Melisandre's ritual before he awakens), and nor are the changes in his character—as previously mentioned, he is reluctant to cede significant responsibility to Sansa. When they do occur, however, they are far more definitive than before, most emphatically demonstrated in willingly bending the knee to Daenerys (7x6 "Beyond the Wall"). Doubly significant here is that this occurs directly after Daenerys has rescued Jon from certain death, a reversal of the common theme within fantasy fiction of "women in need of rescue" (Westfahl 2005:709). Jon's foray beyond the Wall with Thoros, Gendry, Sandor, Beric, Jorah, and Tormund is initially evocative of the archetypal outnumbered male "fellowship" that battles seemingly insurmountable odds to overcome evil, so the inglorious culmination of this mission is another example of the subversion of gender norms and heroic tropes within Jon's arc. This, then, marks the ultimate conclusion in his trajectory as an agent of disruption of hegemonic norms within the series.

Conclusions

Archetypes of hegemonic masculinity are prominent throughout *Game of Thrones*, part of an embattled culture in violent flux and increasingly struggling to endure as the story progresses. Jon Snow functions within this context as a vehicle through which Martin reconfigures the traditional male "hero." At once hegemonic and resistant, he is a contradictory figure—the embodiment of the symbolic union of Stark "ice" with Targaryen "fire"—who promises change even as he typifies the heroic archetype. Death, here, functions not only to suggest a break with the past, but also the possibility of renewal. Though other young men in the story struggle to leave behind the burden of history, and so must die in order for these lingering influences to be exorcised, Snow's trajectory after resurrection suggests a more flexible embodiment of masculinity, one in which deference does not equate to weakness or subordination, and heroism is malleable rather than unyielding.

NOTE

1. On numerous occasions, I refer to George R.R. Martin's storytelling or characters, though I use a combination of examples from both the books and TV series to illustrate my points. Because of certain talking points that concern parts of the story which have not yet been reached within the novels, it is necessary to adopt this multimedia approach to my analysis, and any references to Martin as author which seem to conflate these divergences reflect my trust that these representations constitute a faithful interpretation of his intention for as yet unpublished works.

REFERENCES

Connell, R.W. 1985. *Which Way Is Up? Essays on Class, Sex and Culture*. Sydney: Allen and Unwin.

Connell, R.W. 1995. *Masculinities*. Cambridge: Polity.

Connell, R.W., and James Messerschmidt. 2005. "Hegemonic Masculinity: Re-thinking the Concept." *Gender & Society* 19:829–59.

Donaldson, Mike. 1993. "What Is Hegemonic Masculinity?" *Theories and Society* 22, 5 (October):643–57.

Foucault, Michel. 1979. *Discipline and Punish*. New York: Vintage.

Hackney, Charles H. 2015. "Silk Ribbons Tied Around a Sword: Knighthood and the Chivalric Values in Westeros." In *Mastering the Game of Thrones: Essays on George R.R. Martin's A Song of Ice and Fire*, edited by Jes Battis and Susan Johnston, 132–49. Jefferson, NC: McFarland.

Johnson, Catherine. 2005. *Telefantasy*. London: BFI.

Mitchell-Smith, Ilan. 2011. "American Medieval: Hybrid American Masculinity in Medieval Popular Film." In *Americanization of History: Conflation of Time and Culture in Film and Television*, edited by Kathleen McDonald, 2–21. Newcastle: Cambridge Scholars.

PageSix.com. 2015. "Kit Harington: Being Called a Hunk Is 'Demeaning.'" Accessed 21 December 2017. https://pagesix.com/2015/03/30/kit-harington-being-called-a-hunk-is-demean ing/.

Vulture.com. 2014. "George R.R. Martin on What Not to Believe in *Game of Thrones*." Accessed 15 December 2017. http://www.vulture.com/2014/11/george-rr-martin-new-book.html.

Westfahl, Gary, ed. 2005. *The Greenwood Encyclopedia of Science Fiction and Fantasy: Themes, Works and Wonders*, Westport, CT: Greenwood Press.

Young, Helen, ed. 2015. *Fantasy and Science Fiction Medievalisms: From Isaac Asimov to A Game of Thrones*. Amherst, NY: Cambria.

Zipes, Jack. 2006. *Fairy Tales and the Art of Subversion*. London: Routledge.

A World Without Us
The End of Humanity

Michail Zontos

Throughout the episodes of *Game of Thrones*, many characters, some of them beloved, others not so much, die in a variety of mostly brutal ways. Death is essentially the game changer that moves the plot forward, leading to rebellions, wars, acts of revenge, and shifts in the balance of power in Westeros. Despite the frequent depiction of killings in the saga, death is frequently unexpected. In fact, the series tends to use death as a tool to subvert our expectations and shatter our supposed knowledge of how the world works or should work. Initially, we only hope that Ned Stark will cut the Gordian knot of power politics that threatens to sink the Seven Kingdoms into endless warfare, only to have our hopes destroyed during Ned's execution at the steps of the Great Sept of Baelor, a few days after his discovery of Joffrey Baratheon's true parentage. Later on, we believe that Robb Stark will manage to restore justice by avenging his father, only to go through the traumatic experience of the Red Wedding. Prince Oberyn's attempt to punish the man who savagely raped and murdered his sister, Elia, concludes in a similarly bitter way as he ends up brutally killed by the perpetrator of that heinous crime. George R.R. Martin's trope of killing off most of the characters that we root for is well recorded and has led, in our era of social media frenzy, to the creation of many related memes that humorously celebrate the author's sadistic tendencies and his habit to mock the long-established sense of morality in the traditional genre of fantasy literature.

The unpredictability of death in *Game of Thrones* is closely related to another frequently explored theme in the series: the apparent failure of the keepers of knowledge to really comprehend the complexities of the world. Ygritte's famous line "You know nothing, Jon Snow," cleverly comments on the supposed wisdom of the "civilized" who tend to ignore or suppress those they perceive as "uncivilized." In the novels, the inhabitants of Westeros perceive the wildlings, the people who live beyond the Wall, as barbaric tribes, with little to separate them from wild animals. The maesters, the scholars of Westeros, do not dissent from the popular opinion about the wildlings and slam their stories of giants, children of the forest, or creatures of ice that dwell beyond the Wall. To his surprise, during his time with Mance Rayder's people, Jon Snow discovers that many of the wildlings tales are true and there are things in the remote parts of the world that most educated people of Westeros would not be able to understand or explain, despite their supposed mastery of crafts such as history and science. The inability of the educated to fully explain the mysteries of the universe is an important element in the series—one closely related to the tactic of death as an element of surprise. Both tropes, in combination with Martin's technique to narrate the story in third-person limited through the point-of-view of one character, creates an eerie sense of instability which makes the reader constantly question the validity of the events described in the books. As Brian Cowlishaw notes, "Like Jon Snow, we readers of (any) fiction know nothing" (Cowlishaw 2015:67).

The most radical combination of death and humanity's failure to comprehend the universe, however, is achieved by the inclusion of the White Walkers, the supernatural entities that threaten the world of the living and whose ultimate purpose is yet unknown to the reader. It is remarkable that although Martin's saga has been praised for its realism, the story basically begins with the supernatural. The appearance of the White Walkers paints the narrative with an essence of Lovecraftian horror. Most of the acts of violence and brutality that occur throughout the series are caused by humans. They may defy our expectations and our standards of morality, but the motivations behind these actions can be logically explained. The creatures that live beyond the Wall, however, defy logic. Not only is their objective unknown, but their very existence subverts reality. Although their shape is human, they seem to be ethereal creatures made of ice that possess otherworldly magical abilities. They are able to resurrect the dead, which is the most radical act against any common understanding of life. It is also not clear whether the White Walkers seek harsh climate and move towards the direction of the winter or if it is their presence that alters weather conditions. In every sense, the terror the White Walkers represent is cosmic; it is beyond human understanding. Their existence implies the unimaginable: the possibility of a posthuman world, one that will keep moving forward without a single living human being on it—or, worse, a world inhabited by animated corpses.

Moreover, while the White Walkers advance towards the Wall to, presumably, bring about a second Long Night, there are only a few who warn against this unexplained force of destruction. Old Nan, telling stories about living dead to Bran Stark; Sam Tarly, by reading old forgotten volumes and surviving an encounter with a White Walker; the wildlings, who live on the wrong side of the frontier; and Jon Snow himself, who, in the HBO series, survives Hardhome. Yet, these people and populations are outsiders who have not been able to alter the common belief that the White Walkers are a fairytale, or at least, a tale of the distant past. In a way, Martin points to the fact that the most threatening thing in his world of ice and fire is a force that does not care about human affairs and whose very existence cannot be comprehended by the living who prefer to ignore it.

This idea of the world as a primordial force that ignores humankind is an essential element in Howard Phillips Lovecraft's literature. Lovecraft's unique terror was essentially based on his ability to establish a universe in which human beings are threatened by forces they cannot understand and by ancient creatures that human language cannot really describe because their nature is beyond any concept known to humankind. Lovecraft's entities ruled the world long before the arrival of humans. It is implied, in Lovecraft's works, that they will rise again and walk upon this earth long after the last human is gone. As the headline of a 2013 *Los Angeles Review of Books* review of the collection *The Classic Horror Stories*, a critical edition of Lovecraft stories, stated, "To understand the world is to be destroyed by it" (Nevins 2013). Similarly, main characters in Martin's saga, such as Jon Snow, eventually come to realize that the only war that matters is the one related to the threat from the North—that is, the war against the supernatural entities that defy logic and appear determined to exterminate humankind. Sadly, this realization occurs at a moment when the likelihood of human extinction appears to be high, as the constant conflict in Westeros leaves humankind unprepared. A reading of the posthuman world as it appears in *Game of Thrones* through Lovecraft's concepts of horror literature and the theories of pessimist philosopher Eugene Thacker reveals that the saga is preoccupied with the idea of humanity's vain efforts to survive in an indifferent universe.

Lovecraft's Cosmic Fear and Game of Thrones

Howard Philips Lovecraft is considered one of the most influential authors of horror literature. Although he did not achieve much fame during his lifetime (1890–1937), which ended in poverty, he is now considered one of the founders of modern horror. In his most important nonfiction essay, "Supernatural Horror in Literature" (1923), the author presents a historical study of the genre and explains the prerequisites a story should fulfill in order to be considered a proper narrative of horror (or, in Lovecraft's definition, a story of weird fiction or, even better, of cosmic fear).

For Lovecraft, weird literature's appeal is based on the fact that it triggers feelings of primordial dread: "The oldest and strongest emotion of mankind is fear, and the oldest and strongest kind of fear is fear of the unknown" (Lovecraft [1923] 1973:12). An essential element of the genre is the combination of uncertainty and danger which "are always closely allied; thus making any kind of an unknown world a world of peril and evil possibilities" (14). *Game of Thrones*, which possesses both qualities, seems to qualify as a story of cosmic fear, although it is much easier for us to categorize it as a work of fantasy.

Yet, *Game of Thrones* belongs equally to the horror genre as it occasionally evokes that fear of the unknown that Lovecraft considers as the most essential element of the genre. It is possible, then, for a story that belongs to a completely different genre, such as fantasy, to be able to reach excellent moments of cosmic fear. Indeed, there are many such instances in the series: the appearance of the White Walkers in the pilot of *Game of Thrones* (1x1 "Winter Is Coming"), the birth of the shadow killer by red priestess Melisandre of Assai (2x5 "The Ghosts of Harrenhal"), Daenerys's visions in the House of the Undying (2x10 "Valar Morghulis"), Beric Dondarrion's resurrection after being killed by the Hound (3x5 "Kissed by Fire"), and the massacre of a wildling village by an army of White Walkers and wights (5x8 "Hardhome"). In comparison to the human horrors of the series, such as the killings of favorite characters such as Ned and Robb Stark, the cases mentioned above fulfill Lovecraft's criteria:

> The true weird tale has something more than secret murder, bloody bones, or a sheeted form clanking chains according to rule. A certain atmosphere of breathless and unexplainable dread of outer, unknown forces must be present; and there must be a hint, expressed with a seriousness and portentousness becoming its subject, of that most terrible conception of the human brain—a malign and particular suspension or defeat of those fixed laws of Nature which are only safeguard against the assaults of chaos and the demons of unplumbed space [Lovecraft [1923] 1973:15].

The dreadful element in *Game of Thrones*, closely connected to the element of uncertainty, establishes the series, or at least part of it, as a modern Lovecraftian classic. As such, the series occasionally advances Lovecraft's philosophical pessimism: there is a perennial sense of cosmic indifference to the whereabouts of humanity and the ever-present possibility of mankind's destruction. A constant reminder of the possibility of humanity's end is the story of the Doom of Valyria. Once a great civilization in the continent of Essos, which was ruled by dragonlords and boasted great cultural advancements, the Valyrian Freehold virtually vanished due to a cataclysm that took place approximately a hundred years before Aegon's conquest of Westeros. Although there were survivors, such as the Targaryens, whose ancestry can be traced back to Valyria, the Valyrian civilization disappeared and with it many of the elements that made it unique, such as its command of magic. "For thousands of years the Valyrians were the best in the world at almost everything and then...," Tyrion tells Jorah Mormont while they are sailing through the ruins of Valyria, to which Jorah responds, "And then they weren't" (5x5 "Kill the Boy"). Eventually they both find out that only stone men live there now—zombie creatures that have lost their humanity due to the leprosy-like Greyscale disease. The Doom of Valyria reminds audiences of similar cases in literature such as the legend of Atlantis, the destruction of Sodom and Gomorrah, the flood survived by Noah in Genesis, or substantiated events such as the destruction of Pompeii, all tales that describe human annihilation at the hand of forces that humans seem unable to comprehend or prevent. This element of cosmic indifference, which is strong in the series, hints to the idea of a posthuman world—a world without us.

It is interesting that, in the relevant literature, concepts of the posthuman tend to focus on hybridity or human enhancement. As William S. Haney II puts it, "posthumanism envisions a biology/machine symbiosis that will promote this extension by artificially enhancing our mental and physical powers" (Haney 2006:viii). This branch of posthuman theory is often called transhumanism. Other theorists have focused on the problem of the human/animal binary (Wolfe 2003). In *Game of Thrones*, we view elements of both. Consider for example, Beric Dondarrion and Jon Snow's resurrection. In both cases, the magic of the Lord of Light is a form of technology that allows two dead bodies to come back to life. In comparison to the wights, both characters retain their humanity, although we are told by Beric Dondarrion that each time he returns to the world of the living he is "a bit less" (3x5). The Mountain's resurrection at the hands of disgraced former maester Qyburn is another example in which science seems able to end the consequences of dying. Warging, the ability of certain humans to enter the body of animals (or other humans), experience the world through their senses, and control their actions, is another example of hybridity in the series. Certain characters, such as Melisandre, have managed to achieve one of transhumanism's essential tenets, namely the prolonging of life, while, in a more abstract level, Arya's ability to bring back dead people (or, at least, their shape) by wearing their faces is another example of hybridity.

All these cases represent examples of both hybridity and human enhancement: the merging of the human with the posthuman seems to make the characters stronger. The dead come back to life and, on some occasions, with greater physical strength, while wargs have superhuman abilities. These cases are also horrific as they constitute anomalies that subvert the normal order of things. Dead are not supposed to come back to life and humans should not be able to control the lives of animals. Moreover the series deepens the relevant discussion by stressing a more pessimistic version of the posthuman:

the idea of the complete extinction of the human element from the earth as the greatest example of the posthuman in the series is the White Walker threat and the Walkers' ability to transform the dead into animated corpses. In this sense, while *Game of Thrones* cleverly comments on several branches of the posthuman theory, it focuses strongly on the idea of posthumanity, which is closely related to the pessimism of Lovecraft and Eugene Thacker's concept of a world without us.

Thinking the Unthinkable: A Posthuman World

Events such as the Doom of Valyria, the greyscale disease, and, more importantly, the advance of the White Walkers towards Westeros, has led many commentators to explain *Game of Thrones* as a metaphor for climate change. This idea became popular in 2012, when political scientist Charli Carpenter published an article in *Foreign Affairs*, in which she argues that:

> environmental disaster, meanwhile, threatens all even as it is ignored by most. Far from being an allegory for immigration reform, the story of the Northern Wall and the forces it holds at bay is about the mistaken belief that industrial civilization can stand against the changing forces of nature. The slogan "Winter Is Coming" is meant literally as well as metaphorically: planetary forces are moving slowly but inexorably toward climactic catastrophe as the infighting among kings and queens distracts them from the bigger picture [2012].

In this sense, Carpenter considers *Game of Thrones* "a collective action story" in which a common danger requires all to unite against a greater enemy, and comments on the inability of humans to leave their differences behind in order to prepare themselves against forces of nature that threaten their very existence. Similarly, historian Rebecca Rideal, by focusing on the greyscale disease that has inflicted characters such as Princess Shireen and Jorah Mormont, argues that the important element in the story is the historical fear of disease (Rideal 2017). Greyscale, like the transformation of the dead to wights by the White Walkers, is contagious and threatens, if it expands, to create a world of stone men—similar to the world of animated corpses that will become a reality in the case of the White Walkers' expansion.

The possibility of great catastrophes caused by diseases or climate change have led recent pessimistic philosophers to study horror in order to come to terms with the unthinkable idea of a posthuman world. Eugene Thacker, a leading figure in this school of thought, has occasionally returned to Lovecraft's ideas in order to establish a concept of the world without us. In his influential study *In the Dust of This Planet* (2011), Thacker argues that "the world is increasingly unthinkable—a world of planetary disasters, emerging pandemics, tectonic shifts, strange weather, oil-drenched seascapes, and the furtive, always-looming threat of extinction" (Thacker 2011:1). This very idea, Thacker believes, forces us to "confront an absolute limit to our ability to adequately understand the world at all" (1). Thacker underlines that as human beings we tend to explain the world in anthropocentric terms and philosophy, an existential discipline, has a great difficulty in comprehending a world in which existence—at least human existence—becomes obsolete. For this reason, Thacker notes that we reach a stage he terms the horror of philosophy:

> the isolation of those moments in which philosophy reveals its own limitations and constraints, moments in which thinking enigmatically confronts the horizon of its own possibility—the thought of the unthinkable that philosophy cannot pronounce but via a non-philosophical language [Thacker 2011:2].

In order to expand our horizons and be able to think of the unthinkable, Thacker divides the world into three distinct concepts that can help us understand his idea of cosmic pessimism: "a pessimism of the world without us" or "of primordial insignificance" (Thacker 2012:68):

- The world-for-us (or the World), which is "the world that we, as human beings, interpret and give meaning to, the world that we relate to or feel alienated from, the world that we are at once a part of that that is also separate from the human."
- The world-in-itself (or the Earth), which is "the world in some inaccessible, already-given state, which we then turn into the world-for-us." For Thacker this is a paradoxical concept, for when we think of the world-in-itself then it becomes the world-for-us. Yet, he underlines that "we are most reminded of the world-in-itself when the world-in-itself is manifest in the form of natural disasters." The concept of extinction that is always present in conversations about natural disasters leads to the third concept, which is
- The world-without-us (or the Planet), which "cannot co-exist with the human world-for-us; the world-without-us is the subtraction of the human from the world" [Thacker 2011:4–9].

The third concept is the most challenging, according to Thacker, for although it is important to comprehend, it is also, somehow, impossible, as it requires the comprehension of the incomprehensible. Horror, then, for Thacker "is a non-philosophical attempt to think about the world-without-us philosophically" (Thacker 2011:9). It is in horror literature, in writers such as Lovecraft, whose writings are filled with unexplained terrors that language cannot really describe, and in the indifference of these terrors towards humanity where we can find an attempt to understand the world-without-us. As Graham Harman notes, Lovecraft's writing style makes clear a "tension between a real object and its real qualities" (Harman 2012:36). Such moments, Harman writes, are evident "whenever there is talk of outermost regions of the cosmos ruled by deities or forces so bizarre that an empty proper name is all that can be used to designate something for which no tangible qualities are available" (36). Lovecraft, for example, never makes clear what his primordial monsters, the Cthulhu, look like. "If I say that my somewhat extravagant imagination yielded simultaneous pictures of an octopus, a dragon, and a human carica-ture, I shall not be unfaithful to the spirit of the thing ... but it was the general outline of the whole which made it most shockingly frightful," Lovecraft writes in his description of the creature in *The Call of Cthulhu* ([1928] 2005:125–26). *Game of Thrones'* terrors similarly challenge us to think about such forces that we cannot entirely comprehend, and yet, we have to encounter. Although the show's depictions of the White Walkers are much more solid than Lovecraft's descriptions of his monsters, the creatures are shrouded in ambiguity. They appear to be like mummified humanoid crea-tures, yet they are ethereal. It is, however, in the motives of White Walkers where the series excels in providing the frightful ambiguity that challenges our perceptions of the world. What, really, do the White Walkers want? Are they a force of nature, indifferent about humanity and the concepts humanity understands, or do they have human needs and feelings? It is important to note that the White Walkers in the novels remain more ambiguous in their description and motives than in the series: While in the series we have a Night King who seems to lead the rest of them, in the novels no such figure exists—a Night's King is mentioned as a character who lived in the Age of Heroes, a legendary commander of the Night's Watch who apparently fell in love with a female White Walker, yet there is no evidence in the books that the story of the Night's King is anything more than an old folk tale. Although in the series it is explained that the White Walkers were created by the Chil-dren of the Forest to protect them from men, this has not been discussed in the books—even then, we should note that the Children of the Forest are creatures that transcend the human element. In both the novels and the series, we can never be sure about what the White Walkers are exactly or what they want—and this is what makes them so scary.

As the story in the TV series has advanced beyond Martin's books, we now know that Jon Snow has managed to convince at least the people of the North, who have proclaimed him King, and one more leader of Westeros, namely Daenerys Targaryen, about the importance of preparing against the White Walker invasion. He also attempts to convince Cercei Lannister, albeit unsuccessfully. This means that Carpenter's correct assertion that the story is a call of collective action is also a sad one, because the rivalries of Westeros may not allow such unity to take place. It is true that as the threat of the White Walkers becomes more apparent, an impressive alliance has been formed among former enemies—the fact that Jon Snow may end up fighting alongside Jaime Lannister is a case in point. Yet, we are at a point where the White Walkers have penetrated the Wall, while, at the same time, Cercei still plots against her human enemies. It may be that the forming of the alliance has come too late and that this very alliance will still have to deal with Cercei's hostilities. If this is the case, then we are much closer to Thacker's ideas of Lovecraftian pessimism. In the end, the whole known world in *A Song of Ice and Fire* may well end up like the ruins of Valyria.

Conclusion: "The things we love destroy us every time"

Lovecraft has frequently been described as a misanthrope. French author Michel Houellebecq has written a long essay on Lovecraft, whose subtitle is "Against the World, Against Life." Houellebecq notes:

> Few beings have ever been so impregnated, pierced to the core, by the conviction of the absolute futility of human aspiration. The universe is nothing but a furtive arrangement of elementary particles. A figure of transition toward chaos. That is what will finally prevail. The human race will disappear. Other races in turn will appear and disappear. The skies will be glacial and empty, traversed by the feeble light of half-dead stars. These too will disappear. Everything will disappear. And human actions are as free and as stripped of meaning as the unfettered movement of the elementary particles [Houellebecq 2005:32].

The above sentence captures Lovecraft's (and probably Thacker's) pessimism; however, it cannot totally apply in Martin's work. Although his text shares many of the elements of cosmic horror, Martin retains some element of hope, albeit small. It is virtually impossible in Lovecraft's stories to find a character who views the world in a positive or optimistic way. In virtually all of his stories, the main characters, who in many cases are the narrators themselves, end up irrelevant in the grand scheme of things—their lives are nothing more than footnotes in the unknown story of an indifferent cosmos. Although *Game of Thrones* seems to be heading in the same direction, the series allows some form of optimism in a few characters. Jon Snow's struggle to arrange an alliance of the living against the dead is the prime example, while the same optimism is shared by Daenerys Targaryen. Bran Stark's transformation to the Three-Eyed Crow also allows some hope as he has the ability to see the past, the present, and the future. It is still a question, though, if he has the ability to influence what is to come.

Yet, we should remain alert regarding *Game of Thrones*' crumbs of optimism. Even the most religiously optimistic characters in the series, such as Melisandre, have been shown to misuse their self-confidence and ability to partially foresee the future in directions unknown even to them. Optimism requires certainty and certainty is a dangerous quality in an uncertain, incomprehensible world. The end of the story, of course, is still untold and its direction may surprise even the most perspicacious readers. Martin's writings, and this is well adapted in the series, tend to suggest that at his most realistic moments, he accepts the brutality of life, while in his more fantastic ones, the indifference of the cosmos. The combination of unexpected death and the inability to understand the machinations of the world will remain constant elements in the TV series if the creators decide to remain true to the spirit of the so far published volumes. It may be, though, that due to the constant harassment he endures from fans, in order to finish the series, Martin will decide to leave the story unfinished, and inform us after the finale of the TV series that the ending he had in mind was radically different from that of the show—an ending we will not be able to read. This would be a great statement on cosmic indifference, as the world of ice and fire would end without being concluded—giving, in this way, a great blow to our human-centric notion that the end should necessarily have a meaningful conclusion.

REFERENCES

Carpenter, Charli. 2012. "Game of Thrones as Theory." *Foreign Affairs*, 29 March. Accessed 6 April 2018. https://www.foreignaffairs.com/articles/2012–03-29/game-thrones-theory.
Cowlishaw, Brian. 2015. "What Maesters Knew: Narrating Nothing." In *Mastering the Game of Thrones: Essays on George R.R. Martin's A Song of Ice and Fire*, edited by Jes Battis and Susan Johnston, 57–69. Jefferson, NC: McFarland.
Haney, W.S., II. 2006. *Cyberculture, Cyborgs, and Science Fiction: Consciousness and the Posthuman*. Amsterdam: Rodopi.
Harman, Graham. 2011. *Weird Realism: Lovecraft and Philosophy*. Alresford: Zero Books.
Houellebecq, Michel. 2005. *H.P. Lovecraft: Against the World, Against Life*. Translated by Dorna Kazheni. London: Gollancz.
Lovecraft, H.P. [1923] 1973. *Supernatural Horror in Literature*. Mineola, NY: Dover.
Lovecraft, H.P. [1928] 2005. "The Call of Cthulhu." In *H.P. Lovecraft: Against the World, Against Life* by Michel Houellebecq, 121–57. London: Gollancz.
Martin, George R.R. 1996. *A Game of Thrones*. New York: Bantam.
Martin, George R.R. 1999. *A Clash of Kings*. New York: Bantam.
Martin, George R.R. 2000. *A Storm of Swords*. New York: Bantam.
Martin, George R.R. 2005. *A Feast of Crows*. New York: Bantam.
Martin, George R.R. 2011. *A Dance with Dragons*. New York: Bantam.
Nevins, Jess. 2013. "To Understand the world is to be destroyed by it: On H.P. Lovecraft." *Los Angeles Review of Books*, 5 May. Accessed 6 April 2018. https://lareviewofbooks.org/article/to-understand-the-world-is-to-be-destroyed-by-it-on-h-p-lovecraft/#!.
Rideal, Rebecca. 2017. "Forget the Big Historical Names, It's Historic fear of disease that Game of Thrones nails." *New Statesman*, 6 July. Accessed 6 April 2018. https://www.newstatesman.com/culture/tv-radio/2017/07/forget-big-historical-names-it-s-historic-fear-disease-game-thrones-nails.
Thacker, Eugene. 2011. *In the Dust of This Planet*. Horror of Philosophy, vol. 1. Alresford: Zero Books.
Thacker, Eugene. 2012. "Cosmic Pessimism." *Continent* 2, 2:66–75.
Wolfe, Cary. 2003. *Animal Rites: American Culture, the Discourse of Species, and Posthumanist Theory*. Chicago: University of Chicago Press. http://www.hplovecraft.com/writings/texts/fiction/cc.aspx.

Raven: End of Days

Lindsey Mantoan

Critics and fans describe *Game of Thrones* a number of different ways; some view it as a modern-day War of the Roses, some as contemporary politics masquerading as a medieval drama. Alexis Nedd writes that it "began as a murder mystery that morphed into a political thriller, *then* became a war epic and high-fantasy romp" (Nedd 2017).

Game of Thrones is all these things, but it is also an apocalypse story—an impending doom threatens all of humanity, potentially creating a posthuman world, as Michail Zontos describes in the previous essay. In 2015, Marnie Cunningham argued, "It could be said that the underlying theme of 'winter is coming' actually refers to the real-world plight of our warming planet" (2015). Apocalypse narratives, which formerly focused on nuclear disaster, are more and more focused on potential for the end of days to be ushered in via melting glaciers, rising seas, and increasingly disastrous storms (in 2017, *The Verge* put out a list of the 14 best science fiction books about climate disaster). Those who view *Game of Thrones* as a warning about the dangers of climate change focus on the Stark words "Winter is coming," and the threat they hold: with the change in weather comes starvation, chaos, war, violence, death.

And the danger doesn't end there. Encapsulated in the phrase "Winter is coming" is what comes *after* death. If the White Walkers break through whatever defense Dany, Jon, and their alliance can construct, they stand poised to transform remaining life—human and animal—into the *undead*. With the conclusion of Season Seven, Cunningham finds that "it's become clear that all of these genres have come together to make *Thrones* the show it's been trying to become for years: A zombie showdown" (2017).

But I would argue that rather than *GoT* evolving into a single genre of narrative, its great strength comes from bending previously distinct storytelling modes. In terms of the looming end of Westeros, what makes *Game of Thrones* so compelling is its marriage of zombie apocalypse and eco-apocalypse. The White Walkers seem to possess magical ability to change the climate—or is it that climate change has brought about the White Walkers? Either way, these terrifying monsters are harbingers of eco-disaster. The army of the undead threatens the people of Westeros, but they also *are* the people of Westeros. The show draws a direct line between people and climate change during an era when some politicians call human-made climate change "a hoax."

Zombies are (regardless of the climate they live in) so hot right now. The zombie industry generates upwards of "$5 billion a year (a conservative estimate)" (Murali 2013:ix). In *Thinking Dead: What the Zombie Apocalypse Means*, Balaji Murali says of zombies: "they relate to our fear of Others, insecurities over self-reflection and the deep-seated paranoia over the possibility of an apocalyptic event" (2013:7). And, significantly, George R.R. Martin calls the White Walkers "Others" (with a capital C) in the books. Zombies are us, but different—the worst, most base versions of ourselves. Zombies are the ultimate test for humanity, for defining what is human. Plus, zombies have an especially bleak disposition toward the future—and this quality captures the shortsightedness of the dominate contemporary disposition toward climate change. Zombies don't care about the future and are focused on swallowing up more life; capitalists' concerns about the future are focused maximizing profit, not protecting the planet for new generations. Both futures reek of death.

When the Wall came down at the end of Season Seven, it inspired dozens of hilarious memes, including Ronald Reagan at a podium in front of it saying, "Mr. Night King, tear down this wall," and comparisons to Donald Trump's proposed border wall, such as "They're going to build a wall and the Night King will pay for it" (Gonzales 2017). Certainly, the wall served a very political function of separating "proper" citizens of Westeros from so-called wildlings.

But the collapse of the Wall also represents a melting of the climate's status quo, caused by what's left of the people who were meant to safeguard it, who have turned into walking drones manipulated by a centralized force controlled by, and controlling, the weather. The popular fan theory R + L = J (Rhaegar + Lyanna = Jon) has been borne out. Now we'll see if Z + CC = OF (Zombies + Climate Change = Our Future).

REFERENCES

Cunningham, Marnie. 2015. "Winter Is Coming ... Is Game of Thrones Actually About Climate Change?" *Global Citizen*, 27 November. Accessed 2 April 2018. https://www.globalcitizen.org/en/content/winter-is-coming-is-game-of-thrones-actually-about/.

Gonzales, Erica. 2017. "Twitter Is Losing It Over the Last Scene in *Game of Thrones*'s Season 7 Finale." *Harper's Bizarre*, 27 August. Accessed 4 April 2018. https://www.harpersbazaar.com/culture/film-tv/a12102462/game-of-thrones-season-7-finale-episode-reactions/.

Liptak, Andrew. 2017. "14 Sci-Fi Books About Climate Change's Worst Case Scenarios: Your Earth Day reading list." *The Verge*, 22 April. Accessed 2 April 2018. https://www.theverge.com/2017/4/22/15386776/earth-day-best-sci-fi-books-bacigalupi-atwood-ballard.

Murali, Balaji. 2013. *Thinking Dead: What the Zombie Apocalypse Means*. Lanham: Lexington Books.

Nedd, Alexis. 2017. "Is *Game of Thrones* Basically a Zombie Show Now?" *Elle* 18 August. Accessed 8 April 2018. https://www.elle.com/culture/movies-tv/a47494/is-game-of-thrones-a-zombie-show-now/.

"I should wear the armor and you the gown"
Costuming Queens

ROSE BUTLER

In 2017, Jessamyn Conrad observed that "HBO's [*Game of Thrones*] is surprisingly stylish," and asserted that the show's characters "inhabit a world with a fully realized aesthetic, created, in part, by their clothing." In a richly woven plot spanning several years, the series features a number of intertwined narratives and follows kings, queens, bastards, and usurpers as they each vie for their place on the coveted Iron Throne of the Seven Kingdoms. Set in the pseudo-medieval regions of Westeros and Essos, the show's look has clearly been inspired by the Middle Ages, including the costumes worn by its power-hungry characters. In fact, costume in *Game of Thrones* is a constant indicator of the pursuit of status and control in a narrative that is, according to Chris Longridge, "all about power … seeking it, holding it, using it and losing it" (2017).

In *Game of Thrones* costume design denotes identity, psychological motivations, and power shifts, especially in relation to three female characters: Margaery Tyrell (Natalie Dormer), Cersei Lannister (Lena Headey), and Daenerys Targaryen (Emilia Clarke), each of whom have assumed the title of queen throughout the series. By exploring how these female characters utilize dress in order to wage physical and psychological warfare this essay interrogates the idea that the show's medieval setting restricts female autonomy; the series has long been criticized for foregrounding male characters while depicting the brutalization and humiliation of several women. In 2014 this led Danielle Henderson to ask: "How much misogyny … are we expected to put up with in the name of entertainment?" Since then, critics have argued that the series affords both male and female characters compromised positions of status; as Sarah Churchwell notes, "The story recognizes that power is dark, corrupting, necessary and impossible. And it allows women the same problematic relationship to power as it does men."

However, in a narrative where female agency is necessarily hard-fought—women must battle and strategize constantly to obtain and maintain authority—dress becomes a key way that female characters express themselves, displaying their emotions and drives through the very clothes that they wear. By "sculpting their identity through visual display" (Batty and Waldeback 2008:50), the costume designs in the series—often dictated by the societal norms of Westeros and Essos—frequently make considered statements about the identity of female characters; noblewomen in particular are expected to wear gowns and robes adorned with emblems of their family sigil and fashioned from locally sourced textiles. Indeed, as Batty and Waldeback suggest in a discussion of visual storytelling, "if the character has to wear a particular type of dress enforced by others, it can be interesting to see how he or she may appropriate this outfit" (50).

According to Valerie Estelle Frankel, *Game of Thrones*'s treatment of women is "currently one of the most hotly debated issues in popular culture" (2014:1). Since the publication of Frankel's monograph, discussion of women in the series remains conflicted; Churchwell (2017) and Joanna Robinson (2016) have highlighted the complexity of the show's female protagonists as they obtain power while Anne Gjelsvik and Rikke Schulbart (2016) assert that the difficult relationship between the series's female characters and power suggests "that the women in [*Game of Thrones*] are psychologically complex, sexually transgressive, ideologically ambiguous, and intimately grounded in human emotions" (2016:9).

With that in mind, the case studies in this essay will explore how, over the course of the series, dress functions as a disguise, an act of defiance, a symbol of allegiance or an overt representation of status: an essential demonstration of how women appropriate their costumes to assert their dominance, display their sexuality, or claim their heritage. In this way, their very identity is stitched into the clothes they wear.

Growing Strong: Costuming the Rise and Fall of Margaery Tyrell

First introduced onscreen in Season Two (2x3 "What Is Dead May Never Die"), Margaery Tyrell was a shrewd player in *Game of Thrones* until her death in Season Six (6x10 "The Winds of Winter"). Over the first four seasons, Margaery deftly navigates the ruthless aristocracy of Westeros, securing multiple advantageous marriages in order to ensure her position as Queen of the

Seven Kingdoms through her betrothals to Renly Baratheon (Gethin Anthony), Joffrey Baratheon (Jack Gleeson), and Tommen Baratheon (Dean-Charles Chapman). The nature of Margaery's ambition is revealed when Petyr Baelish (Aiden Gillen) queries if she would like to become a queen (2x5 "The Ghost of Harrenhal"). Margaery responds, "No, I want to be *the* queen." A great deal of Margaery's costuming is representative of this shrewd pursuit of power through weddings arranged by her grandmother, Olenna (Diana Rigg). Much like Cersei Lannister, Margaery intends to rule through her control of the King; but where Cersei exploits her children to gain control, Margaery deftly manipulates the Baratheon boy kings and public of King's Landing to become a popular queen and a strong player of the great game.

During the War of the Five Kings throughout Season Two, Margaery wears overtly formal, bold and experimental styles, making clear that she is dressing how she imagines a queen might dress. Margaery's first costume is a symmetrical gold and livid color brocade vest over flowing silk skirts: styles that—later in the season—become synonymous with House Tyrell; this is a strikingly different aesthetic to that adopted by the royal family in King's Landing, where reds, golds and purples are prominent colors and gowns are either carefully fitted or worn in a loose, kimono style. Later, her costume takes inspiration from 21st-century high fashion rather than medieval garb; the dress worn during her scene with Petyr Baelish (2x5) is, according to costume designer Michele Clapton, an homage to Alexander McQueen's bell-adorned funnel dress worn by Björk for her "Who Is It?" music video in 2004 (Clapton in Robinson 2014). Discussing these early costumes for Margaery with Joanna Robinson and *Vanity Fair*, Clapton revealed, "It just felt right that this young ambitious girl would be experimenting with shapes, honing her style skills" (2014). Indeed, the funnel dress, with its detachable sleeves, is a clear indication of her developing style and ambition. The gown is ostentatious and overtly formal with its exaggerated high neck, heavy embroidery and gold beadwork around the shoulders; it is an early display of the status Margaery intends to obtain, and it is significant that she is wearing such a visible suggestion of her desire for power during this particularly revealing exchange with Baelish.

Following Renly's death, Margaery arrives in King's Landing (2x10 "Valar Morghulis") and her overly formal and often experimental gowns are quickly replaced. Once in the capital, her gowns are increasingly revealing, with plunging necklines and cut-out bodices continuing to emphasize her sexuality as she perceptively manipulates Joffrey by feigning interest in his increasingly bloodthirsty hobbies, seducing the boy while ostracizing his mother, Cersei. These alterations to her wardrobe highlight her youthful beauty—key in differentiating her from the queen mother. But her costume also subtly reveals that her true loyalty lies not with the young King but with her own House. She consistently wears colors traditionally associated with House Tyrell: gowns and shawls in shades of gold, green, and teal. She also wears jewelry adorned with roses, the Tyrell sigil.

The rose symbol features heavily in Margaery's costumes throughout the series. In Season Three (3x1 "Valar Dohaeris"), she wears an elaborate—and revealing—teal gown with a plunging gold and blue brocade bodice, and a silk skirt joined at the front with a bronze rose belt. While Joffrey heartily compliments her on the gown, Cersei repeatedly insults her; this is a dress designed to both ensnare men and ward off rivals. Later in the season, during a walk with Sansa Stark (Sophie Turner), Margaery dons the same dress, which stands out in stark contrast to the conservative, mauve-toned gown worn by her friend. This decadent dress is a clear indication of her ruthless and shrewd nature; its colorful design works to elevate her above the other noblewomen in King's Landing. While Cersei dons heavier, wrapped fabrics and ornately decorated armor—becoming increasingly protective and defensive as she becomes more insecure and paranoid—Margaery deliberately wields her youthful beauty as a weapon. The gown is a powerful display of confidence and sexual power, and the rose belt also carries a deep significance. The central flower is adorned with vines and thorns, suggestive of the tightening grip that Margaery—and the Tyrells—have over the Lannister household and the city of King's Landing. The thorny rose is a key motif that continues in the ornate design of her wedding gown in the following season.

Margaery's gown for her wedding to Joffrey (4x3 "The Lion and the Rose") is an unusual silk and linen dress in the same silvery blue tones of her earlier costumes. Moreover, with capped sleeves and a plunging neckline, the dress follows the same style of the gown Margaery wears throughout the third and fourth seasons. Through its simple yet seductive shape, the dress appears relatively traditional. However, detailed embroidery and metalwork reveal a dangerous edge. The gown is embroidered with creeping briar roses, vines, and thorns, made from painted leathers, mesh, and velvet. These thorny stems—much like those that feature in her earlier belt—twist around the entire shape of the dress, gathering at the front before descending in a cascade of tangled, spiked roses in the gown's train, demonstrating the sharp edge to Margaery's beauty. Here, the motif of her household becomes inherently dangerous, with the fall of spiked roses at the back of the dress echoing the spread of Tyrell influence. Similarly, the crowns that both Joffrey and Margaery wear during the ceremony make comparable statements about Margaery's growing power: her brushed silver tiara features prominent Tyrell roses, while Joffrey's Baratheon antlers are choked by twisting thorns, illustrating Margaery's grip over the boy king.

Following Joffrey's death (4x3), Margaery begins to wear heavier, less revealing gowns. While she continues to wear gold brocade bodices and flowing skirts, she shows considerably less skin and adopts a noticeably muted color palette, with dark grays, mauves, and blacks becoming more prominent during a period of respect and modesty. It is apparent that Margaery is no longer interested in dressing to impress the royal court. This assuredness and authority continues with Margaery's wedding to Tommen Baratheon in Season Five (5x3 "High Sparrow"). At the ceremony, Margaery wears a gold brocade sleeveless gown: a much more reserved, traditional and distinctly regal dress. The heavier weight of her gowns and the change of color palette to include Baratheon gold is suggestive of her partnership with the more sweet-natured and easily manipulated Tommen.

However, Margaery's reign as queen is tumultuous and short-lived. In Season Five, she is arrested by the Faith Militant (5x6 "Unbowed, Unbent, Unbroken") and imprisoned in the cells of the Red Keep until late in Season Six (6x6 "Blood of My Blood"). During this time, she is stripped of her royal attire and robed in a simple linen dress. Although Margaery is released after her conversion (6x6), she will never return to the lavish brocade embroidery and regal gowns of earlier seasons, instead opting for plain, shapeless robes to seemingly reflect her newfound faith; her costume is now modest and respectful—and therefore perfectly disguises her still-undying allegiance to her House and reflects the continued game she is playing with the High Sparrow (Jonathan Pryce). She later claims her loyalty to Tommen and the Faith in front of her grandmother (6x7 "The Broken Man"), but as Olenna leaves, Margaery passes her a folded piece of paper with the sigil of House Tyrell inside; her unflattering woolen smock dress and tiara perfectly camouflaging her continuing loyalty to her grandmother.

Margaery Tyrell's costume astutely represents her rise and fall from power and demonstrates her utilization of dress as a method of manipulating and controlling the men and women around her. From her early experimental gowns in Season Two via her youthful, revealing dresses in Season Three, to the traditional, increasingly reserved costumes she wears after her marriage to Tommen, the clothing she adopts consistently reflects her identity and position. Moreover, in a series where female characters are often considered to lack agency and identity, Margaery's costume consistently demonstrates her allegiance to her heritage and depicts her sexual confidence; throughout the series, Margaery repeatedly utilizes dress to wield her girlish power, ensnaring both Joffrey and Tommen and infuriating Cersei. Over the course of four seasons, her costume functions as an expression of her sexuality and status as she finds—and loses—the power she so desires.

Hear Me Roar: The Increasing Isolation of Cersei Lannister

Over seven seasons, Cersei Lannister has become one of the most loved—and hated—characters of the series. From persuading her brother Jaime (Nikolaj Coster-Waldau) to push Bran Stark (Isaac Hempstead Wright) from a window (1x1 "Winter Is Coming") to arranging the death of her husband Robert Baratheon (1x7 "You Win or You Die"), her narrative arc has consistently focused on her struggle to obtain and maintain power at any cost. In Season Six, Cersei arranges for a massive explosion of wildfire to erupt under the Sept of Baelor to destroy her enemies and to avoid a criminal trial at which she almost certainly would have been found guilty (6x10). Victims of the enormous blast include Margaery and most of the Tyrell family, the High Sparrow, and hundreds of noble men and women. Witnessing the death of his wife, Tommen commits suicide, and his mother subsequently claims the Iron Throne and becomes the first Queen of the Seven Kingdoms.

As a prominent figure throughout the series—as queen consort to Robert in Season One, queen regent to her sons Joffrey and Tommen from Seasons Two to Six, and queen regnant as of the final episode of Season Six—Cersei's costuming charts a fascinating journey to power. As queen, and a member of one of the richest families in Westeros, Cersei's costumes are some of the most lavish in *Game of Thrones*: an important reminder of her wealth. Moreover, costume is a vital indicator of Cersei's increasing power and paranoia. In a 2017 interview with Emily Zelmer at *Elle* magazine, Clapton notes that "Cersei has always spoken a lot through her costumes, often because she didn't have a voice." She elaborates: "I use costumes on Cersei to get across her mood and how she's feeling visually. Whether she's feeling powerful or whether she's feeling bereft." Cersei repeatedly laments her position in the Great Game, becoming envious of the men around her, who are knights, advisors, and strategists during times of war; she must find another way to assert her authority and might, and she repeatedly does this through the intricate designs of her costumes.

Before Robert's death (1x7), Cersei's costumes function primarily as a disguise. Often depicted in soft, flowing silk gowns, she wears pastel-hued dresses and delicately embroidered shawls to create a distinctly romanticized aesthetic. From the royal visit to Winterfell (1x1) to threatening Ned Stark in King's Landing (1x7), her sinister intentions and inner feelings are disguised by her pink, gold, and teal gowns. However, the detailed embroidery of these gowns reveals the precariousness of Cersei's position. Her blue kimono, worn repeatedly throughout Season Two, is adorned with delicate Japanese-style embroidery of birds and flowers; while the birds recall her cruel moniker for

Sansa ("Little Dove"), they also show, according to embroiderer Michele Carragher in an interview with Jessamyn Conrad, how "[Cersei] was caught in a gilded cage" (2017).

After Robert's death and the coronation of her son, Cersei's costume changes dramatically, becoming a visual representation of her desire to grasp control. Rather than donning traditional mourning attire after the death of her husband, Cersei quickly opts for sumptuous brocade fabrics in vibrant crimson, greens, and purples. While she still wears her Baratheon tiara, her hair is often swept up into an elaborate style, wrapping around and almost suffocating the last link to her husband. Finally seeing a chance to obtain a position of power through the ascension of her eldest son, Cersei subtly displays this newfound authority through her costume. Dismissing the Baratheon sigil, Cersei frequently starts to wear the Lannister lion on her jewelry and engraved metal bodices, displaying her true allegiance.

Following the Battle of Blackwater Bay (2x9 "Blackwater"), and the subsequent betrothal of Joffrey to Margaery, Cersei's costuming alters again as her position of power is threatened. With the arrival of Margaery, her gowns quickly represent her descent into paranoia, suspicion, and envy; indeed, the more precarious her position becomes as Margaery gains popularity in court, the heavier, more ornate, more embellished, and more armored her gowns become. She uses dress as self-preservation: to project an outward appearance of control and status. As Margaery wears increasingly youthful and revealing styles, Cersei wears progressively formal and heavily layered gowns; her dress becomes an armor to protect her position.

This use of vibrant, sumptuous colors abates in Season Four as her power diminishes. For Joffrey's wedding to Margaery (4x3), she wears a brocade gown in muted purple and bronze tones. Moreover, as a concession to Margaery's influence in King's Landing, the neckline is much deeper than usual for Cersei's gowns, with the round cut bodice exposing her collarbones. Her costume is adorned with the lion sigil: a large gold necklace with three lion heads, presumably for each of her ill-fated children, is worn around her neck—a style similar to the dragon motif chains and brooches worn by Daenerys. The dress itself features open-mouthed lions embroidered on to the shoulders in a design that imitates a military uniform. Appearing as though they are roaring, the Lions' crimson tongues are visible in the detailing; again Cersei's gown is an external representation of her inner defensiveness.

After Joffrey's death, Cersei switches to mourning attire, returning to loose, kimono-style gowns in deep blue and black tones. During this period, a number of motifs are visible in Cersei's costume design which are particularly revealing of her emotional state and inner motivations. In a Season Four episode (4x5 "First of His Name"), she wears a black kimono gown with long, billowing sleeves, and delicate bronze ribbons fastened across the chest.

Although simple in design, it is through delicate embroidery that the dress reveals Cersei's torment: the shoulders of the gown are embroidered with tiny brass skulls, symbolic of death. Later in the same episode, Cersei wears a black and gold–brocade kimono during Tommen's coronation. The black gown, with its gold-dagger pattern, recalls a fabric worn twice by Joffrey. And so as her grasp on her control continues to slip, Cersei's costumes reveal her increasingly troubled mind and foreshadow that Tommen will soon die like his brother.

Indeed, after her walk of atonement (5x10 "Mother's Mercy"), and the death of her daughter (6x1 "The Red Woman"), Cersei is crowned queen in her own right in the Season Six finale following Tommen's suicide. During this episode, Cersei's pursuit of power at any cost is mirrored in her elaborate costumes: two black gowns which both emulate the black, leather doublet that her father, Tywin Lannister (Charles Dance), once wore. Once again, the shoulders are heavily embroidered in a militaristic style: silver thread, crystals and beads form the shape of an open-mouthed lion. But while she is still wearing the Lannister sigil, she no longer dons the colors of her house. As Cersei has gained power at the cost of her children's lives, her costumes grow darker and thicker to represent her autonomy and increased isolation from her own family.

During her coronation at the end of the episode, Cersei wears a gown featuring a gold brocade with leather armor overlay: another clear emulation of her father and a further suggestion of her alienation. The shoulders are armored with silver plates, engraved in a style that is similar to Jaime's golden prosthetic hand: a link, perhaps, to the only familial connection she has left in her incestuous relationship with her brother. However, her crown is the greatest indicator that she is now truly alone. Forged from silver rather than gold, and featuring a twisted, knotted base, it appears to be decorated with an abstract lion at the center front. However, the silver prongs of the lion's mane are more reminiscent of the melted swords of the Iron Throne than the Lannister sigil; Cersei is now all-powerful—but entirely alone.

Cersei's transformation into an all-powerful ruler is displayed in her costuming for the seventh season. When Euron Greyjoy (Pilou Asbæk) arrives in King's Landing (7x1 "Dragonstone"), Cersei greets him in the throne room wearing a black silk gown adorned with shoulder embellishments that embody both danger and fragility. Silver beads and sharp metal spikes decorate both shoulders; she is now untouchable, but there is an obvious brittleness to the gown. Like Cersei, these embellishments could easily snap and break. The spread of the embroidery across the chest and towards the neck of the gown indicates Cersei being consumed by power; the silver designs creep up towards the neck, as if to choke her. The pattern evokes twisting roots or vines, suffocating any familial connections she has left and indicating the fragility and precariousness of her position. While Margaery's gowns charted her shrewd ambition and loyalty to her own House, Cersei's costumes illustrate her long-held desperation for power at any cost, using dress as a disguise, a defense, and a brazen display of authority once she has paid the ultimate price to become queen.

Fire and Blood: Costuming the Mother of Dragons

Over the course of seven seasons, Daenerys Targaryen has transformed from an exiled adolescent to Mother of Dragons. She has conquered cities, overthrowing Astapor, Yunkai and Meereen, and in the finale of Season Six, led her armada of Dothraki horsemen and Unsullied armies across the Narrow Sea to help her claim the Iron Throne. As such, perhaps more than any other female character in *Game of Thrones*, Daenerys's costumes articulate her struggle for identity; in contrast to Margaery and Cersei, whose costumes represent familial loyalty and absolute isolation respectively, as Daenerys has travelled across Essos, her dress has consistently developed to incorporate the various cultures and communities she has experienced, all the while reflecting her desire to return to Westeros and claim the Seven Kingdoms.

In the first episode of *Game of Thrones*, Daenerys is little more than a commodity. She belongs to two men: first her brother Viserys (Harry Lloyd), who then arranges her marriage to Dothraki warlord Khal Drogo (Jason Momoa) in exchange for his allegiance. Her two costumes during this episode—her "viewing dress" and wedding gown—both reflect her lack of agency. Daenerys's "viewing dress" is given to her by Viserys. A sleeveless, gauze gown held up by two silver dragon pins at the shoulders, the almost-transparent material reveals her body underneath, showing Drogo exactly what he is buying. In stark contrast to her brother's costume, comprised of heavy, regal fabrics, her transparent gown underlines how little control she has. Later in the same episode, Daenerys marries Drogo in another revealing gown made from layers of pale grey fabric, with a halter-neck strap, silver pin and engraved armbands. As Frankel notes, "her wedding dress is ... nearly skin coloured, emphasising her nakedness and vulnerability" (2014:149). After the ceremony, Drogo rapes Daenerys, a controversial deviation from Martin's original material. He first undresses her by removing the pins holding her gown in place and untying the lengths of fabric; this is a dress that "[invites] Drogo to unwrap it" (149). The implication here is that she has been given to Drogo merely as a gift, a thing to be used.

Once married, Daenerys adopts multiple costume elements from the Dothraki. As they travel across the grasslands, she wears leather riding chaps underneath loosely woven skirts and starts braiding her hair in a style typical of Dothraki Khals. At the end of the season, when Daenerys kills a comatose Drogo (1x10 "Fire and Blood") and climbs onto his funeral pyre with her dragon eggs, she is once again wearing her wedding dress. That she burns in her wedding gown and emerges naked from the ash with her newly hatched dragons is symbolic of Daenerys's rebirth at the very end of the season; the young girl sold into marriage in the first episode is dead, and the dress that symbolizes that event is, fittingly, Daenerys's funeral attire. By burning an item of clothing representative of her powerlessness, she is, as Frankel notes, "shedding her life with Drogo and reincarnating as Mother of Dragons" (2014:149).

After Drogo's death and the hatching of her dragons, Daenerys's costuming changes dramatically to reflect her newfound independence and power; the two men who once controlled her have died and she now has three dragons and the remaining khalasaar to assert her position. From Season Two onwards, Daenerys and her followers lead a mostly nomadic lifestyle, travelling across the numerous cities of Essos. After spending much of Season Two in the city of Qarth, Daenerys forges a new identity mostly comprised of Qartheen styles; she wears long, flowing gowns paired with filigree armor in a scaly, reptilian pattern. However, maintaining her connections to the Dothraki, she combines these Qartheen elements with leather armor and switches from wearing a woman's gown on the lower half of her costume to wearing leather riding chaps, trousers, and boots underneath her cloaks: important signifiers of her increased authority and assertiveness. She has had to learn to always be ready to run and to fight, and these pieces of costume suggest a practicality to her clothing—a stark contrast to the gowns worn by Cersei and Margaery.

During Season Three, as Daenerys travels to Astapor, Yunkai, and finally Meereen, a number of different colors and textiles are incorporated into her dress. The color blue features heavily in her costume throughout this season. A precious color in Dothraki culture, blue dye, like purple, is expensive, and therefore corresponds with Daenerys's rise to power. Similarly, as she conquers each city, acquiring an army of Unsullied soldiers and a group of mercenaries named the Second Sons, her costumes gradually to start to incorporate more of her Targaryen heritage. High necks and cuffed shoulders evoke the costume of her brother—and recall the militaristic look of Cersei's later costumes—whilst complex lock-stitch embroidery creates a detail that emulates reptilian scales. The more followers Daenerys acquires, the more her costume incorporates traditional Targaryen elements and particularly dragon-themed jewelry; she combines these with her braided Dothraki hairstyles, which, like those of Khals who are successful in battle, become increasingly elaborate with each city she takes.

After the conquest of Meereen (3x10 "Mhysa"), Daenerys acquires new wealth and a permanent home. During this time, as she decides to stay in the city to practice ruling, her costume reflects an increased formality. However, she also displays her sympathy to the former slaves of the city by wearing simple, flowing gowns that connect to a metal collar, imitating the restraints worn by those kept in servitude. In Seasons Five and Six, however, she increasingly begins to wear gowns with plunging necklines in white or grey, evoking a sense of strength, confidence and remoteness. As Clapton notes in an interview with Nicole Lyn Pesce at *New York Daily News*, "I wanted to show a sense of this divine right that Dany seems to feel she has, an overwhelming belief that she is beyond question" (2015). While her more revealing gowns recall the costumes of Margaery—attractive and youthful, yet authoritative—Daenerys's increasing adoption of large metal jewelry, armor, and neck pieces evokes the costume of Cersei Lannister as they both become more powerful. But while Cersei's costuming repeatedly underlines her progressively individualistic approach to power, as Daenerys adopts more and more Targaryen motifs, she retains a rather eclectic style, consistently incorporating cultures and styles from her travels.

When Daenerys finally sets foot on Westeros (7x1), her costume firmly evokes her Targaryen heritage. Throughout the season, she mostly wears long cloaks over her trousers, all in shades of blacks and greys with accents of red. Discussing these choices with HBO, Clapton notes, "I wanted to start going towards charcoal and red because those are [Targaryen] sigil colors" (HBO 2017). Clapton explores the connection between Targaryen colors and Daenerys finally seizing power in an interview with Emily Zelmer: "there's a creeping of red within the scaling embroidery of her coat. It's like she's finally beginning to grasp power and she feels closer to the idea of taking the throne, of coming home" (2017). Similarly, Daenerys's jewelry, as a development from the neckpieces and armor throughout previous seasons, begins to encompass her Targaryen roots. In Season Seven, she wears a silver chain with a three-headed dragon, a piece which, Clapton explains to HBO, "signified status … I wanted her to have authority" (2017).

In the Season Seven finale, Daenerys flies north of the Wall to rescue Jon Snow (Kit Harington) and his comrades (7x6 "The Dragon and the Wolf"). Donning a gray and white fur coat, her costume marks a pivotal moment in her life. As Clapton discusses in an interview with Julie Kosin, "I can't think of another time she's gone to the aid of someone who is also, to some extent, a rival.… It had to be a real statement piece. It looks very warrior queen" (2017). It also reflects her fledgling relationship with Snow, as she adopts fabrics associated with House Stark: leather and fur. Daenerys's regal ascension, then, has consistently been explored through her intricate costumes, from an exiled princess to be bought and sold to a "warrior queen."

Through costumes that emphasize her connections to the nations of Essos and her adoption of colors and styles—reds, blacks and dragon motifs—that recognize her Targaryen heritage, Daenerys's costume reflects her experiences and relationships and references allies that will no doubt become crucially important as *Game of Thrones* nears its climax.

Conclusion: Costuming Queens
   in Game of Thrones

Anne Gjelsvik and Rikke Schubart assert that a portion of *Game of Thrones'* success derives from the inclusion of so many "female characters who have generated praise, intense attention and fascination, heated debate, controversy, and have been read as both feminist and antifeminist, as subversive and repressive" (2016:1). From queens to smallfolk, "women are everywhere" (1) in *Game of Thrones* and ultimately its narrative has come to be one interested in "women and power" (Churchwell 2017).

In comparing *Game of Thrones* to the historical period upon which it is loosely based, Eliana Dockterman notes that "The women had to deal with the misogyny inherent in a Medieval society, but, forced to the sidelines, they found creative ways to seize power" (2015). As this essay has explored, costume is a vital device through which their increasing status and authority is expressed; as Clapton claims to Megan Townsend, "they want to be taken seriously, they want power, so they are dressing powerfully" (2018).

The details of Margaery's costume mirror her journey from Renly's bride to a broken woman, via her time as queen of the Seven Kingdoms. Similarly, Cersei's costuming changes as her power ebbs and flows and becomes an external manifestation of her traumas, the dark colors she comes to embrace in Seasons Six and Seven a representation of the grief she feels for her lost children and her detachment from her family. Finally, Daenerys's costume has functioned as a manifestation of her sense of identity and the vast journey she has been on as she moves ever closer towards staking her claim to the Iron Throne; her costumes have repeatedly reflected the various cultures she has experienced, before finally incorporating her regal heritage at the end of Season Six.

And so, in a series so often discussed in terms of its sexual politics and treatment of women, costume becomes a vital way through which female identity and power is explored; in a world where women have been brutalized and even dehumanized, costume is repeatedly utilized as a physical representation of shifting allegiances, psychological motivations, and traumatic struggles. Perhaps some of the criticism of *Game of Thrones'* treatment of women is not entirely unfounded; in the show's early seasons, its women are undoubtedly oppressed. However, many of those women have since risen to positions of enormous power, as evidenced by their changing costumes. In short, a comment uttered by Cersei in an argument with King Robert in "A Golden Crown" (1x6)—"I should wear the armor and you the gown"—as proven to be not just a witty retort, but a metaphorical prophecy.

References

Batty, Craig, and Zara Waldeback. 2008. *Writing for the Screen: Creative and Critical Approaches*. Basingstoke: Palgrave Macmillan.

Churchwell. Sarah. 2017. "Drama Queens: Why It's All about Women and Power on Screen Right Now." *The Guardian*, 22 July. Accessed 12 January. https://www.theguardian.com/books/2017/jul/22/game-of-thrones-handmaids-tale-wonder-woman-female-power.

Conrad, Jessamyn. 2017. "Embroidering 'Game of Thrones." *The New Yorker*, 20 August. Accessed 12 January 2018. https://www.newyorker.com/culture/culture-desk/embroidering-game-of-thrones.

Dockterman, Eliana. 2015. "*Game of Thrones*'s Women Problem Is about More Than Sexual Assault." *Time*, 11 June. Accessed 12 January 2018. http://time.com/3917236/game-of-thrones-woman-problem-feminism/.

Frankel, Valerie Estelle. 2014. *Women in Game of Thrones: Power, Conformity and Resistance*. Jefferson, NC: McFarland.

Gjelsvik, Anne, and Rikke Schubart, eds. 2016. *Women of Ice and Fire: Gender, Game of Thrones and Multiple Media Engagements*. London: Bloomsbury.

HBO: Making of *Game of Thrones*. 2017. "To Dress a Queen: The Season 7 Costumes of Daenerys and Cersei." HBO, 27 August. Accessed 12 January. http://www.makinggameofthrones.com/production-diary/to-dress-a-queen-the-season-7-costumes-of-daenerys-and-cersei.

Henderson. Danielle. 2014. "Game of Thrones: Too Much Racism and Sexism So I Stopped Watching." *The Guardian*, 29 April. Accessed 12 January 2018. https://www.theguardian.com/tv-and-radio/2014/apr/29/game-of-thrones-racism-sexism-rape.

Kosin, Julie. 2017. "Michele Clapton on How Dany's Coat Hints at Her Relationship with Jon Snow." *Harper's Bazaar*, 24 August. Accessed 12 January. http://www.harpersbazaar.com/culture/film-tv/a12090109/daenerys-coat-inspiration-game-of-thrones/.

Longridge, Chris. 2017. "Is There a Giant Allegory Behind *Game of Thrones* That We All Missed?" *Digital Spy*, 7 September. Accessed 12 January 2018. http://www.digitalspy.com/tv/game-of-thrones/feature/a837470/game-of-thrones-allegory-metaphor/.

Pesce, Nicole Lyn. 2015. "'Game of Thrones' Costumers give Emilia Clarke, Sophie Turner, Natalie Dormer & Others Some Elegant Designers on the Crown." *New York Daily News*, 7 May. Accessed 12 January 2018. http://www.nydailynews.com/entertainment/tv/game-thrones-leading-ladies-outfits-rule-article-1.2212870.

Robinson, Joanna. 2014. "How Do You Dress the Kate Middleton of Westeros? *Game of Thrones* Costume Designer Tells All." *Vanity Fair*, 22 February. Accessed 12 January 2018. https://www.vanityfair.com/hollywood/2014/02/game-of-thrones-fashion.

Robinson, Joanna. 2016. "*Game of Thrones*: How Women Went from Victims to Conquerors." *Vanity Fair*, 26 June. Accessed 12 January 2018. https://www.vanityfair.com/hollywood/2016/06/game-of-thrones-winds-of-winter-recap-finale-women-power.

Townsend, Megan. 2017. "Game of Thrones Season 7: Costume Designer Michele Clapton Talks Female Power Dressing, War and 'The Crown.'" *The Independent*, 27 August. Accessed 12 January 2018. http://www.independent.co.uk/arts-entertainment/tv/game-of-thrones-season-7-costume-designer-michele-clapton-talks-female-power-dressing-war-and-the-a7912736.html.

Zelmer, Emily. 2017. "Game of Thrones Costume Designer Michele Clapton Explains the Details You Missed." *Elle*, 4 August. Accessed 12 January 2018. http://www.elle.com/culture/movies-tv/news/a47144/game-of-thrones-costume-designer-michele-clapton-easter-eggs/.

Game of Thrones
as *Gesamtkunstwerk*
Adapting Shakespeare and Wagner

Dan Venning

"I am hungry for revenge,
And now I cloy me with beholding it."
            —Margaret of Anjou, in *Richard III*
                (4.4.61–62)[1]

Game of Thrones abounds with Shakespearean resonances and adaptations—an internet search for "'Game of Thrones' AND Shakespeare" leads to over a million results, many of which go into great detail analyzing these connections. A few central analogues bear mentioning. The fictional houses of Lannister and Stark sound unmistakably like the real Lancaster and York families immortalized in dramatic literature by William Shakespeare. Perhaps the fiercest character in all of Shakespeare's plays is Margaret of Anjou, the foreign-born warrior Queen of England who is one of only three characters to appear in four of Shakespeare's plays.[2] Margaret is a sort of Cersei and Daenerys in one. When we first meet Margaret, she is, like Daenerys, a girl who has become a sexual victim of a war she herself had no part in causing. Like Cersei, she becomes an unfaithful wife to a king who has no real interest in ruling his country. Margaret wears the pants (or rather, armor) in her marriage, leading the Lancastrian forces of Henry VI. Margaret, like Daenerys in Westeros, is a foreigner in England who nonetheless inspires people to fight for her. Like Cersei, she is viciously cruel, delighting in the mental torment of her enemies. Margaret's soldiers kill Rutland, the young son of the rebellious Richard of York, and then capture Richard. She taunts him, offering to dry his tears at the death of his son with a napkin stained "with the blood /

… made issue from the bosom of thy boy" (*3H6*, 1.4.80–82), puts a paper crown on his head, knocks it off, and stabs him, becoming one of the few female Shakespearean characters to commit violence onstage. Cersei's torture of her imprisoned enemies Septa Unella in "The Winds of Winter" (6x10) and Ellaria Sand in "The Queen's Justice" (7x3) evokes Margaret's vengeance against York.

Shakespeare's English history plays frequently illustrate the dictum that, in civil and political strife, one either *wins or dies*—a fact understood best by Shakespeare's usurper Henry IV, clearly a model for Tywin Lannister. Tywin, who betrays the Mad King, wins the War of the Five Kings not with battles but with letters and plots, and tries to instill his political wisdom in his children, who rarely seem to listen. He does not usurp the throne himself, having intuited that there may be more power in being Hand of the King. He understands all too well, like Shakespeare's Henry IV, how "uneasy lies the head that wears a crown" (*2H4*, 3.1.31). Robert Baratheon seems modeled most after Shakespeare's King John, the titular character from a little-staged work written in the mid–1590s about the tumultuous reign of the English monarch from 1199 to 1216. Shakespeare's King John has neither the aptitude for nor interest in ruling his country. Tellingly, the hero and central character of *King John* is a character given the speech prefix "Bastard." Philip Falconbridge, a bastard who is welcomed as a full member of his family, fights honorably (unlike King John) for England throughout the play, and is eventually recognized as the illegitimate son of Richard I: a man who, like George R.R. Martin's Jon Snow, at least on the strength of his character, if not his lineage, should be the king. The Bastard has the last lines in *King John*, arguing for an honorable society and saying, "Naught shall make us rue / If England to itself do rest but true" (*Jn.* 117–18).

Numerous such adaptations of and allusions to other literary sources can be enumerated and analyzed in more or less depth, whether from Shakespeare, J.R.R. Tolkein's *Lord of the Rings* (1954), Robert Jordan and Brandon Sanderson's *Wheel of Time* books (1990–2013), or other works of fantasy or English historical fiction. Moreover, *Game of Thrones*—David Benioff and D.B. Weiss's soon-to-be-complete HBO television show—is *itself* an adaptation: of Martin's currently unfinished *A Song of Ice and Fire* (1996–) novels. However, more illuminating than enumerating such analogues is addressing the questions of *why* such adaptations work and *how* they deploy references to earlier material in order to create a particular new kind of pleasure, provoking readers' and viewers' imaginations.

To explore such questions, I turn to another source for Martin's work: Richard Wagner's *Ring* cycle (1876) of operas. Martin, Benioff, and Weiss have deployed archetypal characters, narratives, and resonances from foundational Western authors such as Wagner in order to highlight themes of gender, power, and performance that are simultaneously historical and profoundly relevant today, doing so in a way that not only relies on Wagner as a source, but replicates his dramatic theories. Furthermore, by relying on works that have attained a mythic status in Western culture such as Wagner's *Ring* cycle, the creators of *Game of Thrones* have created something similar to what Wagner himself called a *Gesamtkunstwerk*, or "total work of art," combining poetry, music, dance, painting, and all of the arts, designed to fill the "common and collective want" of the "Volk" (Wagner 1892:778).

Other critics have examined connections between *Game of Thrones* and Wagner, but largely in terms of plot. In a recent column entitled "Wagner, Incest, and 'Game of Thrones,'" Alex Ross, the classical music critic for *The New Yorker*, aptly compares the HBO series *Game of Thrones* to Richard Wagner's *Ring of the Nibelung* cycle, highlighting shared themes of incest, critiques of conservative mores presented through archetypal allegories, and powerful female characters like Brünnhilde and Daenerys (Ross 2017). Ross points out that Wagner's *Ring*, like *Game of Thrones*, was immensely popular when it first appeared, stirring the imaginations of a young generation. Simon Williams describes the 1876 opening of the *Ring* cycle as one of the most notable theatrical events of the entire 19th century (Williams 1990:154).

In his essay "The Art-Work of the Future" (1849) in which he describes his concept of the Gesamtkunstwerk, Wagner describes how he sees art as an "immediate vital act" that provides spiritual fulfillment to both individuals and a populace as a whole, through poetry, which inspires love, tone, which connects to a natural wellspring of spiritual energy, and dance and acting, which make these abstract elements corporeal. He describes the orchestral music that accompanied his operas as providing a "loam of endless, universal Feeling" (Wagner 1892:778, 789). Wagner spent his career working towards creating such a work with his *Ring* cycle.

While the operas were first performed as a cycle at the opening of the Bayreuth Festspielhaus in 1876, Wagner had been working on his *Ring* operas for over a quarter of a century. After fleeing from Dresden in 1849 in the wake of the failed revolutions he had passionately supported, Wagner lived in Zurich, writing a number of noteworthy essays that signaled his dissatisfaction with contemporary art and his plans to create his own epic masterpiece. In "Art and Revolution" (1849), an essay that is simultaneously leftist and elitist, Wagner explains that modern, mid–19th-century "art," whether theatre, literature, or music, is debased and not really art at all because it is tied to the commercial viability of the work through ticket sales and must thus cater to the unrefined tastes of the general public. Of course, such a theory might have been motivated by the fact that Wagner's major works of the 1840s, *The Flying Dutchman* (1843) and *Tannhäuser* (1845), had been coolly received by audiences and critics. In "Art and Revolution," Wagner argues that by separating art from business, whether through patronage or state subsidy, a more authentic art, along the lines of that experienced by the ancient Greeks, could be achieved. In *Opera and Drama* (1851) he builds on "The Art-Work of the Future," articulating how music and verse can organically intertwine and support one another. He describes these as "melodic moments" that could recur and highlight various elements. In his 1876 work *Thematic Guide through the Music to Richard Wagner's Festival Drama The Ring of the Nibelung*, the critic and composer Hans von Wolzogen coined the term *Leitmotiv* to describe such repeated melodic moments (Grey 2008:85–114 and Thoreau 2009:133–50). The anglicized term "leitmotif" has of course become a central term in musicology, but is often especially associated with Wagner. Finally, in his 1851 essay "A Communication to My Friends," Wagner describes his intention to produce his own Gesamtkunstwerk: a prelude and trilogy of mythological works (Treadwell 2008:179–91). As is the case with Martin's still unfinished series *A Song of Ice and Fire* (the first book of which was published in 1996, with the sixth and seventh books, *The Winds of Winter* and *A Dream of Spring* still forthcoming), this was a lengthy process that took Wagner the next 25 years to complete.

In his *Ring* cycle, Wagner was consciously creating an adaptation of primal archetypal myths. The story Wagner chose to adapt is the *Nibelungenlied*, a medieval Austro-Germanic saga, which Elizabeth Magee calls the "greatest and most widely-known German literary version of the native Nibelung saga" (Magee 1993:29). The story concerns the hero Siegfried, who slays a dragon and is eventually murdered through the treachery of his in-laws. Wagner combined this story with the pre–Christian Norse Eddas, turning Siegfried into a demi-god, the grandson of Wotan (Odin), king of the gods. The central "ring" of the title, forged by the Nibelung dwarf Alberich from gold stolen from the Rhine, is a talisman that offers the power to rule the world. The ring's eventual return to the Rhine by the Valkyrie Brünnhilde at the funeral pyre for Siegfried prompts the destruction of Valhalla and the old gods. Brünnhilde is the daughter of Wotan and the goddess Erda; her lover Siegfried is the son of Siegmund, Wotan's son by a mortal mother. This makes Brünnhilde not only Siegfried's lover, but also his aunt.

As Ross notes in his *New Yorker* article, this aunt/nephew incest is precisely the relationship of Daenerys Targaryen and Jon Snow, who was born Aegon Targaryen. In final episode of Season Seven (7x7 "The Dragon and the Wolf"), Bran uses his greensight to discover Jon's origins. We see him watch the marriage of Rhaegar Targaryen and Lyanna Stark, as he says in voiceover, "Robert's Rebellion was built on a lie. Rhaegar didn't kidnap my aunt, or rape her. He loved her." As Bran utters the words "He loved her," we see Jon approach Daenerys's chamber and knock. "And she loved him," Bran says, as Dany opens the door. As the two make love, we hear Bran say, "He's never been a bastard. He's the heir to the Iron Throne." Thus, the incest is high-lighted as genuine love, something Martin had explored from the beginning of his series through the incestuous twins Cersei and Jaime Lannister—whose own relationship hearkens back to that of Siegfried's incestuous twin parents, Siegmund and Sieglinde.

Beyond the theme of incest, Ross notes that both Wagner and Martin created their masterpieces from leftist impulses; writing that "Wagner intended an allegorical assault on modern capitalist society [... and] bourgeois restrictions on sexuality" (Ross 2017). Martin, like Wagner, is an unabashed leftist—in an article published in *Esquire*, he was quoted comparing President Donald Trump to his own sadistic and self-centered child King Joffrey: "I think Joffrey is now the king in America, and he's grown up just as petulant and irrational as he was when he was thirteen in the books" (Hill 2017). Beyond bashing the insanity and cruelty of the Trump presidency, on his personal blog Martin has called the Tea Party "Teabaggers" and described Republicans as "corrupt ... oligarchs and racists clad in the skins of dead elephants," while praising Democrats' support for "economic recovery, peace in Iraq, gay rights, Wall Street regulation, tax reform, women's reproductive freedoms, and ... especially ... health care" (Martin 2012). Martin's progressive bent is mainly seen in *ASoIaF* through the way abject characters gradually take center stage, transforming themselves from marginalized others into heroic subjects. It is not Eddard Stark, the Warden of the North, Head of House Stark and Lord of Winterfell, who is the hero of the series, nor is it his son Robb, heir to his father's title and would-be avenger of his death. Instead the heroes are a young girl who is sold as a bride in exchange for political capital and becomes every inch a queen (Dany), a bastard (Jon), a dwarf (Tyrion), a female knight (Brienne of Tarth), a paraplegic boy (Bran), a crippled warrior (Jaime Lannister), victims of sexual assault (Sansa) and of slavery (Missandei), and a knighted smuggler missing his fingers on one hand (Davos Seaworth), among others (Massie and Mayer 2014). Benioff and Weiss have worked to intensify this focus in *Game of Thrones*, granting even more subjectivity to marginalized figures like the prostitutes Shae and Ros or the eunuch Varys than Martin affords them in the books—Martin depicts Shae and Varys as schemers, and the tragic figure of Ros was invented for the television show. In the very first episode of the series, when Tyrion and Jon first meet, Tyrion offers what could be seen as a manifesto for the abject: "Let me give you some advice, bastard: never forget what you are. The rest of the world will not. Wear it like armor, and it can never be used to hurt you" (1x1 "Winter Is Coming").

Of course, neither Wagner nor *Game of Thrones* can be seen as a paragon of progressivism. Wagner, despite creating a number of extremely powerful female characters, was by no means a feminist, espousing a hyper-masculine understanding of history and culture in his essays. Furthermore, his choice of the *Nibelungenlied* as the archetypal myth to adapt indicates his extreme Eurocentrism: he did not just want to create a new art for the German Volk, but saw German and Nordic culture as the ultimate and universal expression of high culture. It is no accident that his works were celebrated by the Nazis and remain unofficially banned in Israel; in 1850, in the period when he was writing his essays in Zurich and beginning to plan his *Ring* cycle, he published "Das Judentum in der Musik," an essay that he revised, expanded, and republished in 1869. In this essay, which is often translated "Jewishness in Music" or "Judaism in Music," but is perhaps best articulated as "Jewry in Music," since *Judentum* is a slur, Wagner argues that Jewish culture, with, as he characterizes it, a greedy capitalistic focus on usury and business, can never create true art. The false art of the mid–19th century, Wagner says, was "Jewish" in spirit. In an essay written less than a decade after the Jewish composer Felix Mendelssohn created his "Wedding March" (1842), and only a century after celebrated German authors Gotthold Ephraim Lessing and Friedrich Schiller pleaded for religious tolerance and an end to anti–Semitism, Wagner wrote an essay that paved the way for Hitler and the Nazis in the 20th century (Conway 2012:1–13, 143–202).[3] In a sense, all of Wagner's other essays from the Zurich period must be read through the anti–Semitic lens of "Jewry in Music," since when Wagner articulates in "The Art-Work of the Future" how those who do not appreciate art "*feel no Want*; whose life-spring therefore consists in a need which rises not to the potence of a Want, and thus is artificial, untrue, and egotistic" (Wagner 1892:779; emphasis in original) we can see he is using the same sort of language he will apply one year later to Jewish artists.

Similarly, *Game of Thrones* has been repeatedly critiqued for overt orientalism, with few characters of color and tropes of white saviors and noble savages, with the Dothraki as a particularly problematic example of the voracious and rapacious Middle Eastern barbarian and the Dornish exoticized into Don Juan–esque pseudo–Spaniards, or hot-blooded lover/brawlers like many characters in Shakespeare's Italian plays. Mat Hardy analyzes such troubling trends in his essay "The Eastern Question," where, drawing upon Edward Said's *Orientalism*, he argues that "*Game of Thrones* inherits some of our real-world baggage in its imagining of the orient [… with] natives prone to treachery, dark mysticism, fanatic religious cults, slavery, and arbitrary slaughter" (Hardy 2017:98). Perhaps even more troubling is the way rape has been used in the show. As Danielle Alesi argues, at times rape is utilized positively in *Game of Thrones* for subject-focused character-building, to demonstrate the traumatic ordeals countless "women have suffered throughout history," allowing figures such as Sansa to develop a strength that is based in their utilization of "traditional feminine qualities [… of] 'courtesy,' courtly manners and carefully chosen words—polite lies—in order to survive" (Alesi

2017:165, 168–69). But at least as frequently, rape is used quite literally as scene dressing: such as when the Orientalized Dothraki are raiding, or when the mutinous Knight's Watch rape Craster's daughter-wives. In an article for *IndieWire*, Katie Walsh describes the latter scene as "a ridiculously gratuitous portrayal of the rape and abuse of women" (4x4 "Oathkeeper"; Walsh 2014).

However, beyond the thematic resonances involving incest, mythological adaptations, and imperfect progressivism, one especially crucial connection between *Game of Thrones* and *The Ring of the Nibelung* remains: music. It is surprising, however, that Ross, *The New Yorker*'s music critic, in his article on *Game of Thrones* and Wagner, does not even mention Ramin Djawadi's musical compositions that underscore the television series. They are, in my estimation, the most Wagnerian element of the show. Stewart Spencer's English translation of Wagner's *Ring* cycle contains, adapted from von Wolzogen's seminal study, a "thematic guide" to Wagner's leitmotifs—from the unmistakable Valkyrie theme to themes for the Rhine, the Ring itself, the World-Tree, and others (Wagner 1993:17–24). Djawadi has similarly composed notable leitmotifs, from the theme for Daenerys's dragons, which was first heard faintly at their birth in Season One and increasing in grandeur with their growth, to Queen Cersei's chilling theme featuring cruel-sounding string instruments. Notably, Djawadi has allowed these themes to intermingle, revealing the individual motifs to be part of long-hidden compositions; the music underscoring the scene where Bran reveals Jon's true identity while we see Jon and Dany have sex blends themes heard throughout the series. It is a song of ice and fire. The many motifs are most fully on display in "The Dragon and the Wolf," when most of the major characters in the series come together for the first time since the very first episode. Djawadi's compositions serve to highlight the mythic themes of the series, and demonstrate his skill as a contemporary popular classical composer. Indeed, like film composer John Williams, Djawadi's music has been presented at major venues; the "*Game of Thrones* Concert Experience" played to sold out venues such as Madison Square Garden in 2017.[4]

One final historical connection is worth mentioning. Wagner's *Ring* was not just a landmark composition: the very theatre that he had built for it, the Bayreuth Festspielhaus, marked a total transformation of theatrical aesthetics. Wagner pioneered the practice of dimming the lights over the audience, so that the performance, as opposed to fellow theatre-goers, would be the primary focus. Bayreuth's fan-shaped auditorium allowed for "democratic seating," where all seats had an equally good view and ticket prices were the same throughout the house. And Wagner was also the first to hide the orchestra in a pit so that the music would arise as if from the ether (Williams 1994). In a similar sense, HBO transformed the very medium of television in the beginning of the 21st century, with prestige shows like *The Sopranos* and *The*

Wire that featured superb acting, novelistic and self-contained storylines as opposed to a more literally episodic structure. On September 4, 2017, *The New Yorker*, for the first time in the magazine's storied highbrow history, published an entire issue devoted to television. HBO's success in the revitalization of television led to a wide array of similar shows, from AMC's *Mad Men* to the binge-worthy programming on Netflix. *Game of Thrones* can certainly claim a position at the apex of this relatively new era of prestige television series, at least in terms of budget and viewership (see Adam Whitehead's afterword in this volume).

Wagner's concept of the Gesamtkunstwerk thus extends beyond the artistic melding he describes in "The Art-Work of the Future." His design for the Bayreuth Festspielhaus and the reception of his *Ring* cycle as an era-defining cultural touchstone at its 1876 premiere are part of what make the cycle a Gesamtkunstwerk, encompassing literary sagas, music, dance, theatrical performance, architecture, and national mythology. *Game of Thrones* can be seen in a similar light: it is spectacle-filled prestige television. It has made the careers of young actors like Emilia Clarke, Kit Harington, Sophie Turner, and Maisie Williams, and features established stars of the British stage and screen such as Diana Rigg, Iain Glen, Charles Dance, and Julian Glover. *Game of Thrones* has built the career of Djawadi into that of a popular classical composer who can be seen as an heir to John Williams. The show has become such a cultural touchstone that real-world figures are routinely compared to characters from the series.

Furthermore, part of the reason that *Game of Thrones* can be seen as a Gesamtkunstwerk is that Martin, Benioff, and Weiss have consciously adapted sources that are such crucial cultural touchstones for Western dramatic performance. As Linda Hutcheon notes in *A Theory of Adaptation*, utilizing the resonances available through adaptation creates a great deal of potential for artistic pleasure, brought about by "repetition with variation, from the comfort of ritual combined with the piquancy of surprise." She reads an adaptation as necessarily palimpsestic, "a derivation that is not derivative—a work that is second without being secondary. It is its own palimpsestic thing" (Hutcheon 2006:4, 9). Hutcheon's model is particularly applicable to *Game of Thrones*: Martin and the showrunners deploy Shakespearean and Wagnerian resonances and allusions, but not derivatively. Westeros is not England, and Jon/Aegon and Daenerys are not Siegfried and Brünnhilde. But these resonances help *Game of Thrones* to take on archetypal and mythic qualities, just as Wagner and Shakespeare have in our culture. Graham Holderness, examining Shakespearean myths through the lens of cultural materialism, argues that "myth" is "a real and powerful form of human consciousness … the process by means of which the creative mind makes its own objective reality" (Holderness 2016:7). He articulates the ways in which Shakespeare has been mythologized, transformed from a poet, actor, and shareholder in a theatrical troupe into a symbol for Western culture. Deploying such myths through the process of adaptation or allusion can give new cultural products, such as *Game of Thrones*, more cultural weight, helping to bridge the gap between popular fiction and literature and cinematic spectacle and aesthetic film. In other words: Martin, Benioff, and Weiss's crafting of a compelling work that can stand on its own accounts for the massive popular success of *Game of Thrones*, but these allusions and references to works of mythic status in the Western canon—even when only grasped subconsciously by viewers or readers—have helped the show and books gain traction with audiences and critics who might not normally have tuned in to epic fantasy.

Indeed, some might argue that as a work of sprawling fantasy, *A Song of Ice and Fire* and *Game of Thrones* owe far more to Tolkein's *Lord of the Rings* (which of course itself owes an obvious debt to Wagner and the *Nibelungenlied*) and Jordan/Sanderson's *The Wheel of Time* than they do to Shakespeare's plays or Wagner's operas. Such works, often discussed as "genre fiction" have been seen, at least until quite recently, as significantly less suitable for academic study than Shakespeare's dramas or Wagner's operas. But while *Game of Thrones* certainly is designed to appeal to fans of fantasy, it is also a series watched by both scholars and their students, both opera aficionados and attendees of John Williams and Ramin Djawadi in concert. In his book *Highbrow/Lowbrow: The Emergence of Cultural Hierarchy in America*, Lawrence W. Levine articulates how Shakespeare once had a similarly broad audience, before elitist discourses made his works seem unapproachable to less educated audiences that had previously flocked to his plays (Levine 1990). Today, *Game of Thrones* similarly bridges the cultural divide between highbrow and lowbrow. Furthermore, as a sort of televisual Gesamtkunstwerk, it is already transforming our understanding of what television can do, and, in future generations, could itself become the model that other artistic works adapt. For example, Pulitzer Prize–winning television critic Emily Nussbaum, writing about HBO's new series *Westworld*, argues that the show is specifically designed to build upon the model of *Game of Thrones*—presenting sexy and spectacular entertainment with a diverse cast of superb actors, strong central female characters, and a complex, morally challenging storyline (Nussbaum 2016). Even once the Winds of Winter are past and audiences and readers have experienced *A Dream of Spring*, the Mother of Dragons and the Sword in the Darkness will, like Wagner's Valkyrie, certainly hold a place in our cultural memory for some time to come.

NOTES

1. All quotations from Shakespeare are taken from the Oxford Second Edition of *The Complete Works*, ed. Stanley Wells, Gary Taylor, John Jowett, and William Montgomery (Shakespeare 2005), and citations and further Shakespearean quotations will be identified

in the text using the standard abbreviation for the play followed by the act, scene, and line numbers; thus this would be (*R3*, 4.4.61–62).

2. This is a debatable statistic. Margaret of Anjou appears in all three *Henry VI* plays, as well as in *Richard III*. The other two characters are the Hostess (Mistress Quickly) and Bardolph, both of whom appear in *Henry IV, Part 1* and *Part 2*, *Henry V*, and *The Merry Wives of Windsor*. Other Shakespearean names (such as Balthazar) and speech prefixes (such as Soldier) appear in four or more plays, but these can reasonably be assumed to represent different characters with the same name. Other characters do appear in more than one play, such as Falstaff (three plays), Marc Antony and Octavius Caesar (two plays), and Shakespeare reused character archetypes to fit the talents of his company of actors. See Gurr (2009:100–38).

3. Lessing's *The Jews* (1749) and *Nathan the Wise* (1779) are Enlightenment dramas that significantly critique anti-Semitic ideology and rhetoric. The German Library translation of selected works by Lessing features a preface by Hannah Arendt (Lessing 1991). In "The Stage as a Moral Institution" (1784), Schiller writes that universal religious tolerance is a crucial feature of a moral society (Schiller 1902:250–54).

4. In contrast to his lack of mention of Djawadi or music in his article on *Game of Thrones* and Wagner, following the release of *Star Wars Episode VIII: The Last Jedi*, Ross published an article comparing the musical work of Wagner and John Williams, noting that "the *Star Wars* corpus has increasingly attracted scholarly scrutiny," arguing that Williams's music help *Star Wars* "step out of the adolescent-adventure arena and into the realm of modern myth" (Ross 2018).

REFERENCES

Alesi, Danielle. 2017. "The Power of Sansa Stark: Female Agency in Late Medieval Agency." In *Game of Thrones versus History: Written in Blood*, edited by Brian Pavlac, 161–70. Hoboken, NJ: Wiley Blackwell.

Conway, David. 2012. *Jewry in Music*. Cambridge: Cambridge University Press.

Grey, Thomas S. 2008. "Leitmotif, Temporality, and Musical Design in the *Ring*." *The Cambridge Companion to Wagner*, edited by Thomas S. Grey, 85–114. Cambridge: Cambridge University Press.

Gurr, Andrew. 2009. *The Shakespearean Stage 1574–1642*, 4th ed. Cambridge: Cambridge University Press.

Hardy, Mat. 2017. "The Eastern Question." *Game of Thrones versus History: Written in Blood*, edited by Brian Pavlac, 97–109. Hoboken, NJ: Wiley Blackwell.

Hill, Logan. 2017. "Kit Harrington Already Died Once." *Esquire* June/July.

Holderness, Graham. 2016. *Shakespeare and Venice*. London: Routledge.

Hutcheon, Linda. 2006. *A Theory of Adaptation*. New York: Routledge.

Lessing, Gotthold Ephraim. 1991. *Nathan the Wise, Minna von Barnhelm, and Other Plays and Writings*, edited by Peter Demetz. New York: Continuum.

Levine, Lawrence W. 1990. *Highbrow/Lowbrow: The Emergence of Cultural Hierarchy in America*. Cambridge: Harvard University Press.

Magee, Elizabeth. 1993. "In Pursuit of the Purely Human: The 'Ring' and Its Medieval Sources." *Wagner's Ring of the Nibelung: A Companion* by Richard Wagner, translated by Stewart Spencer, 29–32. London: Thames and Hudson.

Martin, George R.R. 2012. "Show Us Your Papers" (11 August) and "A Great Night for the USA" (7 November). *Not a Blog*. Accessed 7 February 2018. https://grrm.livejournal.com/.

Massie, Pascal J., and Lauryn S. Mayer. 2014. "Bringing Elsewhere Home: *A Song of Ice and Fire*'s Ethics of Disability." *Studies in Medievalism* XXIII: 45–59.

Nussbaum, Emily. 2016. "Second World." *The New Yorker* 24 October 2016. 82–83.

Ross, Alex. 2017. "Wagner, Incest, and 'Game of Thrones.'" *The New Yorker*, 29 August. Accessed 20 December. https://www.newyorker.com/culture/cultural-comment/wagner-incest-and-game-of-thrones.

Ross, Alex. 2018. "A Field Guide to the Leitmotifs of *Star Wars*." *The New Yorker*, 3 January.

Accessed 4 January. https://www.newyorker.com/culture/culture-desk/a-field-guide-to-the-musical-leitmotifs-of-star-wars.

Schiller, Friedrich. [1902]2000. "The Stage as a Moral Institution (1784)." *Theatre / Theory / Theatre: The Major Critical Texts from Aristotle and Zeami to Soyinka and Havel*, edited by Daniel Gerould, 250–54. New York: Applause.

Shakespeare, William. 2005. *The Complete Works* (Oxford Second Edition). Ed. Stanley Wells, Gary Taylor, John Jowett, and William Montgomery. Oxford: Clarendon Press.

Thoreau, Christian. 2009. "Guides for Wagnerites: Leitmotifs and Wagnerian Listening." *Richard Wagner and His World*, edited by Thomas S. Grey, 133–50. Princeton: Princeton University Press.

Treadwell, James. 2008. "The Urge to Communicate: The Prose Writings as Theory and Practice." *The Cambridge Companion to Wagner*, edited by Thomas S. Grey, 179–91. Cambridge: Cambridge University Press.

Wagner, Richard. [1892]1974. "The Art-Work of the Future," translated by William Ashton Ellis. *Dramatic Theory and Criticism: Greeks to Grotowski*, edited by Bernard F. Dukore, 777–94. South Melbourne: Thomson Heinle.

Wagner, Richard. 1993. *Wagner's Ring of the Nibelung: A Companion*, translated by Stewart Spencer. London: Thames and Hudson.

Walsh, Katie. 2014. "Recap: 'Game of Thrones' Season 4 Episode 4, 'Oathkeeper' Needs a Trigger Warning." *IndieWire*, 28 April. Accessed 7 February 2018. http://www.indiewire.com/2014/04/recap-game-of-thrones-season-4-episode-4-oathkeeper-needs-a-trigger-warning-86676/.

Williams, Simon. 1990. *Shakespeare on the German Stage, Volume 1: 1586–1914*. Cambridge: Cambridge University Press.

Williams, Simon. 1994. *Richard Wagner and Festival Theatre*. Westport, CT: Greenwood Press.

A Girl Is Arya
Acting and the Power of Performance

CAROL PARRISH JAMISON

Game of Thrones presents complex layers of performance. Until the sixth season, the HBO series has itself been a performance based on the novels. Within both the novels and the series are numerous performances, some obvious (such as those by singers and mummers) and others less so (such as the various disguises of Varys and the deceptive manipulations of power-hungry Littlefinger). Foremost among Martin's performers is Arya Stark. Early in the series, Arya engages in various kinds of role-playing and disguise as she crafts new identities for herself. Heavily influenced by theatrical performance, she emerges not merely as a master of disguise, but also a masterful performer. Although she is repeatedly told that the most effective performances require her to abandon her strong identity as a Stark, Arya creates a new kind of performance that combines her training and experiences but never necessitates a loss of identity. Throughout, she uses performative deception as a tool in her quest to exact vengeance against those who harm her or her family.

Raised in the isolated North, Arya likely would not have had much exposure to mummers' shows, as these professional troupes are typically portrayed as performing in more populated areas. Nonetheless, her early childhood is rich with oral performances that are instrumental to her development as an actor. Arya has been immersed in the lore of Westeros through songs and stories, dramatically recited to her by her Septa, Old Nan. These stories have shaped her perception of the world and her early identity. When we first meet her, Arya is struggling to find a suitable role for herself in her family's household. She compares herself unfavorably to her older sister, noting her own imperfections such as her hair, which she finds "a lusterless brown." She also recognizes that she is not beautiful. Her long face earns her the nickname

"Arya Horseface," and her sister's friend Jeyne Poole insults Arya by neighing at her (Martin *G of T* 2011:70).[1]

Before she leaves for King's Landing, Arya's difficulties stem from the fact that she does not fit easily into the social role she is expected to play. She has difficulty acting the part of proper young lady, and she is met with resistance when she tries to recast herself according to her natural inclinations as a tomboy. Season One first presents Arya awkwardly sewing imperfect stitches under the watchful and disapproving eyes of her Septa. The scene then shifts to show her shooting an arrow and hitting the bullseye as her younger brother practices (with much less success) (1x1 "Winter Is Coming"). Although it suits her natural inclinations, the role of tomboy is difficult for Arya because her Septa, Cat (her mother), and Sansa expect her to adhere to gendered conventions. Her half-brother Jon and her father Ned, on the other hand, support and accept Arya's unconventional behavior. Jon, who as a bastard is similarly ostracized, and Ned, who sees in Arya shades of his dearly-loved late sister, both have special connections with Arya that allow them to empathize with her.

Once Jon gives her a sword (which she names Needle in an ironic reference to her failed sewing lessons) and her father finds a swordsman to train her properly, Arya becomes more comfortable in the role of tomboy. These gestures by male family members signal their acceptance and encourage her not only to embrace being a tomboy, but also to strive towards a new identity: female warrior. Arya cherishes the small sword her brother gives her, and she takes the training seriously. She knows that the role of a warrior cannot be fulfilled without training and equipment, and once Arya acquires these necessities, she can learn the requisite skills and behaviors that should accompany this role. This process is accelerated once she moves with Ned and Sansa to King's Landing and finds herself in a series of dangerous situations.

In King's Landing, Syrio Forel, Arya's sword master, trains her to become a water dancer, a particularly graceful type of sword fighter. Even though this role comes somewhat naturally to her, she must learn the part. Unlike the arduous and unsuccessful sewing lessons which Arya resisted mightily, this training transforms Arya into an enthusiastic student who immerses herself completely into the role of water dancer. Forel repeatedly calls her "boy," acknowledging that she is taking on an unconventional role for a female. He also encourages her, telling her that she must forget any other identity in order to succeed: "you are a sword, that is all" (Martin *G of T* 2011:224). This is the first instance in which Arya is encouraged to forget her identity as a Stark, and it is a critical moment in her early development as an actor. Forel encourages her to try a number of roles to enhance her training. For example, he trains her to be stealthy, "like a cat," and Arya repeats this advice as a mantra. She observes and emulates the behaviors of alley cats in King's Landing. Arya thus begins acquiring the tools and experience required to perform new identities convincingly.

When Forel is killed by Lannisters, Arya's sword training ends. She is never able to become a female knight. Arya might here be contrasted with Brienne of Tarth, who succeeds in this role despite social resistance. Arya faces obstacles that cut short her formal training. Thus, she never has a chance to develop fully the skills and knowledge of chivalry that may have set her on a similar path to becoming, like Brienne, a female knight. Despite her gender, Brienne is made part of Renly Baratheon's Rainbow Guard and eventually earns the respect of Jaime Lannister, an infamous knight. Arya's early inclinations imply that she might like to follow a similar path. Rather, she is thrust into situations that force her to act various parts in order to survive. She must hide from those pursuing her and conceal her identity as a Stark. Her natural inclinations to become a fighter prevail, though she must become a fighter of a different nature than she originally envisioned.

At her father's beheading, Arya is snatched away by Yoren, a man of the Night's Watch. Yoren instructs her to assume the role of "Arry," a low-born boy on his way to the Wall. Whereas Arya has long been called a boy because of her rough appearance, at this point, she must assume the role of a particular, fictitious boy. This is her first true acting role. To ensure that she will look the part, Yoren chops off her hair and warns her that she must behave as if she were male. The disguise proves effective. She not only fools the Lannister scouts, but she also effectively convinces the recruits with whom she travels of this new identity. A natural tomboy, Arya has rehearsed this role most of her life, and she finds it easy to perform. This role frees her from the strictures imposed upon her when her Septa and her mother had tried to make her conform to the role of proper young lady. The role of Arry is complicated only by the fact that she must relieve herself and bathe in private.

When Yoren is killed and Arya is held captive at Harrenhal, Needle is taken from her, so Arya must reconsider how she might protect herself. Tywin Lannister, who rules at Harrenhal, recognizes that she is female, and she must assume a new persona. When she explains that she has disguised herself as a boy so that she might travel safely, he tells her that this is "smart" and assigns her to work (2x4 "Garden of Bones"). At Tywin's request, Arya takes on the role of a cupbearer to the Lannister patriarch. She identifies herself as a low-born girl named Nan, and she works in close proximity to him, all the while gathering information about the political climate in Westeros and her brother Robb's campaign against the Lannisters. Her performance as Nan is threatened when Tywin recognizes Arya's accent and manner of speech as Northern and highborn. Arya does not yet realize that a convincing performance requires attention to details, including mannerisms and speech. By pointing out flaws in her performance, Tywin unknowingly provides Arya with essential training. Fortunately, the quick-thinking Arya invents an excuse to explain her accent: that her mother served Lady Dustin and taught her high-born speech (2x7 "A Man Without Honor").

Arya's life depends on her performing the role of Nan convincingly, yet she cannot resist breaking out of character and making comments that threaten to reveal her true identity. When Tywin asks her for the opinion of Northerners about Robb Stark, she responds by relating the rumors that Robb rides into battle upon a giant direwolf and that he cannot be killed. Tywin asks if she believes this account, and her response is ominous: "Anyone can be killed." In this moment, although Tywin does not see her motives, Arya breaks out of the role of Nan and subtly makes clear her desire for vengeance. Again, she breaks out of character when Tywin questions her about her father's death, claiming that he is a blacksmith who died of "loyalty" (2x5 "The Ghost of Harrenhal"). Tywin recognizes these and other small cracks in her performance, but fortunately he cannot pinpoint them. The television audience, however, delights in these moments of dramatic irony as Arya slyly deceives the Lannister patriarch.

Except for these moments when she breaks out of character, Arya quietly plays the role of Nan and then uses her wits to trick Jaqen, a skilled assassin who owes her a favor, into helping her and her friends escape. Her survival at Harrenhal evidences that her acting skills are developing. Once she and her friends escape, she travels anonymously with the Brotherhood without Banners until the Hound unveils her identity and then kidnaps her. She then resumes her performances as the two must pose as father and daughter. Arya's ease at slipping into roles is highlighted by the Hound's gruff and unmalleable character, yet the two are convincing enough to gain entry to the Tully / Frey wedding.

Despite her growing skill at performative deception, Arya is not always such a willing or convincing performer. In the novels, when she encounters the Brotherhood and is mistaken for a boy, she corrects them, but she hides her true identity, telling Tom of Sevenstreams to call her "Squab, if you want … I don't care" (Martin *S of S* 2011:177). Arya has again neglected a key aspect of effective performance; this time, appearance and wardrobe. Tom is able to discern an important fact that she had hoped to hide: he recognizes that she has escaped from Harrenhal, for Arya still wears the Bolton sigil on her smock.[2] Arya, thus, is essentially unveiled of her character by a costume malfunction. She also refuses to play the part of Clegane's son when they are on the run: "'I'm not his stupid son!' said Arya furiously. That was even worse than being taken for a boy" (Martin *S of S* 2013:653).

Further, Tywin and Tom are not the only characters who see cracks in her performances. When Gendry first recognizes her true identity not only as a female, but also as a Stark, Arya must reestablish herself in the more comfortable role of tomboy. Gendry addresses her as "m'lady," making her embarrassed and uncomfortable, as this is a role she has never wanted. She explains to him: "My mother's a lady, and my sister, but I never was" (2x2 "The Night Lands"). Yvonne Tasker and Lindsey Steenberg note that Arya's identity does not significantly change after she is revealed to be a girl: "the revelation is not narratively significant as it is in other tales of cross-dressing: instead the most important disguise is that she is a very particular girl (Arya Stark) rather than simply a girl" (2016:184). Once Gendry uncovers her identity, Arya denies the role of "lady" and reasserts her true identity as Arya Stark, tomboy, by pushing Gendry to the ground.

Jaqen not only pinpoints Arya's true identity as a Stark, but also the various roles she has played: "Some men have many names. Weasel. Arry. Arya" (Martin *C of K* 2011:684). Jaqen is much more adept at performance than Arya, and he is also highly skilled in seeing through the performances of others. He recognizes her potential talents and hands her a coin, which, much later in the series, leads her to join the House of Black and White. Like herself, Jaqen is a role player and performer, but of a different variety: he can literally shed his skin and assume new physical identities. Arya is intrigued by Jaqen's shapeshifting abilities, and they inspire her once she makes her way to Braavos and enters the House of Black and White, where she trains to become one of the Faceless Men.

One of Arya's first tasks in the House of Black and White is to remove all vestiges of her identity. She is initially confused that none of those she meets in the House of Black and White seem to have names. Once she pledges her desire to join, she learns that she, too, must begin the process of undoing her strongly ingrained family identity. When she first arrives, she is surprised to find that Jaqen denies his own identity. He tells her that he is "no one, and that is what a girl must become" (5x2 "The House of Black and White"). With no place to go, she must find a way to fit in, so she immerses herself in training. Here, she moves from assuming identities as a means of survival to becoming a master of theatrical performance. Most difficult of all, she must convince her fellow assassins that she has successfully become "no one." Becoming "no one" is an extremely complicated role to which Arya is never fully able to commit. However, through this training, she does learn critical skills about acting and ultimately perfects her own method of performance.

Arya undergoes extreme training in method acting to prepare for the role of "no one." Each day in the House of Black and White, Jaqen and the Waif question Arya's identity. She reviews in her mind the various roles she has performed: "Arya Underfoot, Arya Horseface, Arry, Weasel, Squab, Salty, Nan the cupbearer, a grey mouse, a sheep, and the ghost of Harrenhal" (Martin *F for C* 2011:446). Still, in her heart, she adheres to her identity as Arya Stark of Winterfell. As her training intensifies, Arya finds it challenging to mask her true identity. The Waif, who helps train Arya, repeatedly strikes her when she unconvincingly claims that she is no one. Arya's response to her repeated question "Who are you?" reveals her frustrations and confirms her adherence to her Stark identity. She reaches for Needle and responds, "you are about to find out" (5x3 "High Sparrow").

In the novels, the Waif slaps Arya for chewing her lip, explaining afterwards, "It is Arya of House Stark who chews on her lip whenever she is thinking. Are you Arya of House Stark?" (Martin *F for C* 2011:736). This gesture reveals to the Waif that Arya is not succeeding in becoming "no one." The Waif wants Arya to immerse herself completely into the roles assigned to her, abandoning any ticks or subconscious gestures that might break believability, even such a minute gesture as lip chewing. As the Waif notes, Arya's identity, largely shaped by her devotion to the Stark family, is difficult to discard. Noting her belongings, Jaqen asks her, "How is it that No One came to be surrounded by Arya Stark's things?" (5x3 "High Sparrow"). Arya subsequently disposes of her belongings, but she finds herself unable to part with Needle, so she hides rather than gets rid of the sword. For Arya, Needle represents the most honest representation of herself and of the family she holds dear.

As an early step towards becoming one of the Faceless Men, Arya must prove that she can act. She does so by convincing a sick girl that drinking from the temple's well will cure her. Subsequently, she and the Waif begin playing "the lying game," training for Arya to emerge as a master actor. They each must guess if the other is lying, basing their judgment on facial control and vocal tone. Arya not only must learn to keep her face still, but she also devotes time to trying to alter her expressions: "Arya puffed up her cheeks and stuck out her tongue. 'There. Your face is changed'" (Martin *F for C* 2011:463). Once her training has sufficiently progressed so that she can control her facial gestures and mask her emotions, she is asked to perform her first major role as an assassin.

She becomes, first, an ugly fishmonger, Lanna (Cat of the Canals in the books). This theatrical performance requires method acting. Arya strives to identify completely with this role, not merely donning a physical costume, but also changing her mannerisms and appearance. In the novels, she chastises herself even for dreaming out of character: "I should not be dreaming wolf dreams, the girl told herself. I am a cat now, not a wolf. I am Cat of the Canals" (Martin *F for C* 2011:719). Her close ties to her family may help her to immerse herself in this role, for her mother is named Cat (short for Catelyn). She enjoys and strongly identifies with the role of Lanna / Cat and plays it convincingly, yet "try as she might … she could not rid herself of Arya" (719). Like a stage actor after a performance, when Arya returns to the House of Black and White, she transforms back into herself:

> Down in the vaults, she untied Cat's threadbare cloak, pulled Cat's fishy brown tunic over her head, kicked off Cat's salt-stained boots, climbed out of Cat's smallclothes, and bathed in lemonwater to wash away the very smell of Cat of the Canals. When she emerged, soaped and scrubbed pink with her brown hair plastered to her cheeks, Cat was gone [Martin *F for C* 2011:735].

Once she has removed her costume and washed away the vestiges of her life as Cat, she falls out of character and resumes her identity as Arya Stark. Thus, she does not obey the dictate of the Faceless Men to become "no one"; nevertheless, she succeeds in theatrical performance, convincingly playing the role of "someone else."

At this point in the storyline, Arya is not only undergoing intense acting training, but she is also on the verge of being profoundly influenced by theatre. Perhaps to emphasize this influence, her storyline begins to converge, through subtle allusion, with that of Shakespeare's *Hamlet*.[3] Both Arya and Hamlet have in common an overwhelming urge to avenge the deaths of their loved ones that invites audiences to compare the two. Following her father's death, Arya, not unlike Prince Hamlet, has become increasingly obsessed with vengeance to the point that this becomes the overriding aspect of her identity. Ironically, the grueling training that she undergoes to join a group of assassins eventually strengthens, rather than erases, Arya's identity. It also allows her to cast herself in a new role and to shed the role of victim. No longer disguising herself for protection against those pursuing her, she herself becomes a pursuer with the sole goal of avenging the deaths of her loved ones.

In the novels, the influence of theatre, specifically Elizabethan-style theatre, intensifies when Arya, playing the role of Cat, meets mummers who give her acting tips, showing her "how a hero stands" and teaching her speeches from plays with titles that are evocative of Shakespeare, such as "The Conqueror's Two Wives" and "The Merchant's Lusty Lady" (Martin *F for C* 2011:725). Arya's stint as Lanna / Cat is enjoyable and instructive, but it ends when she kills one of the enemies on her personal vendetta list.[4] Caroline Spector writes that women in the series frequently use sexuality as lure, but "Arya [and a few others] have other means at their disposal" (2012:175). Arya does however lure Meryn Trant with sexuality. When Arya kills Trant, she wears one of the faces of the dead to disguise herself as one of three girls whom Trant hopes to use for his perverted pleasure. As she kills him, she pulls off her mask to reveal her true identity and motive.

The murder of Trant directly defies the dictates of the Faceless Men who must kill anonymously and without motive. When she returns from this kill, Jaqen tells her that breaking the rules has consequences. He then appears to die, whereupon Arya removes from his body a series of death masks and finds that Jaqen, disguised as the Waif, is standing behind her. Arya is then blinded and, out of necessity, assumes the role of a beggar, Blind Beth. During this period of her training, she learns to rely upon her other senses to enhance her performances. She also perfects another distinctive kind of skill that may aid her ability to act: she explores her powers as a warg (one who can transfer consciousness into an animal). Doing so, she is able to enter the mind of her lost direwolf, Nymeria. During her stint as Blind Beth, Arya finds that she can also use her powers on an alley cat that she finds while begging. Though blind, she can see through the eyes of the cat. Although warging is a special skill that might only arguably be called theatrical performance, the experience allows Arya to see from a different perspective, a skill that would surely help her as an actor.

In the novels, once Arya's vision is returned to her, she earns the privilege of discovering how the Faceless Men are able to transform themselves. The Kindly Man (not portrayed in the series) who trains her explains the differences between mummers, who "change their faces with artifice" and sorcerers, who use optical illusions. He explains to her that she will use these techniques in her performances, but, he tells her, "what we do here goes deeper. Wise men can see through artifice, and glamors dissolve before sharp eyes, but the face you are about to don will be as true and solid as that face you were born with" (*D with D* 2011:922). To prepare her for wearing wigs that will go along with these "theatre masks," Arya's head is shaved. She is thus physically and mentally prepared to immerse herself in any role required of her.

In Season Seven of the HBO series, Arya's increased exposure to theatre enhances her acting abilities. When she is assigned to kill an actress, Lady Crane, Arya becomes more closely associated with mummers. She adopts the role of Mercy, an actress. As Mercy, she sees three productions that duplicate events in King's Landing and that mildly evoke the "play within a play" in *Hamlet*. The first of these plays reenacts both Robert Baratheon's and her father's deaths. At the actual death of her father, Yoren shielded Arya from seeing the beheading by placing his hands over her eyes. She does not arrange the production of the play as does Hamlet; however, like "The Murder of Gonzago" which replicates the death of Hamlet's father, this mummers' play forces Arya to re-live her father's death and even to witness it through the lens of dramatic performance.

Well aware of the impact performance can have on audiences, Arya witnesses the stage production with a discerning eye. She carefully watches not just the play itself, but also the audience's reactions. The production begins humorously, but when she sees the action turn to her father's death, she grows somber. She is disturbed by the fact that her father is portrayed as a buffoon who does not understand the intricacies of the court and that the audience enjoys, and buys into, this portrayal. Then, she witnesses the actress playing Sansa, whom she blames, unsuccessfully pleading for her father's life, and she sees a wooden head roll on the ground to symbolize the beheading. Again, the audience is amused by what was, for Arya, perhaps the most traumatic and unjust occurrence of her young life. The performance not only forces Arya to see the event unfold, but it also reignites her anger over the injustices done to her family and the shame wrongly brought to them. Sam Adams explains the effect this production has on Arya: "Arya begins to see that avenging her father's death won't be enough. It's not simply a matter of killing those who've wronged her but of restoring the Stark family's honor, and that will take more than putting a sword through Cersei Lannister's heart" (2016). This production affects her profoundly. It gives her insight into how performance can be shaped to influence audience. Further, it alters, but certainly does not erase, her plans for exacting vengeance. Arya recognizes that she cannot let go of her identity or her personal vendettas.

Empathy is a critical trait for actors, and with the second of the mummer's performances, Arya shows that she has developed this trait. In this performance about King Joffrey's death, Lady Crane plays Cersei Lannister. The skilled actress effectively portrays a mother grieving for her son, but Arya, who understands the Lannister court much better than the cast performing the play, immediately sees that something is lacking from this performance. Arya knows that Cersei would not grieve for long but would soon turn to thoughts of vengeance, and she instructs Lady Crane to act accordingly. With this guidance, Arya is empathizing with her intended target, which will complicate her mission of murder. Additionally, her acting skills have evolved to the point that she can identify the emotions of her sworn enemy, Cersei. Thus, she gives Lady Crane sound acting advice that will authenticate the role of Cersei Lannister.

Specifically, Arya instructs Lady Crane to change her performance so that the action and the word will reflect Cersei Lannister: "Change it. She wouldn't just cry. She would be angry. She would want to kill the person who did this to her" (6x6 "Blood of My Blood"). Arya evokes Prince Hamlet as he advises and directs the players in "The Murder of Gonzago" to "suit the action to the word, the word to the action" (3.2). Arya thus becomes simultaneously an actor and, briefly, a director. Lady Crane is a seasoned actress, well acclaimed for her skills, yet Arya, at this point, is equally skilled and has insider knowledge that helps Lady Crane perfect this role in the next performance.

This production not only reflects real events that Arya has witnessed, but it also gives her news about events that occurred after she left King's Landing. She learns from the play that her sister Sansa has been forced to marry the dwarf Tyrion Lannister. Arya shapes the performance to reflect the actual Lannister court, and equally, the performance shapes both her perceptions of the court and her role in the House of Black and White. As she becomes better acquainted with the actress she is assigned to kill, Arya has second thoughts. Though motivated by vengeance and disturbed by Lady Crane's performance, Arya is able to separate the skilled actor who is portraying Cersei from Cersei herself. She holds an affinity with the good-natured actress. The two bond over the shared practice of acting. At their first meeting, Lady Crane insightfully asks her, "Do you like pretending to be others?" (6x5 "The Door"). When Arya realizes that one of Lady Crane's fellow actors, a jealous rival, has commissioned the murder, she decides not to go forward with the death.

Although the assassination of Lady Crane is an assignment from the House of Black and White, this murder goes against Arya's identity as a Stark. Adams explains her reluctance to fulfill this duty:

> She's dedicated herself to avenging the murders of her father, her mother, and her brother and very nearly lost herself in the process: Had she cold-bloodedly murdered Lady Crane, betraying her father's determination to only dole out death as merited punishment and never in anger, she would truly have become No One [2016].

When Arya does not go through with murdering Lady Crane, she finds herself in a battle with the Waif, whom she kills. Jaqen praises her, believing that she has now succeeded in erasing her identity: "Finally a girl is no one." Arya rebuts, evidencing that she has deceived even Jaqen: "A girl is Arya, and I am going home" (6x8 "No One"). She does not, however, abandon her talent for performing. In fact, her best performances occur once she leaves the House of Black and White.

Arya leaves the House of Black and White to reclaim her identity as Arya Stark of Winterfell. However, she is a transformed Arya, now fully capable of using performance as a means to exact personal vengeance. Ironically, she is now more convincing when she is performing than when she is not. When she stumbles upon a band of warriors and straightforwardly reveals to them her intention to kill Cersei Lannister, they laugh at her, unable to believe that this "nice young girl" could be serious (7x1 "Dragonstone"). On her journey back to her home, Arya takes on various roles as she retaliates against those who have wronged her family. She assumes the identity of a Frey maid. She avenges the deaths of her brother and mother by killing Walder Frey, feeding him a pie made of his own sons, and then slitting his throat. She subsequently dons Frey's mask to poison his men and family. Walder Frey's death is portrayed in a particularly gripping scene in that viewers of the series are completely immersed in Arya's performance, unaware of her true identity until the moment she unveils herself.

Arya plays on the reactions of her own audiences as the Freys are also completely duped by her performance. For Arya, vengeance would be unsatisfying unless she can identify herself to her victims. Otherwise, the blood feud would not be successfully concluded. Thus, as she has done when killing Trant, she breaks character in the moments before she makes her kill by taking off her mask. Her last words to Frey are to identify herself as Arya Stark. She tells him that the last thing he will see is "a Stark face smiling down at you" (6x10 "The Winds of Winter"). And again, as the Frey men are dying of poison, she rips off Frey's mask to reveal herself. Such an act is strictly forbidden by the Faceless Men and confirms that Arya, whose identity as a Stark is indelible, is unwilling to assume the role of "no one" as dictated by the Faceless Men. Ultimately, though, she surpasses these assassins. Vengeance, it appears, is for Arya an excellent motivation for performance. She does not need to deny her own identity in order to act convincingly. She is able to dupe the Faceless Men into believing that she can become "no one" and then use the skills they have taught her for purposes of vengeance.

Once back in Winterfell, performance, for Arya, becomes a means of acclimating to a greatly altered political climate. When she first returns, her sister Sansa is puzzled by who Arya has become and dismayed to find Arya's suitcase full of masks. Lingering resentments and tensions between the two erupt, intimating that they might turn against one another. In the end, Sansa comes to terms with the changes in her sister. They join forces with their brother Bran, all participating in a performance to defeat a formidable enemy, Littlefinger. Each of the Stark siblings calls on a special talent for this performance. Sansa uses her charms to convince Littlefinger that she can be easily swayed by his machinations; Bran uses his power of sight to determine Littlefinger's motives; and Arya, in a scene that leaves audiences stunned, uses her theatrical abilities to murder this enemy of her family.

In the final episode of the season, we see Arya in perhaps her greatest role as she plays the part of victim to Littlefinger, only to reveal that she has outsmarted him. For this role, Arya does not require a death mask. She must play a naïve and fearful version of herself as she is brought to a hearing in which it appears that her sister Sansa will accuse her of treason. She approaches the court hearing tentatively, looking as if she is terrified of these accusations and of Sansa's impending judgment. Her mouth slightly open and with a nervous expression, Arya glances over her shoulders at the armed men who surround her. Then, Sansa reveals that Littlefinger is actually the accused. Although Littlefinger is a skilled manipulator who identifies and preys on the weaknesses of those around him, he is completely taken in by this performance. He has failed to see how the Stark children, particularly Arya, have changed. Arya transforms back into her new role as assassin, as revealed by the slightest of smiles, just before slitting Littlefinger's throat (7x7 "The Dragon and the Wolf").

This performance evidences that Arya, though a misfit, has an unbreakable bond with family that extends even to her least favorite family member,

Sansa. Because this performance occurs in Winterfell, it highlights her evolution from a rebellious tomboy to an immensely successful actor, and also her indelible identity as a Stark. Whereas the Faceless Men believe that the most convincing performances occur when one completely loses sense of self, Arya shows that she can effectively play any number of roles while maintaining her identity. Arya can not only change her physical appearance, but also take on all the subtleties of someone else, their mannerisms, speech habits, and personality traits. She masters elements of acting that allow her to perfect her various performances and thus becomes an effective assassin in a wide range of circumstances. By the conclusion of Season Seven, Arya's skills are so finely honed that she has duped or outwitted almost everyone she encounters. Because the list of those whom she seeks to kill is still incomplete, fans of the series can surely expect more vengeful performances by this masterful actress.

NOTES

1. This citation and those that follow come from the five-volume set of George R.R. Martin's *A Song of Ice and Fire* (2011). Citations will be to individual novels in the series, abbreviated as follows: *A Game of Thrones* (*G of T*); *A Clash of Kings* (*C of K*); *A Storm of Swords* (*S of S*); *A Feast for Crows* (*F for C*); and *A Dance with Dragons* (*D with D*).

2. In the HBO series, Arya and her companions are recognized as Harrenhal escapees by their castle-forged swords.

3. Martin's novels share some other recognizable motifs with Shakespeare. Astute readers may note a reference in *A Dance with Dragons* that evokes Act 5, Scene 5 of *Macbeth* in which Macbeth's enemies carry branches while marching. Macbeth has been warned, "Fear not, till Birnam wood. Do come to Dunsinane." Stannis's men adopt a similar disguise when they march on Deepwood Motte carrying branches in order to take Asha Greyjoy and the Ironmen by surprise. Twice, Martin borrows a motif from Shakespeare's violent play Titus Andronicus, in which the title character bakes the sons of his nemesis into a pie and serves them to her. Martin shapes this motif into the Westerosi legend of the Rat King and again when Wyman Manderly bakes Walder Frey's sons in a pie (*D with D* 2011:544). In the HBO series, this latter scene is reworked as Arya kills Walder Frey.

4. In the novels, Arya kills Dareon, a singer of the Night's Watch who has neglected his duties. Arya's own sense of duty and her devotion to her half-brother, a man of the Night's Watch, compel her to commit this murder.

REFERENCES

Adams, Sam. 2016. "What the Scenes Performed by Lady Crane's Theater Troupe Revealed About Where Got Is Headed." *Slate*, 14 June. Accessed 21 December 2017. http://www.slate.com/blogs/browbeat/2016/06/14/what_the_scenes_performed_by_lady_crane_s_theater_troupe_reveal_about_where.html.

Martin, George, R.R. 2011. *A Song of Ice and Fire*. 5 volumes. New York: Bantam.

Spector, Caroline. 2012. "Power and Feminism in Westeros." *Beyond the Wall: Exploring George R.R. Martin's A Song of Ice and Fire*, 169–88. Dallas: Benbella Books.

Tasker, Yvonne, and Lindsay Steenberg. 2016. "Women Warriors from Chivalry to Vengeance." In *Women of Ice and Fire: Gender, Game of Thrones, and Multiple Media Engagements*, edited by Anne Gjelsvik and Rikke Schubart, 177–92. London: Bloomsbury Academic.

Avatars and Identity Performance
Disembodied Self in Virtual Spaces

IAN ROSS

With the introduction of outsider heroes such as Tyrion Lannister, Bran Stark, Jon Snow, and Arya Stark at the outset of HBO's *Game of Thrones*, the series shows viewers that this is not a story about handsome knights, damsels in distress, and chivalrous adventure. While these familiar archetypes may seem to be present in this world (especially if you don't look too closely), *Game of Thrones* is instead a series about the unexpected power wielded by the forgotten, the ignored, and the cast aside. Within the feudal worlds of the series, the audience slowly learns that those who remind us most of the medieval heroes of our childhood stories are often the most corrupt, and that perceived deviation from the hegemonic norm within this world is met with exclusion, oppression, indifference, and outright violence.

Game of Thrones establishes early on that deviation from the norm is much more punishable when attached to one's socially constructed identity than it is when attached to one's actions. For instance, the poorly kept secrets of Jaime and Cersei Lannister's incestuous affair or Ramsay Snow's sadism are overlooked or even rewarded by those in power when it serves them. Between Cersei, Jaime, and their three children, three members of their family sit on the Iron Throne at some point in the series. Ramsay Snow's gleeful deconstruction of Theon Greyjoy causes his father to upgrade him from bastard to legitimate heir. However, embodied deviation from hegemony seems to function much differently. As Tyrion states to Jon Snow in the second episode of the series: "All dwarves are bastards in their father's eyes" (1x2 "Kingsroad"). Despite his talents and credibility, Tyrion's size causes his father to see him as a stain on the pride of the Lannister name. Maimed characters like the scarred Hound, one-handed Jaime, or castrated Theon are consistently mocked, underestimated, or shunned for their physical deformities by those in power, while Ramsay, physically whole and male, is rewarded for his psychological sadism. Arya and Brienne, as women attempting to engage in the fluency of Westeros's "might makes right" systems of conflict, are consistently dismissed or ignored by their male counterparts. In fact, the series repeatedly reminds us that women have very little power that they do not seize from behind the scenes, like Margary and Cersei (in fact, it could be argued that in many ways, Cersei's "walk of shame" in Season Five is a socially accepted punishment for her perceived political ambition). Embodiment and perceived embodiment, either in reference to patriarchal limitations imposed upon gender or in reference to physical lack, play a vast role in one's social agency within the series.

Therefore, we see that instead of creating a world of shining knights for us to cheer, David Benioff and D.B. Weiss (and of course George R.R. Martin) create a world that punishes physical deviation from hegemony in the extreme. However, much more importantly, the series also props these characters up as the secret heroes and architects of this world by providing characters with new means of wielding power. Through these means, characters subvert their physicality and perform their agency through processes that ignore, erase, or replace that physicality. Most specifically through Arya and Bran Stark, the world of *Game of Thrones* creates for us several virtual spaces in which agency is wielded effectively by the physically othered. Critically mapping these virtual spaces illustrates the power and agency (and the effects thereof) wielded through them.

The virtual, often, is used within literary criticism as a term to discuss digital spaces: game spaces, social media interactions, and other forms of digital communication. However, the word is in no way specifically tied to notions of digital or analog. In *Bergsonism*, Gilles Deleuze argues against the inherently fallacious problem which maintains that the physical is "more" than the possible and that the possible is retroactively given significance in the past by the present. For Deleuze, the virtual instead inherently already exists, and has only to become actualized in the present to come into being. Therefore, not only is the present a constant state of "becoming" actualized rather than static existence, the infinite possibility of the virtual informs this present rather than the commonly assumed reverse (1981:55–56). In other words, what exists (the actualized) is informed by future potential (the virtual), rather than potential being informed by what exists. Analytically, I will be approaching the virtual here through a critical lens informed by Deleuze and Felix Guittari's *A Thousand Plateaus* (1987), where the virtual or actualized can be identified through the conceptualizations of the smooth and the striated. The narratologically smooth refers to moments when embodiment is in flux or retains the potential to change drastically, whereas the striated represents a solidification of embodiment and identity into materiality and permanence.

So, while it might be surprising on the surface to discuss a series like *Game of Thrones* in terms of its virtual spaces, a closer look will reveal these spaces throughout the series. Bran's growing ability to mind-walk as a Warg emerges directly from his ability to interact with nature's flora and fauna and "plug into" avatar bodies (an ability mirrored early on, aptly enough, with an intersection between nature and mechanical apparatus in the form of his custom saddle from Season One). Arya's emerging ability to embody different forms for her own vengeful needs, through her training with the Faceless Men, allows her to outpace the patriarchal restrictions she feels so confined by at the start of the series. Her engagement with an embodiment that is *smoothed*, i.e., outside of materially static (*striated*) embodiment, allows Arya to ignore the social restrictions of her young and female embodiment, while simultaneously causing her to question whether she can, or should, give up who she is in order to do so. This understanding of the virtual, with Bran and Arya engaging with fluid embodiment and therefore taking control of the corresponding social identity politics, can coarsely then be observed to contain similarities to the digital as understood in cyberpunk fiction, such as the apparent lack of materiality/embodiment and the possibility inherent in the pre-actualized. However, the two must be understood as separate conditions, most importantly because of the following: while the virtual appears as a smooth materiality in these narratives, it is still a materiality.

Technological posthumanism and digital identity studies asks one to consider the degree to which an embodiment smoothed by Arya and Bran's emerging skills allows for an escape from the previously striated self. Beginning with an examination of posthumanism, N. Katherine Hayles in her text *My Mother Was a Computer: Digital Subjects and Literary Texts* (2005), discusses the coevolution of human identity and technology, arguing that "making, storing, and transmitting can be thought of as modalities related to information; they also help to constitute the bodies of subjects and texts" (2005:7). Hayles describes how this constitution of bodies through intersections with technology and the flow of information allows subjective experience to move beyond embodiment, and calls this "'intermediation,' that is, complex transactions between bodies and texts as well as between different forms of media" (7). Interestingly, Hayles does not conceive this process as a means by which to erase embodiment, but instead as a means by which to circumvent embodiment's limitations. The question becomes, to what degree does the virtual function as an escape from striated embodiment for Arya and Bran, if at all.

Both Bran and Arya Stark, through the virtual spaces of hidden magics and alternative technologies which run as an undercurrent throughout Westeros, attempt to redefine embodiment in a world where they are defined socially and culturally by embodiment. However, given the theoretical foundations above, that engagement with virtual space does by no means successfully *erase* embodiment. In fact, Hayles argues that, paradoxically, embodiment becomes even more important to one's understanding of self when one engages with agency in virtual spaces. Therefore, a more complete articulation of this project's goal might be to ask the following: is the virtual within the world of *Game of Thrones* a kind of cure for the embodied trauma of the actualized world (the harshly patriarchal and ablest world of Westeros), a means by which othered embodiment is reconfigured and weaponized, both, or neither?

In many ways, Bran's "accident" in the first episode of the series, where he becomes paralyzed from the waist down, becomes the inciting incident which unleashes the massive chain of events upon which *Game of Thrones* focuses. Bran, of course, spends the months immediately following this fall bedridden and furious, sick of the pity he sees from others and the helplessness he feels in himself. In a world where Bran sees (and has been taught) that power is defined physically, even by those who need not actually wield that physical power personally, Bran's loss as a lord of his house is profound. However, Season One curiously gives Bran his first return to mobility through an intersection of nature and technology. As an early sign of good will, Tyrion Lannister designs a saddle for Bran that will allow him not only to sit upright on a horse successfully, but also to steer the horse entirely with a combination of his upper body and vocal commands. This return to mobility through a weaving of natural flora and technological innovation is especially interesting when one considers the roles Donna Haraway feels nature and technology play in informing our understanding of the posthuman. In *When Species Meet*, Haraway argues that the posthuman form is not only a cyborg, but is also a biological hybrid, defined by interspecies relationships with animals which she refers to as "companion species" (Haraway 2008:5). In order to define the companion species relationship, she invokes Derrida's philosophical engagement with the social shame he felt at his nakedness when visually acknowledged by his pet cat. Haraway argues, using Derrida's semiotic contemplation of a cat's acknowledgment from "The Animal That Therefore I am (More to Follow)" as a jumping off point, (Derrida 2002:379) that

> to respond to the cat's response to his presence would have required his joining … to the risky project of asking what this cat on this morning cared about, what these bodily postures and visual entanglements might mean and might invite … delving into the developing knowledges of both cat-cat and cat-human behavioral semiotics when species meet [2008:22].

Unlike Derrida's fascination with his shameful response to his nakedness upon the cat's acknowledgment, Haraway furthers this examination of socially constructed interspecies interaction and calls for a true relational understanding of the companion species. Bran's horse is not steered through force but through vocal commands, through communication, through a mutual understanding, an innovation upon the technological apparatuses (i.e., a traditional saddle and traditional reigns), which came before. Bran's mobility is reliant upon this hybrid of bodies and motivations. In fact, when Bran's saddle is broken and his horse taken by wildlings in Season One, we feel the same way we might if a blind man's seeing eye dog had been taken away: Bran has lost a piece of himself, a piece of his embodiment.

Bran's embodiment is further (and much more recognizably) defined when, accompanied by Meera and Jojen Reed, Bran continues the companion species relationship with his direwolf, Summer, in his training as a warg. Within the mythology of the series, very few humans have an innate ability to enter the minds of animals and take control of their physical forms, and the series suggests that a combination of Bran's Stark heritage and the lack felt through his injury causes Bran to develop this potential. As Bran's relationship with Summer strengthens, he begins to unconsciously manifest this ability, eventually training in it actively. Like Bran's relationship with his horse in Season One, his relationship to Summer develops into a true mutual understanding. Bran *becomes* Summer, feeling, smelling, tasting through the direwolf's senses. When they separate again, Bran understands Summer better and Summer understands Bran better. The young lord's ability to warg becomes a new technological interface by which the bridge between bodies creates a symbiotic relationship of embodiment and through this relationship both demonstrated skill and ability they could not individually. Haraway refers to this as a "biotechnology" and notes the ways in which this process alters future evolution for both species as they move towards the posthuman (Haraway 2008:72).

Interestingly, this relationship between technology and flora and fauna functions quite similarly in another pop culture artifact: James Cameron's *Avatar* (2009). The world of Pandora presented in the film functions, the audience learns, through a kind of naturally occurring data network, an "internet" housed within rare and large "spirit trees" located throughout the world. The native Na'vi have evolved a biological means through which to "plug into" this network during physical interactions with both flora and fauna, which they understand through purely spiritual terms. *Game of Thrones*, like *Avatar*, engages in the concepts of avatar forms through Bran's ability to warg, and later (perhaps more importantly) in a plant-based network of memory housed in weirwood trees, and more specifically the "heart tree," a mystical central hub of universal memory. Bran's journey throughout the series to find the source of this network takes him to the roots of a Weirwood where he finds a human man, the so-called "Three Eyed Raven" for whom he has been searching, entangled in the roots, entangled in a network of memory.

Avatar and *Game of Thrones* both engage in a conversation about virtual spaces and their social and philosophical significance. Like the digital spaces of the internet, the networks of memories and histories seen in both examples exist outside of embodiment, and yet require physical central hubs to access these naturally (or magically, depending on your interpretation) occurring virtual spaces. Before his full transformation into the newest incarnation of the Three Eyed Raven, Bran needs to physically hold onto the roots of the Weirwood, just as Jake Sully (also without the use of his legs in his natural body) must physically merge with the Spirit Tree in *Avatar*. Bran and Jake are "jacking in" as much as any cyberpunk character might be. As James Tobias states in his essay "Going Native with Pandora's Tool Box":

> The closing sequence goes beyond the transhumanist fantasy of uploading one's con-sciousness into a computer network; Jake's consciousness is transplanted and trans-formed via a ritual that allows his Terran body to die and his consciousness to occupy his Na'vi body. Now, Jake's every action will be a sacred act of uploading and downloading natural, memorial data … gaining access to pristine nature, social belonging, and pre-individual, even primordial, memory-as-data-one and for all [2012:342].

And with the engagement between consciousness and new physical identity comes interesting questions of agency, knowledge, and how embodiment alters one's sense of self. Like *Avatar*, this "jacking in" accompanies physical and psychological transformation. Jake Sully's merging with the Spirit Tree leads to his eventual transition from human to Na'vi, both physically and spiritually. The question becomes, in what ways are virtual spaces capable of true transformation? Is Jake no longer informed by his human experiences upon transformation into Na'vi? Is Bran no longer informed by his human experiences upon transformation into the Three Eyed Raven?

Bran's merging with the Weirwood's roots and his time spent warging within Summer's form are presented within *Game of Thrones* as an unhealthy escape for Bran from his physical embodiment. On his journey to the "heart tree" with Meera and Jojen, especially after his near reunion with Jon at Cras-tor's Keep in Season Five, Bran begins to ignore the needs of his physical form in favor of spending time as Summer. As his companions drag his unconscious body on a sled towards their destination, Bran spends his time hunting and exploring through the eyes of his direwolf, and becomes increas-ingly irritable and closed off when he returns to his body. At one point, Jojen points out how long it has been since Bran ate, to which Bran replies simply that he just did, as Summer. We see this same overly eager reaction to Bran's ability to "plug into" memories in the roots beneath the "heart tree," as the Three Eyed Raven warns him during one vision, "It's beautiful beneath the sea, but if you stay too long, you'll drown." Bran replies, "I wasn't drowning. I was home" (6x2 "Home"). In both of these situations, Bran's eagerness is entirely informed by his psychological relationship with his disability, and his unresolved anger towards his physical embodiment. Thomas Foster, in his book *The Souls of Cyberfolk* (2005), talks about the kind of disconnect between virtual and actual illustrated here within a conceptualization of "citizenship" of social value and belonging. Foster argues that the citizen is made up of two parts: the physical/performative and the discursive meaning put onto the first by social structures (139). Therefore, we see that the virtual is not meant to function as an erasure of embodied self, nor as a separation from that self, as embodiment informs the very motivations by which the virtual is accessed. Instead, Bran's engagement with the virtual does not become entirely successful until Bran allows it to alter his understanding of self, and perhaps more importantly, his understanding of the historical context of that embodiment (discussed below). As the Three Eyed Raven says to Bran upon their first meeting, "You will never walk again…. But you will fly" (5x10 "Mother's Mercy").

Bran's engagement with the virtual memory network of the "heart tree," like his engagement with Summer, allows him to walk again briefly within memory. However, to use Foster's language, Bran may redefine his performative embodiment through access to the virtual, but his physical self remains part of the equation (in fact, the times when he forgets this become counterproductive, perhaps most obviously through Jojen's death protecting a warging Bran on the frozen lake in the finale of Season Five). Instead, Bran's access to memory transforms his understanding of the context of his embodiment. The Three Eyed Raven walks Bran through his ancestral history, examining the early stories of his father Ned Stark, his relationship to King Robert, and the mysterious circumstances surrounding the death of his Aunt Lyanna, the undercurrent of which informs the entire series. Bran's attitude towards the loss of his legs has always been understood within the context of a very specific image of his father, and a very specific idea of his own role within the Stark family and society itself. His entry into these memories recontextualizes these expectations for Bran. Additionally, with the death of the Three Eyed Raven, and Bran's ascension into that role in Season Six of the series, the context in which Bran understands his embodiment shifts. As the Three Eyed Raven, he has (or wants) no claim to Winterfell. He has no need to perform physical power in order to obtain or hold that role.

While Bran's renegotiation of self takes place through a redefinition of embodiment, Arya brings the virtual to the actual, literally blurring the borders of her physical embodiment entirely. Arya, like many other characters throughout *Game of Thrones*, is a warrior in a body that this culture will not recognize as capable of wielding power. Like Brienne of Tarth, Tyrion Lannister, and Daenerys Targaryen, Arya yearns from the start of the series to be seen for more than her embodiment. From the start of the series, female characters lack agency even when presented positively to the audience and those who have some, such as Margaery Tyrell, wield that agency primarily through sexuality, unofficial manipulation, and relation to powerful men. Cercei, the Queen of Thorns, and even Septon Unella are portrayed this way. When we first meet her, Arya is chastised for her rejection of the trappings of "ladyhood," unlike her sister Sansa, who is mesmerized by tales of white knights and beautiful princesses. Arya's rejection of these social expectations allows her to recognize the true nature of characters like Cersei and Joffery Lannister far before many of the other main characters, and when her father is killed at the end of the first season, Arya's survival is entirely dependent on her complete rejection of traditional royal femininity. She spends the majority of the second season disguised as a boy, and the majority of Seasons Three and Four in the company of the Hound, witnessing firsthand what traditional masculine agency affords those who embody it, as the Hound survives on the road almost exclusively through the threat his stature and sword represent. Interestingly enough, it is not until after the Hound's apparent death at the hands of Brienne of Tarth, arguably the most prominent example of female embodied physical power and agency in the series, that Arya understands how possible this agency actually is for her. In response, she abandons her homeland completely and looks outside of Westerosi hegemony for answers that will allow her to access agency and power in this world (outside of Brienne, the majority of socially and physically powerful women presented in the series who directly wield this power are marked as "foreign" to Westeros: Daenerys, Ellaria, and the Sand sisters are all examples of this). Upon seeing the true possibility of agency and power for those who attempt to exist outside Westeros's socially oppressive expectations (the virtual's discursive meaning which Foster pairs with embodiment in his construction of the apprehensive citizen), Arya exits that social structure completely, traveling to the strange and foreign Braavos in search of a means of revenge she can bring back with her.

The House of Black and White represents several important things to Arya. Firstly, Braavosi culture offers Arya her first interaction with a type of power and agency that ignores her young female embodiment. Syrio Forel, Arya's water dancing teacher in Season One, sees Arya as a capable and determined warrior in training, and this experience drastically informs Arya's survival in the several seasons that follow. Secondly, Arya's first and only interactions with a member of the House of Black and White up to this point is Jaqen H'ghar, a "faceless man" able to change his physical identity at will. Here, Arya trains in this same art, learning that the House of Black and White is a kind of assassination guild in Braavos, whose victims become new identities/faces into which its members can transform. For Arya, the House of Black and White offers both the means by which she can wield power and agency outside of her physical embodiment, but also the means by which to potentially erase and/or blur that very embodiment.

Judith (now Jack) Halberstam's *Female Masculinities* examines the various ways in which social expectations of femininity and masculinity can be reappropriated and redefined through their connection to the embodied and to the technological, a process entirely important to understanding the shift in embodied self which Arya experiences. Halberstam's female masculinity examines the necessary balance between cognition and body within Hayles's posthuman in the creation of a productive alternative (to cis straight male) masculinity. Hayles acknowledges that it is through a mastery of the cognitive self that the posthuman can move past a passive interaction with information and meaning which makes up these spaces and instead take part in a proactive redefinition that meaning (2008:3). Importantly, while Hayles and Foster do not hold to the fallacious concept that the mind can exist separately from the body within virtual space, this construction frames the means by which Arya is able to fully access power when she returns to Westeros.

Halberstam's construction of alternative female masculine identities, which function through a reappropriation of embodied gender signifiers, is illustrated most powerfully through her survey of photographer Catherine Opie, whose work includes well known examples of Drag Kings (female-identified individuals who perform/satirize male identity through a series of traditionally hypermasculine signifiers such as exaggerated body hair and military dress). Of Opie's photos of Drag Kings, Halberstam writes, "The close-up [in an early project called "Being and Having"] articulates what feels like an intimacy between the model and the artist, an intimacy, moreover, not available to the viewer. The person looking at the photograph is positioned simultaneously as voyeur, as mirror image, and as participant" (1998:33). And while Halberstam's female masculinity engages with the technological, it does not rely on an engagement with the technological apparatus. Therefore, unlike Bran's reliance on his saddle, his direwolf, and his physical "jacking in" to the "heart tree," Ayra's performance of power and agency here takes place through proficiency in a technique, a skill. By the time her training at the House of Black and White comes to a close, Arya has become a kind of cyborg, engaging in an emergent alternative masculinity (masculinity here is not in reference to male-ness, but to the rhetorical coding of social and physical power as masculine traits).

Arya's training as a "faceless man" allows her to function outside of the actualized/striated, transforming her body at will to what the situation demands and therefore effectively bringing the virtual *onto* her own embodiment. If we return to the construction of the apprehensive citizen laid out by Foster, we see that Arya becomes capable of taking control of the discursive meaning attached to her embodiment. However, like Bran, this process questions the connection her original embodiment has to these new interpretations of self. While training at the House of Black and White, Arya is taught to become "no one," engaging in a "game of faces" with other members which asks her to blur the concrete reality of her own experience. Early in her training, Jaqen points out that it is impossible for her to be "no one" if she is still dressed in the clothing of Arya Stark. And this is where the question of Arya's embodiment and how strongly it is connected to her understanding of self becomes complicated. While Arya obediently abandons most of her belongings, she hides her prized sword Needle to return for it later. When she steals a face from the House of Black and White in order to assassinate one of the names on her list of revenge for her own reasons, she is stricken with blindness and punished. Arya slowly learns that to become a "faceless man" is not just to alter one's physical embodiment, nor is it to bask in the changes to social discursive meaning which take place through this alteration of embodiment. Instead, she must fundamentally abandon her past, her trauma, her lived experience, and this becomes an impossible achievement for her. Like Foster argues, the virtual may be capable of altering the context by which embodiment is understood, both by the self and society, but it cannot *erase* the self, nor the traumas and limitations which accompany the self into the virtual. Arya falls so completely into the new physical embodiment that her body experiences loss. The cognitive cannot be productively overridden or erased by a restructuring of the physical.

While concepts of the virtual, the cyborg, and the posthuman are perhaps more traditionally prevalent within genres such as cyberpunk, *Game of Thrones* creates various means by which bodies, identities, and conceptualizations of self are transformed and redefined within its fantasy-based world. However, as Hayles and Foster make clear, and through the narrative structure of the series, while the virtual may redefine or reinterpret embodiment, the virtual as a means through which to *erase* embodiment cannot truly function. While both Bran and Arya at times may wish to erase that embodiment entirely and replace it with something new, they both function most effectively throughout the series when they acknowledge that embodiment, as well as the history of experience attached to that embodiment, and use the emergent technological intersections available to them to redefine its discursive meaning, becoming true forces of power and change within the series.

REFERENCES

Cameron, James. 2010. *Avatar*. 20th Century Fox. DVD.
Deleuze, Gilles. 1981. *Bergsonism*. Translated by Hugh Tomlinson and Barbara Habberjam. New York: Zone Books.
Deleuze, Gilles, and Felix Guattari. 1987. *A Thousand Plateaus: Capitalism and Schizophrenia*. Translated by Brian Massumi. London: Continuum.
Derrida, Jacques, and David Wills. 2002. "The Animal That Therefore I Am (More to Follow)." *Critical Inquiry* 28, 2 (Winter):369–418.
Foster, Thomas. 2005. *Souls of Cyberfolk: Performativity, Virtual Embodiment, and Racial Histories*. Minneapolis: University of Minnesota Press.
Halberstam, Judith [Jack]. 1998. *Female Masculinities*. Durham: Duke University Press.
Haraway, Donna. 2008. *When Species Meet*. Minneapolis: University of Minnesota Press.
Hayles, Katherine. 2005. *My Mother Was a Computer*. Chicago: University of Chicago Press.
Tobias, James. 2012. "Going Native with Pandora's Tool Box." *Acting and Performance in Moving Image Culture: Bodies, Screens, and Renderings*, edited by Jorg Sternagel, 339–62. Bielefeld: Transcript Verlag.

"Let there be no more woe for Jon Snow"
The Dramaturgy of Spoilers

Sarah Beck

Warning! This essay contains spoilers.

Dramatis Personae

Dallas—*The Over-Sharer.* Eagerly discusses *GoT* episodes on social media.

Marie—*The Eye Roller.* Perplexed by friends who publicly make *GoT* references online.

Broda—*The Seeker.* Spoiler enthusiast, who purposefully reads *GoT* social media posts before watching the episode.

Ryan—*The Spoiler-in-Denial.* His references to plot twists are not intended to spoil, but in fact, they do.

Susanna—*The Self-Restrained.* Her fingers itch to share, but she knows it's wrong.

Katie—*The Corrections Officer.* Chastises her mother for unacceptable *GoT* etiquette on social media.

Emma—*The Passive Aggressive.* Publicly complains about spoilers without pointing fingers at the spoiler/offender

Jason—*The Curator.* The actor who posts about *GoT* performances and casting choices for vocational reasons.

Yu-kei—*The Night Watcher.* Watches episodes at the moment of release, no matter the time zone

Beth—*The Analyst.* A script developer, who observes/reflects upon *GoT* posts on social networks.

John and Duncan—*The "So Passé" Guys.* They were huge fans of *GoT* … until everybody else was.

Chris—*The Pseudo Intellectual.* Who read the "superior" book series, and scoffs at the TV audience and their "spoilers."

The Art of the Spoiler

In 2014, the story of a frustrated math teacher and his unruly class in Belgium went viral. Having read all of George R.R. Martin's books to date, the math teacher threatened to list one-by-one the major *Game of Thrones* characters killed off in the novels with detailed descriptions of their demise on the chalkboard if the students continued to misbehave (Conner 2014). The teacher's method of wielding the power of spoilers over the student fans of the *GoT* television series worked, highlighting the trials some fans endure to preserve their unadulterated narrative enjoyment of the television series.

The global reach and popularity of HBO's *Game of Thrones* television series continues to be significant. Lotz (2017) has charted its international appeal, reporting that from 2015 HBO had a global release across 170 countries, meaning that episodes are aired simultaneous to the U.S. broadcast. The opportunities for a transnational audience to view the live broadcast simultaneously has created what Lotz terms a "global water cooler" whereby fans around the world partake in "a shared media culture that transcends national boundaries." Furthermore, social media is the conduit that enables this global water cooler chat to ensue, offering fans the opportunity—irrespective of the boundaries of time and geography—to tease, share, decipher, or even disclose spoilers about *GoT* episodes to fellow fans in their social networks. *The Guardian* reported that #GameofThrones "was the 10th most discussed topic in the world in 2015, and Season Six conjured '3,900 tweets per minute'" (Hunt 2017).

Inevitably, the global consumption of the *Game of Thrones* television series, coupled with the capacity to react via live-tweeting and Facebook, make the simple act of opening a web browser risky for fans unable to keep up with each episode's debut. My own experience of the Season Five finale was spoiled by clicking on an email from my father, who lives 3,500 miles away on the east coast of the U.S., the content of which simply read, "Be there no more woe for poor Jon Snow! Good night and God bless" (he doesn't even watch the show). Elsewhere, another Facebook friend expressed a lack of sympathy for *GoT* fans not fully up to date with Season Five, adding a caveat to his *GoT* post, "Spoiler alert … wait a minute no … if you haven't read the books … you deserve to have all of the good stuff ruined for you!" The following year my narrative enjoyment was hindered yet again by a Facebook post from a childhood friend, hinting at the finale of Season Six, which stated, "'Not Today Satan'—Cersei to the High Sparrow."

The scenarios outlined above beg the question: what pleasure do *GoT* fans derive from instantaneously sharing their knowledge of the show with their social networks? Furthermore, what do those who share *GoT* commentary gain from these exhibitions, and what, if anything, might such posts cost them in terms of social relations? Analysis of *GoT* social media posts on Facebook and Twitter and interviews with *GoT* fans show that these microperformances are underpinned by a complex dramaturgical process whereby users negotiate their *GoT* fandom with the ideal image of themselves they wish to project to their wider social media audience.

Spoiler Consumption

While the term spoiler has become a part of the media studies lexicon, finding a robust definition for it is difficult (Perks and McElrath-Hart 2016:2). Jenkins (2006) equates spoiling with the act of dedicated fans—"a contingent known as 'spoilers'"—who "go to extraordinary lengths to ferret out the answers ... they call this act the process of 'spoiling'" (25). He uses this term to assess the actions of extreme *Survivor* fans, who work together using their shared knowledge, or what Jenkins refers to as "collective intelligence" (28), to ascertain how a series will play out before it airs. Nevertheless, Jenkins' narrow conception of spoiling focuses on the act of seeking out locations, plot points, and evictions mainly in the case of reality shows, activities pursued by hard-core fans rather than the average *Survivor* audience member. Sharing a similar viewpoint on spoiler culture, Gray (2010) considers spoilers as

> includ[ing] any information about what will happen in an ongoing narrative that is provided before the narrative itself gets there. To tell someone who will die on next week's show, what a film's key plot twist is, or what to expect next is to "spoil" the person and/or text [147].

However, this definition of spoiling is limiting in scope as it overlooks how general audiences interact with one another in relation to the object of fandom. Moreover, focusing on spoiling as a kind of sport dismisses those everyday social media interactions where a user can, quite by accident, encounter posts about major plot twists, character mentions, or memes that can spoil their enjoyment of the given show. Elsewhere, Perks and McElrath-Hart (2016) argue that the circulation of paratexts—which they define as "spoilers, trailers, spin-offs, parodies, merchandising, and other forms of communication" (2)—can entice potential fans to commit to watching a particular film or television show, despite having prior knowledge as to how a narrative might unfold. Despite this, Perks and McElrath-Hart's optimistic view of spoilers as teasers fails to account for what ways teasers can diminish viewing experiences for fans who have already invested time in a television series.

A more effective way to approach spoilers is Völcker's (2017) broader characterization of the term, namely that "spoilers do not only incorporate information, hints and twists, punchlines and plot development, but may also spoil the enjoyment of a movie" (148), or in this context a television show. Concentrating on *Star Wars* fandom, Völcker highlights a spectrum of participation within the range of spoiler consumption. On the one hand, there are the spoiler avoiders, who attempt to steer clear of paratexts that might disrupt their narrative pleasure, and on the other, there are more hard-core fans reminiscent of Jenkins' categorization, who actively seek out spoilers prior to the premiere of a film or television show as a means of signifying *"their own* fan status" (146).

In the case of the *Game of Thrones* television series, the spectrum ranges from active spoiler avoiders, who might go to extremes to download the "Game of Spoils" Chrome extension (Renfro 2016), which is capable of redacting any Westeros-related jargon on social media, to those dedicated spoiler-sport fans, who purposefully seek out information about *GoT* episodes prematurely. Yet to focus on fans who occupy the opposing poles of this spectrum is reductive in its overshadowing of the general *GoT* audience who may casually post, or observe social media posts about *Game of Thrones* on their social networks.

Indeed, the act of demonstrating one's consumption of *Game of Thrones*, coupled with the framing of one's image for social media, presents the larger question of whether posts are about forming genuine connections with fellow fans on social media, or evidence more self-glorifying displays of cultural knowledge to impress one's audience. As Papacharissi poses, "without an audience—actual, imagined, or a blend of both—who are we telling these stories to?" (2012:2002).

Measuring the micro-performances of *GoT* knowledge on social media, I collected responses from 17 participants in the USA, UK and Taiwan between November and December 2017. I employed Twitter's search function to find tweets that included *"Game of Thrones,"* "spoilers," and "Facebook."[1] Based on search results, I either directly messaged Twitter users or replied to their tweets. In addition to Twitter, I circulated research questions to contacts to be shared on Facebook and email lists in an effort to widen a search for participants.[2] In one case, I conducted a group interview with five *GoT* fans about their experiences with *GoT* social media posts and spoilers.[3]

On Performing GoT *Posts: The Over-Sharer and the Eye Roller*

The desire for fans to perform their *GoT* knowledge on social media could be interpreted as the performer's effort to strengthen social ties based on a shared interest with friends on social media, whereby social bonding "acts as a social glue, building trust, and norms within groups" (Sajuria et al. 2015:710).[4] Reflecting on the intrinsic value of social media, one participant, Beth, expressed: "If social media is about connecting and sharing, which in essence it started out that way, then it's just that … it's about connection." Social media platforms enable spaces for participants to partake in "condensed storytelling" in the form of status updates and tweets whereby "affect and play" become "important elements in integrating fantasy in everyday life" (Papacharissi 2012:2002).

Commenting on the merging of fiction and Facebook posts, Dallas, based in Washington, D.C., writes, "I think it's really kind of fun to see all of your friends get into [*GoT*] together. I don't know of another show that people get as into and feel compelled to share anything on." Dallas performs her enthusiasm to invite commentary from fellow fans, as seen in her evocative Facebook status update posted during the penultimate Season Five episode of *GoT*, which read "Until they show me Jon Snow's decomposed body I still believe he can come back!!" Moreover, Dallas's social media posts exemplify Goffman's (1959) dramaturgy of the self, whereby in social situations we interpret cues from others, assess the setting, and put on a performance with the ultimate goal of "project[ing] a desirable image" of ourselves to others (Bullingham and Vasconcelos 2013:101).[5] Bringing Goffman's work into the digital era, Liam Bullingham and Ana Vasconcelos designate the "front stage" online environment as the public space where social media users are "conscious of being observed by an audience" (2013:101). Take for example Dallas's aestheticized status update "#notabastard" posted "front stage" to her social media audience in response to the revelation in 7x5 "Eastwatch" that Jon Snow's parents were married. Yet in the effort to amuse *GoT* fans and friends, over-sharing can also alienate one's audience.

If the "front stage" online involves the conscious act of posting status updates/tweets for a wider social media audience, the "backstage" environment constitutes the private space where "no performance is necessary" (Bullingham and Vasconcelos 2013:101). Backstage social media users can relax, scroll, or lurk without having to publicly perform their wit, charm, politics, or morality for an online audience. Rather than performing *GoT* knowledge front-stage, Marie, a writer based in south-central Pennsylvania, prefers the security of the backstage environment, adding "[I've] always been mystified by the desire of some to be 'first out of the gate' with the climax of episodes in near-real time." When compelled to engage in *GoT* discussions online, Marie uses private messenger to send "'exclamations' such as 'How bout them dragons'" to close friends only when she knows "the other friend has already seen the episode." Marie's reluctance to publicly post about the show is primarily founded on a concern not to ruin the experience of those who have yet to watch the most current episode, but also as not to appear among her social media audience as the self-gratifying "first to know" or "showoff." As Patrick Lonergan (2016) suggests, "our social media identities are not just a representation of *who we think we are*, but a performance of *how we wish to be seen* by others" (28).

On Fan Etiquette: The Self-Restrained, the Seeker and the Spoiler-in-Denial

Through the observation of social conventions online, *GoT* fans learn how to tailor their performance. Self-conscious of the risks of disrupting the narrative enjoyment of her Facebook audience, Susanna, an actress based in London, avoids posting about *GoT* despite her impulse to discuss elements of the show. She explains, "If I could [post] ambiguously though I would," but adds, "I'm wary of posting about it, because everyone watches things on demand these days and I'd HATE to deliver a spoiler." Susanna's case illustrates the relationship between spoiling another fan's narrative pleasure as a kind of violation of social conventions and the desire to preserve one's own self-image and how they wish to be perceived by others. Accidently spoiling could result in one *"losing face"* and "failing to project the image/persona they wish to create" (Bullingham and Vasconcelos 2013:101). Yet, at the same time, Susanna holds those in her own social network to the same standard of discretion, adding, "I can usually trust my friends won't give anything away publicly!"

In contrast, Twitter user Broda, based in San Francisco, explains he "loves spoilers" and welcomes the circulation of spoilers on social networking sites. Part of the narrative pleasure Broda derives from watching the series is making connections with those who have already commented on episodes, adding "I request more info when I see that someone knows something." Broda explains how actively seeking out spoilers enhances his experience of watching the series, adding that

> spoilers do not change my feelings in the moment I see *Game of Thrones*. In the moment I'm seeing *GoT* I forget even my name. And then, [a] few minutes after the episode ends, I remember the spoilers and I connect them with the episode, but only after the episode. During the episode I forget everything.

Broda's position complicates assumptions that spoilers detract from the enjoyment of audiences' experiences, and correlates with Perks and McElrath-Hart's (2016) argument that audience "engagement with spoilers can be a participatory, exploratory, and evaluative experience" (6). Furthermore, Broda feels compelled to share posts on what he considers to be his private networks, remarking that "Twitter and Facebook were created for that thing (not for spoilers, just for the post [sic] what you are doing)." For instance, when Ygritte was killed, Broda shared the innocuous tweet "I'll miss you red." Rather than viewing the delivery of spoilers on his social networks as a violation of social conventions, Broda contends the responsibility of protecting narrative enjoyment lies with the social media observers in his social network, suggesting, "If you don't like it, do not use Facebook or watch HBO: shrug."

However, Broda recognizes there are suitable and unsuitable places to post about *GoT*, adding that he abides by the rule "no-spoilers on public pages." To some degree, Broda's post illuminates an awareness of fan etiquette as examined in Mayka Castellano, Melina Meimaridis, and Marcelo Dos Santos, Jr.'s (2017) study of *Game of Thrones* fandom on Twitter. Through an analysis of tweets, they discovered commonalities in *GoT* fan's attitudes towards rules for posting online, observing:

> [Fans] contend that posting a spoiler on a Facebook group for *Game of Thrones* fans may be appropriate, but posting on Twitter, where anyone can have access to that content, is unacceptable. The proposal is to restrict these paratexts to certain spaces where fans have the option to consume them, thereby eliminating the risk of coming across them accidentally on social networks such as Facebook, Tumblr or Twitter [80].

Yet, recognizing and adhering to fan etiquette are different activities. Similar to Broda's suggestion that *GoT* posts require a certain fan etiquette, Ryan, a musician based in Lynchburg, Virginia, presents more detailed criteria for what posts are socially acceptable when referring to *GoT* episodes, explaining:

> I know last season [Season Seven], I posted a photo of Jon Snow from an older episode to describe my shocked reaction after a scene. But I try to never indicate names, plot info, or anything that would stop someone from experiencing that same moment. When I post, it's usually just general excitement about the show.

Despite acknowledging certain performance rules, Ryan's posts suggest slight deviations from his own code of conduct regarding plot information. While discussion on 21 August 2017 was dominated by the lunar eclipse in North America, Ryan wrote: "Things I don't care about today: moons blocking suns. Things I do care about today: ice dragons," referencing the final scene of the previous evening's penultimate *GoT* episode of Season Seven. Here, Ryan's Facebook posts exhibits humor and playfulness for the entertainment of his social media audience but at the same time draws attention to a significant plot point. In this way Ryan's actions are more self-serving rather than driven out of concern with social bonding.

On Spoiler Faux Pas: The Corrections Officer and the Passive Aggressor

The act of posting *GoT* social media posts is partly motivated by a desire to build social capital, yet in some cases authors fail to consider, or perhaps choose to ignore, the impact of their micro-blogging on fellow *GoT* fans' experiences on their social network in the dramaturgy of such *GoT* postings. A performer's failure to consider fellow fans in their social network who might have missed the scheduled broadcast, or live in a different time zone (where the show has yet to be aired) can significantly alter the audience's perception of the performer in question, and might alienate the very audience the performer seeks to impress. In the case of performance gaffes, audiences may choose more direct and indirect ways to "correct" fellow social media users' spoiler faux pas.

Blacklisting certain friends on Facebook is a tactic Jason, based in London, employs during the *GoT* season, reserved only for those on his friend's list who purposefully share plot twists. He says:

> One friend does a "Fuck, Marry, Kill" post for every episode and I always avoid their posts. One of my best friends just posts comments that are outright spoilers so I know to avoid his posts…. And yes, my one friend who posts spoilers constantly has altered my attitude towards him.

Furthermore, the activities of some peers as described by Jason—through the repetition and continuation of spoiling plot twists—verge on "anti-fan" behavior whereby trolling by spoiling is done for the entertainment and benefit of the spoiler (Recuero, Amaral, and Monteiro 2012:5).

Taking a more diplomatic approach, Katie, who lived in Utah for the majority of the *GoT* series, and would sometimes encounter *GoT* social media posts prematurely (due to living in a different time zone to Eastern Standard Time), has on occasion expressed her discontent at offending friends directly. She reflected on a post made by her mother (who lives on the east coast) on 16 May 2016, which read, "You simply don't mess with the mother of dragons." Katie considered her mother's declaration to lack the social awareness of those in her social network. Katie's recognition of her mother's unintentional spoiler intersects with Goffman's (1959) explanation of how faux pas influence one's performance. He states:

> Unmeant gestures, inopportune intrusions, and *faux pas* are sources of embarrass-
> ment and dissonance which are typically unintended by the person who is responsi-
> ble for making them and which would be avoided were the individual to know in
> advance the consequences of his activity [205].

Acknowledging her mother's online faux pas, Katie admits, "I scolded my kind mum about a mother of dragons comment" privately offline. Katie's private interaction with her mother in the backstage environment evidences her desire not to embarrass her mother "front stage" in the presence of the former's Facebook friends. This correction illustrates a kind of loyalty between team members of the same in-group. As Goffman (1959) explains, "when a member of the team makes a mistake in the presence of the audience"—in this case Facebook friends—"the other team-members often must supress their immediate desire to punish and instruct the offender until, that is, the audience is no longer present" (94).[6]

Sharing a similar detestation of spoilers, Emma, based in the UK, has on several occasions had her narrative enjoyment ruined by friends on social media, including the "deaths of all the Martells, Littlefinger's death" and Joffrey's poisoning. She laments, "if you know a plot twist it doesn't have the same impact." Despite Emma's displeasure, she does not personally harbor ill feelings towards friends who've spoiled her narrative enjoyment. Nonetheless, unlike Jason and Katie, Emma has publicly posted her discontent front stage regarding spoiler faux pas on her social network. For instance, on 28 August 2017 Emma posted on Twitter, "So me and my housemates sat to watch game of thrones [sic], I was waiting for them to get snacks and got two spoilers from fucking Facebook." Here Emma publicly rebukes spoiler offenders in her social media network front stage, to make friends and followers aware of their performance blunders.

On Networking: The Curator, the Night Watcher and the Analyst

One way of approaching the motivations behind the dramaturgy of *GoT* social media posts is through the lens of social capital conceptualized by Bourdieu (1999), wherein the significance of one's social standing is influenced by "the social capital of relations, connections, or ties" (128). Within the dramaturgy of social media micro-performances of *GoT* lies insight, not only into the performer's cultural consumption, but also their social and professional aspirations. As an actor based in London, Jason's reasons for regularly posting about *GoT* are twofold. One reason Jason posts on Facebook is to amuse his friends and *GoT* fans with playful posts. For instance, in light of the Bran, Arya, and Sansa Stark reunion in the fourth episode of Season

Seven, Jason wrote: "Sansa's like 'Everyone's else's gap years were SO much better than mine.'" The second key motivator for Jason is to exhibit his involvement in the arts, evidencing a merging of professional capital with humor. Take for example his integration of *GoT* ruminations and references to his experiences as an actor in the following post: "In the past month I have been asked if I am Spanish, Italian, Pakistani and Persian. Yet I still haven't been cast as a Dothraki Warlord or a Dornish Prince!!!"

Elaborating further on his pre-meditative reasoning for posting, Jason explains:

> Usually, I will post about my love for the series or how much I want to be cast on it (actor specific post obviously!). I share on Facebook as I have other Facebook friends who are also huge fans of the show and also because I post about other shows, films, entertainment and arts that I enjoy.

In Jason's case, using social network sites to display his cultural consumption of television series, films, music, and plays reinforces his professional image to those in his social network, some of whom are also actors, directors, and writers.

Also using Facebook as a means of acquiring cultural capital is *GoT* fan and media studies scholar Yu-kei, who is based in Taiwan and specializes in "media globalization and audience studies." Because a key element of Yu-kei's research interests includes examining "the roles the official simulcast and the informal sharing of *Game of Thrones* in making the series a global phenomenon," she occasionally posts about *GoT* as a means of connecting with friends, but mostly to monitor fan responses on her social network for research purposes. Having lived both in the UK and Taiwan for the duration of the series, she watches the show simultaneous to the U.S. broadcast explaining:

> I usually watched the latest episode at 2–3.00 a.m. in the UK when it was simulcast globally … none of my friends in the UK/Europe would do so I think. (Not many of them had Sky Subscription [sic] either). That would be 9.00 a.m. in Taiwan, and most of my friends in Taiwan were working so no one would watch it.

Underlying the dramaturgy of Yu-kei's posts is a desire to prompt responses from Facebook friends to gauge who on her social network is watching the show in real time. For instance, posts such as "'#GameofThrones simulcast!!! [sic]'" or "'Winter is Here' #Simulcast Facebook #GoTS7" are employed by Yu-kei to "express [her] excitement (of watching the latest episode/season)." Posts of these kind help Yu-kei determine what series are popular among her Facebook friends—particularly those who are Taiwanese—as a means of monitoring the show's global reach, and at the same time indicate her dedication to watching the series no matter the hour of day.

Also recognizing the value of expressing fandom online as a means of developing professional ties is Beth, who works in script development in London. She reflects on the advantage of live-tweeting (the act of formulating tweets about a television show as it unfolds) for those who work in entertainment as on opportunity to build audiences. She explains,

> [W]hen people tweet about *Game of Thrones* … people do it to gain followers. You tweet about something, and like that, it gets people to follow you. So Adam [a comedian] used to do it a lot to get more followers. So he'd live-tweet about it and people would be like, "oh, ok." It's a business! It's a good way for you to gain followers.

While Beth approaches live-tweeting as a marketing strategy to benefit the entertainer's career, rather than as an altruistic endeavor, live-tweeting can also make the audience feel more connected to fellow fans. Considering this phenomenon, Schirra, Sun and Bentley (2014) suggest, "Live-tweeting can help viewers feel connected to a large online viewing audience, while also helping to strengthen social bonds with real-life friends, providing a context for conversation around shared interests" (2450). Whether the motivations of posters are solipsistic in nature or about making genuine connections with fellow fans, *GoT* micro-performances are value-laden and the success or failure of one's ability to perform for one's social media audience is vital to the maintenance and building of one's social and cultural capital.

On Overexposure: The "So Passé" Guys and the Pseudo Intellectual

On the other side of exhibiting status updates and tweets as a means of acquiring social capital, some fans refrain from posting or reject others' social media expressions of fandom as an indicator of their own cultural superiority. During a group interview, Jon, who works as a web developer in London, evidenced some reflexivity mid-discussion regarding his reception of *GoT* social media posts and his feelings of condescension that followed. He contemplates, "when something becomes really popular, you don't really want it as much anymore. I do that a bit, which is snobbery really. If it becomes too popular, it's like 'oh well, I liked it when no when else liked it.'" Jon's point of view intersects with Bourdieu's (2010) deconstruction of class and taste, whereby he suggests that when cultural objects (such as music and art) become reflective of "popular taste" they subsequently become "devalued in their popularization" (8). Jon's lack of desire to share posts—when he actively shared posts in the beginning of the television series—is based partly on the rejection of mass popularity. Building on this dynamic, Duncan, an IT consultant based in London, added to Jon's point, "It's the act of discovery, 'I'm so glad I found this awesome thing that's hard to find and it's brilliant!' When everyone already knows about it, it's like ugh." These sentiments relegating the *GoT* franchise to the realm of "too passé" indicate a kind of fatigue and rejection of mainstream culture. Sarah Thorton (1995) theorizes to be hip "is to be privy to insider knowledge" (6), and therefore subscribing to the popularity of *GoT*, and performing one's enthusiasm for *GoT* online can diminish one's coolness and credibility in the eyes of their social media audience.

The rejection of *GoT* social media posts based on popularity can also operate to establish one's intellectual superiority, as exemplified by Chris, an actor and barman based in Bosworth, UK, who read the George R.R. Martin's series *A Song of Ice and Fire*. In his response to how social media spoilers alter his consumption of the show, he interpolates a hierarchy of cultural value in regard to the *Game of Thrones* franchise, explaining:

> I get annoyed by people who moan about spoilers, 'cause like I said, either watch it or don't watch it. I read the books ... I loved the books, but the TV show does not appeal to me in the slightest. I think it's shit ... I have no respect for anyone who watches the show. Read the books!

In light of this attitude, an audience member's repudiation of *GoT* social media performances may not simply be about respecting other viewers' narrative enjoyment of the television series, but may also be rooted in the receiver's preoccupation with seeking to present themselves as, in this case, culturally superior.

A Hall of Faces

Approaching *Game of Thrones* social media posts as micro-performances draws critical attention to the complex interplay between performers, audiences, and social status. The performer's approach to the dramaturgical process of *GoT* social media posts may either strengthen or sustain social relations, whereby posts function as a form of social bonding, or indeed diminish an audience's enjoyment of the series and possibly their perception of the performer at the same time. Furthermore, key factors that play a vital role in understanding the intricate but often taken-for-granted dramaturgical and performance processes involved in the creation of paratexts, include impression-management, and the acquisition and exhibition of social and cultural capital.

Despite the range of interpretations as to how spoilers enhanced or diminished participants' enjoyment of the television series, there seemed to be consensus regarding boundaries for which *GoT* posts are socially acceptable, and what kind of micro-performances would violate social conventions. Some participants suggested that they personally adhere to an unspoken fan etiquette, which they expect friends and fellow *GoT* fans to follow. Some respondents purposefully avoided social media if lagging behind on the series, and certain friends who are "repeat offenders" in terms of spoilers within their social network. In most cases, respondents' annoyance when encountering plot twists on social media were not personally directed at those in their social network whose posts had altered their engagement with an episode.

More illuminating were participants' responses where antagonisms were focused towards the popularity of the television series itself, rather than individual *GoT* posters. In these cases, participants' hostility regarding the circulation of *GoT*-related social media sprang from feelings of cultural superiority. In light of this occurrence, a key area for further analysis in terms of the dramaturgy of social media posts and cultural consumption is: what role does cultural snobbery play in the reception of *GoT* posts, and what does this relationship reveal about the politics of the performer/audience dynamic?

Adapting Goffman's work in the context of performing *GoT* fandom on social media offers the opportunity to better understand both the intentions of fans who purposefully or inadvertently spoil online as well as how these micro-performances are received by peers.[7] In turn, the findings from this study demonstrate some of the reasoning behind how and why *GoT* fans choose to perform or refrain from performing their cultural knowledge online. Furthermore, it evidences the ways in which social bonding, social conventions, and cultural capital influence how one chooses to present their fandom online. The findings suggest that the tension between those who actively perform their *GoT* fandom "front stage" on social media and those who prefer engaging with the television series backstage, is not solely based on enhancing or preserving narrative engagement. Instead, conflicting attitudes about performing/receiving *GoT* posts are entangled with social and cultural values, and individuals' preoccupation with the presentation of the self. Or, as Goffman (1959) surmises of this symbiotic relationship between the performer and the audience, "the part one individual plays is tailored to the parts played by the others present" (9).

NOTES

1. My research methodology was informed by Bucher's (2017) research on Facebook and algorithms, where she utilized Twitter to make contact with individuals who had tweeted posts that referenced their recognition of algorithmic profiling on Facebook (30–44).

2. The survey questions included: "Have you ever posted about *Game of Thrones* on Facebook? If so, what was the nature of your post and what/why did you feel compelled to share it with your social network? What *GoT* spoilers or *GoT* posts, if any, have you encountered checking your Facebook feed that have altered your experience of the show? Are there any individual(s) on your feed you purposefully try to avoid or unfollow during a *GoT* season? In what ways, if any, have *GoT* spoilers on Facebook enhanced or hindered your enjoyment of the series or altered your attitude toward Facebook friends who have posted spoilers?" In addition to the main survey questions, participants were asked to distinguish what they considered as a spoiler. The first question of the survey included:

Which of the following do you consider to be a spoiler? Feel free to choose more than one:

A) When a name of a GoT character is mentioned on Facebook but no context is given (i.e., HODOR!);

B) An innocuous Facebook status making some reference to an episode (i.e., "If you're a guest at the wedding and not feeling the love vibes, leave before the first dance #GOT #RedWedding");

C) When a particular plot point is directly mentioned on Facebook (i.e., "Watching Joffrey die was joyful!");

D) None of the above;

E) Write in a type of spoiler if not listed above.

3. The group interview/discussion took place on 17 December 2017 in Nailsworth, UK, lasting 40 minutes. Participants addressed survey questions in a discussion form, interjecting different viewpoints regarding their spoiler experiences.

4. In the context of building and maintaining social capital on social networks, Sajuria, van Heerde-Hudson, Hudson, Dasandi, and Theocharis (2015) draw on Robert Putnam's theory of bonding social capital, explaining that "bonding social capital exists in the strong ties occurring within, often homogeneous, groups—families, friendship circles, work teams, choirs, criminal gangs, and bowling clubs" (710).

5. Goffman defines performance as "all the activity of a given participant on a given occasion which serves to influence in any way any of the other participants" (1959:26).

6. Despite, chastising her mother in private, Katie admits to posting about *GoT* from time-to-time, explaining that "I have posted about Hodor in the context of wishing others a happy birthday or quoting him because he is universally endearing to fans."

7. Reflecting on Goffman's contribution to the field of sociology, Bourdieu wrote that "he regarded social subjects as actors who put on a performance and who, through a more or less sustained *mise en scène*, endeavor to show themselves off in the best light" (1983:113).

References

Bourdieu, Pierre. 1983. "Erving Goffman, Discoverer of the Infinitely Small." *Theory, Culture & Society* 2, 1:112–13.

Bourdieu, Pierre. 1999. *The Weight of the World: Social Suffering in Contemporary Society.* Cambridge: Polity.

Bourdieu, Pierre. 2010. *Distinction: A Social Critique of the Judgment of Taste.* London: Routledge.

Bucher, Tania. 2017. "The Algorithmic Imaginary: Exploring the Ordinary Affects of Facebook Algorithms." *Information, Communication & Society* 20, 1:30–44.

Bullingham, Liam and Ana C. Vasconcelos. 2017. "'The presentation of self in the online world': Goffman and the Study of OnlineI. *Journal of Information Science* 39, 1:101–12.

Castellano, Mayka, Melina Meimaridis, and Marcelo Dos Santos, Jr. 2017. "'Game of Spoilers': Adapted Works and Fan Consumption Disputes in Brazil." *Intensities in the Journal of Cult Media* 9:74–86.

Conner, Megan. 2014. "Teacher Punishes Students with Game of Thrones Spoilers." *The Guardian*, 25 March. Accessed 11 November 2017. https://www.theguardian.com/tv-and-radio/tvandradioblog/2014/mar/25/teacher-punishes-students-with-game-of-thrones-spoilers.

Goffman, Erving. 1959. *The Presentation of Self in Everyday Life.* London: Penguin.

Gray, Jonathan. 2010. *Show Sold Separately: Promos, Spoilers and Other Media Paratexts.* New York: New York University Press.

Hunt, Elle. 2017. "Game of Thrones Spoilers Are Everywhere on Social Media! How Can I Avoid Them?" *The Guardian*, 21 July. Accessed 10 November 2017. https://www.theguardian.com/culture/2017/jul/21/game-of-thrones-spoilers-are-everywhere-on-social-media-how-can-i-avoid-them.

Jenkins, Henry. 2006. *Convergence Culture.* New York: New York University Press.

Lonergan, Patrick. 2016. *Theatre & Social Media.* London: Palgrave Macmillan.

Lotz, Amanda (2017). "How *Game of Thrones* Became TV's First Global Blockbuster." *The Conversation*, 12 July. Accessed 10 December 2017. https://theconversation.com/how-game-of-thrones-became-tvs-first-global-blockbuster-79820.

Papacharissi, Zizi. 2012. "Without You, I'm Nothing: Performances of the Self on Twitter." *International Journal of Communication* 6, 1989–2006.

Perks, Lisa Glebatis and Noelle McElrath-Hart. 2016. "Television Spoilers Recast as Narrative Teasers." *"Qualitative Research Reports in Communication* 18, 1:1–7.

Recuero, Raquel, Adriana Amaral, and Camila Monteiro. 2012. "Fandoms, Trending Topics and Social Capital in Twitter." *Internet Research 13* Conference, Salford, UK, 20 October, 1–24. Accessed 17 November 2017. http:// spir.aoir.org/index.php/spir/article/view/7.

Renfro, Kim. 2016. "If You're Sick of 'Game of Thrones' Spoilers, This Chrome Extension Will Solve Your Problems." *Business Insider*, 27 May. Accessed 11 November 2017. http://uk.businessinsider.com/game-of-thrones-spoilers-block-chrome-extension-2016-5?r=US&IR=T.

Sajuria, Javier, Jennifer van Heerde-Hudson, David Hudson, Niheer Dasandi, and Yannis Theocharis. 2014. "Tweeting Alone? An Analysis of Bridging and Bonding Social Capital in Online Networks." *American Politics Research* 43, 4:708–38.

Schirra, Steven, Huan Sun, and Frank Bentley. 2014. "Together Alone: Motivations for Live-Tweeting a Television Series." *Proceedings of the 2014 Association for Computing Machinery (ACM) Conference on Computer-Human Interaction (CHI)*, 2441–50. New York: ACM Press.

Thorton, Sarah. 1995. *Club Cultures*. Cambridge: Polity.

Völcker, Matthias. 2017. "'Spoiler!? I'm Completely Painless, I Read Everything': Fans and Spoilers—Results of a Mixed Method Study." *Participations: Journal of Audience & Reception Studies* 14, 1:145–69.

Raven: Social Media

LINDSEY MANTOAN

As Sarah Beck writes in the previous essay, fans of *Game of Thrones* post about the show on social media as a way to boost their social capital (or tank it, if they fail to respect codes related to spoilers). Fans in the entertainment industry—actors, directors, costumers, musicians—might post to boost their artist cred. Those people too cool for school will post about *not* watching *Game of Thrones*. There are any number of reasons fans engage social media as a platform for interacting with *Game of Thrones*.

Somehow during Season Six, my Facebook wall became a site for people to work through their intense feelings about the show, and although most of my Facebook friends who participate in this discussion aren't friends with each other, we formed a new a community of fans. It was entirely unintentional on my part. Origin stories are always suspect, and I can't really remember how this one starts—I must have posted something about the show, and various FB friends started responding, first to me, and then to each other. And the posts took on a life of their own. By Season Seven, we'd fallen into a routine. After each episode, I would post a line or two from the show—something more or less innocuous in terms of spoilers. I'd tag friends who had become part of this community. By the time I woke up the next morning, I would have at least a dozen comments, most of which already had a dozen replies. If someone was going to be traveling or otherwise unable to watch the episode the night it aired, he or she would message me in advance and ask me to delay tagging until a set time.

Comments range from processing emotions about awful or wonderful scenes, to positing theories about what might happen next, to reminding each other of little-known Westeros lore (a given human can only ride one dragon, for example). The more literary-minded sometimes draw connections between *Game of Thrones* and other texts or discuss the tactics used to adapt the books to the show. We also gossip about the characters and the real-life

"Well, don't get used to it. You're still very strange and annoying."

20 Reactions 44 Comments

👍 Like   💬 Comment   ↱ Share

👍❤️😆 Jennifer Johnson, Christine Alfano and 18 others

Courtney Shaw Huizar DING DONG, THE WITCH IS DEAD. (More tomorrow.)

Like · Reply · 30w   👍 4

↳ Susanne Shawyer replied · 6 Replies

Juliet Hernandez Eli Now WHY does Bran tell Sam of all people??? Why no one else! I know it's convenient that Sam had the marriage info (which he suddenly remembers?), but is there any narrative reason he confides in Sam?

Like · Reply · 30w

↳ Courtney Shaw Huizar replied · 4 Replies

Ted Brassfield Sam stealing credit from Gilly - Ugh, patriarchy!

Like · Reply · 30w · Edited   👍😆 7

Juliet Hernandez Eli Jamie's puppy dog eyes at the moment his sis is going to order him killed! Almost makes you forget what a louse he was.

Like · Reply · 30w   👍 3

↳ Noa Levanon Klein replied · 31 Replies

Ted Brassfield Another complaint about Varys: Cersei must have put the Golden Company order in ahead of time, because she had no time for a private moment with Greyjoy (tyrion convinced her and walked back a few seconds ahead of her, Jamie was walking next to her)

How did Varys not hear about the Golden Company's new employer? ... See More

Like · Reply · 30w   👍 1

↳ Courtney Shaw Huizar replied · 17 Replies

Processing the Season Seven finale on Facebook.

actors playing them, and there was much gushing when Kit Harington and Rose Leslie got engaged. Commenting is concentrated on Mondays, the day after the episode airs, but continues through the week and spikes again on Sundays in anticipation of that evening's episode. After the new episode airs, people turn their attention to that week's post, but aren't above returning to previous posts to revel in satisfaction (or misery) about earlier predictions.

In addition to the community of international fans who share their predictions and help each other process the events of every episode on my Face-

Lindsey Grzenczyk Mantoan What do we make of Sansa giving the order but Arya swinging the sword, as it were (and then the two of them discussing this)? Very un-Ned and un-Jon-like.

Like · Reply · 30w   🖒 2

^ Hide 11 Replies

    Noa Levanon Klein Because women don't need to do things the way that men do them. That's fine. And, in fact, both Ned and Jon were undermined by LF and by their insistence on doing things their way. New ways of doing things clearly get results.

    Like · Reply · 30w   🖒 4

    Courtney Shaw Huizar The lone wolf dies but the pack survives.

    Like · Reply · 30w   🖒 3

    Courtney Shaw Huizar And this way allowed BOTH girls to use the skills they've learned, which I loved.

    Like · Reply · 30w   🖒 4

    Katie Vroom Duke ^^ I wondered if that quote could be viewed as commentary/foreshadowing on Cersei, who is very lone wolfey right now. She's chased her family away, and her only allies are a hired mercenary army, and a large reanimated man.

    Like · Reply · 30w   🖒🖒 6

    Elie Mystal Sansa swung Arya. Arya IS the sword.

    Love · Reply · 30w   🖒🖒 6

Reflections on Littlefinger's death.

book wall, there's a shadow community, lurking, reading, processing, but never commenting. I had no idea about this shadow community until shortly before the premiere of Season Seven, when someone stopped my wife in the elevator at her office and said he was looking forward to my Facebook posts for that season. He had never participated himself, and I never knew he read them. I've heard whispers from others hinting that they enjoy their position as silent readers. I've occasionally gotten messages from people who don't want to add to that week's thread themselves, but wanted to share their thoughts privately with me. I have no idea how large this shadow community is, or why it prefers to remain anonymous.

During the long winter between seasons, this community supports each other, adding to the last thread of the previous season tidbits of news from HBO about filming, GIFs of our favorite characters, or reminders to each other to stay strong while we wait. Social media was ostensibly launched, at least in part, to foster new communities of people who didn't know each other, and might even be spread across the world, but who share common interests. It wasn't until *Game of Thrones* and this impromptu community that I experienced this use of social media myself. Adam Whitehead's epilogue in this collection talks about the power *Game of Thrones* has had in terms of creating its own watercooler culture. I'm grateful for this culture, and the emotional processing it allows me to do, and I have newfound appreciation for social media as a therapeutic and analytic tool.

Epilogue
A Storm of Shows:
How Game of Thrones
Changed Television

ADAM WHITEHEAD

The Show

In 2001, a young American writer named David Benioff hit it big with his very first novel, *The 25th Hour*. The book garnered critical acclaim and impressive sales on release. It also immediately attracted attention from Hollywood, with actor Tobey Maguire interested in making a film version. Ultimately the rights were picked up by Spike Lee, who released the movie (starring Ed Norton, as Maguire was busy with his *Spider-Man* movies) at the end of 2002. Benioff himself wrote the screenplay and rapidly found himself being offered more script work by Hollywood producers. He was paid $2.5 million to write the script for the 2004 historical epic *Troy*, starring Eric Bana and Brad Pitt (where Benioff made the acquaintance of future *Game of Thrones* actors Sean Bean, Julian Glover, and James Cosmo) and was also hired to write the script for *X-Men Origins: Wolverine* and a Kurt Cobain biopic.

Benioff's experiences with film were ultimately unsatisfying: *Troy* and *Wolverine* were both heavily rewritten before release and his Kurt Cobain script was junked altogether. Although Benioff had garnered additional success with a collection of short stories, *When the Nines Roll Over* (2004), he had not gotten a screenplay made to his full satisfaction since *The 25th Hour*. His friend and colleague Dan "D.B." Weiss was in a similar boat: after a successful novel, *Lucky Wander Boy* (2003), he'd gotten sucked into working in development hell, penning multiple scripts based on the video game *Halo* for a Neill Blomkamp–directed version that never got picked up.

Like many frustrated film screenwriters, they could only look at the freedom and creativity offered to writers in television, where the likes of Joss Whedon (*Buffy the Vampire Slayer*), Damon Lindelof (*Lost*), David Chase (*The Sopranos*) and David Milch (*Deadwood*) had tremendous success in getting their visions on screen with much less interference from studios and focus groups. The latter two also had the impressive financial resources of premium cable giant HBO at their disposal to realize their vision.

In late 2005, Benioff was sent a copy of four large fantasy novels by George R.R. Martin's Hollywood agent who thought they might be interesting to him. Benioff had been a fantasy genre fan (and occasional player of *Dungeons & Dragons*) as a teenager but had not read much fantasy recently. Despite his misgivings about reading four books, each the size of a brick, he was quickly sucked into the world created by George R.R. Martin (himself a former Hollywood scriptwriter). Benioff called in his friend Weiss and they agreed that the story needed to be seen on screen. Initial thoughts about adapting the story for the cinema foundered on the issue of time: to get a movie or even a trilogy made would mean cutting most of the story away and just focusing on a few storylines and characters. They ultimately decided that the story needed to be on the small screen and, because of its vast scope, violence, and sexual content, it needed to be done on premium cable.

HBO was impressed by Benioff and Weiss's pitch and optioned the books in 2007. After delays resulting from the 2008 Writer's Guild of America strike, they finally shot a pilot in 2009 and aired the first season in 2011. The rest, as they say, is history.

The Storm

Game of Thrones is a gamechanger of a kind rarely seen on American television. From more humble beginnings, it has become not only the most expensive ongoing television series in American history[1] but also the most popular television series in the history of the HBO network, outstripping the likes of *The Sopranos*, *The Wire*, *Sex and the City*, and *True Blood* (Beaumont-Thomas 2014).

Game of Thrones demonstrates the impressive foresight of HBO in selling the series to an international audience and insisting on near-parity in broadcast with the United States, both reducing its financial exposure (through early overseas sales)[2] and creating a global phenomenon which, thanks to the internet, everyone can participate in simultaneously. As a result *GoT* has defied the fragmented nature of modern television to become appointment viewing and a proper "watercooler show" to discuss the day after broadcast.

Game of Thrones also furthered the serialization of television, moving away from standalone episodes with discrete storylines to telling large, epic tales spanning the entire series. The show also inspired other networks to snap up genre novels to adapt into their own long-form series. *Game of Thrones* has changed the debate about television budgets, with audiences now expecting far more visual quality from their series than in the past. This has impacted many other shows, such as the new *Star Trek* series, which had a substantial budget increase from its more modestly budgeted forebears to compete.

Finally, *GoT*'s impact on the medium of television has been substantial and transformative, and likely will define the next generation of the medium on almost every level, from storytelling to budget to scope. However, these strategies may not always produce such success especially for those companies not as financially stable as HBO.

Gamechanger

The arrival of *Game of Thrones* on television in 2011 is a watershed moment in the history of television. Future historians of the medium will divide series between those that came before *Game of Thrones* and those that came after. *Thrones* changed the conversation and the perception of what television could be: cinematic, epic, heavily serialized, and made on a scale and scope to rival that of Hollywood blockbusters. It also suggested that in television, as with film, the more resources and money put into a project, the more profits to be made. This trend, however, has both positive and negative consequences for the future of the medium.

With its April 2011 premiere, *Game of Thrones* was seen as a gamble by HBO. The channel had high hopes for the series, which they described as "*The Sopranos* in Middle-earth" (Kachka 2008), an attempt to appeal to both fans of the high fantasy *Lord of the Rings* movies and HBO's own adult crime series. But fantasy had a rough prior history on television. Starz's *Camelot* had crashed and burned just a few months earlier; ABC's *Legend of the Seeker* had been cancelled the previous year after two seasons; and SyFy's adaptation of another popular novel series, *Earthsea*, had completely bombed in 2004. Arguably, fantasy had only succeeded on television when it was set in the present day (as with *Buffy the Vampire Slayer* and *Charmed*) or when it had taken a comedic or camp tone to make up for a low budget (such as *Hercules: The Legendary Journeys* and *Xena: Warrior Princess*).

Game of Thrones was different. HBO wanted to bring seriousness, grit, and high production values to the fantasy genre, just as they had done successfully for the vampire drama with *True Blood* (2008–2014). HBO also wanted a big-budget period drama, something that would appeal to the fans of their prematurely cancelled historical series *Rome* (2005–2007) and *Deadwood* (2004–2006) but wouldn't break their bank balance, as *Rome*—whose 22 episodes had cost HBO over $200 million—had threatened to (Hibberd 2014). When *Game of Thrones* went into production, it had a still-impressive budget of over $6 million per episode, enough to build elaborate sets and feature lavish location filming in locations such as Malta and Croatia, but this still wasn't enough to do everything the writers wanted. An elaborate battle sequence at the end of the first season had to be cut (1x9, "Baelor"), with Tyrion Lannister getting knocked out in the opening seconds of the battle rather than partaking fully, as he does in the novel, and even a montage sequence of hundreds of ravens being sent to rouse the lords of the North to war, written by novelist George R.R. Martin, had to be dispensed with (1x8, "The Pointy End"). From its first season *Game of Thrones* was a big-budget show by the standards of both network television and basic cable (its budget was almost twice that of its AMC rival, *The Walking Dead*), yet it fell short of bringing the full scope of epic fantasy to the screen.

HBO appears to have been as dissatisfied with this shortfall as viewers, but the viewership also responded positively to the characters, the fantasy elements (the direwolves and baby dragons), and the political drama. Season by season, HBO increased the budget of the show significantly, giving producer-showrunners David Benioff and Dan Weiss the resources needed to sell the scale of the story. The difference on screen is palpable: the first season features static background mattes, no aerial establishing shots, and very little CGI. The seventh season has thousands of CG shots, aerial establishing shots (either fully CG or created with the help of filming drones), and elaborate animated backgrounds. It also featured four massive visual effects set-pieces: a castle assault, an attack on a wagon train, a battle on an icefield, and the infamous Wall crashing down in a blaze of undead dragon fire, all of which would have been far beyond the scope of the series in its first year. The budget for Season Seven of *Game of Thrones* came in at an estimated $14.2 million per episode, more than double when the series started; Season Eight budgets are estimated to come in at $2.5 million above that. HBO has not only loosened its purse strings—they've simply cut them altogether. It's now clear that HBO has been willing to let the producers have all the resources they need to deliver their vision onto the screen and filming time has actually been a bigger problem than money.

This has all been possible due to the remarkable global success of the series. Over the course of its first three seasons, *Game of Thrones* rapidly became HBO's most-watched television series of all time, eclipsing previous records set by series such as *The Sopranos*, *Sex and the City*, and *True Blood*. This success was on a global scale, with the show's ratings around the world increasing year after year. HBO's decision in 2011 to try to get the series seen by as many people in as many countries as close in time to the initial U.S. broadcast as possible added greatly to the show's success. HBO directed its international subsidiaries, such as HBO Latin America and HBO Europe (which operates in Eastern European countries), to show each episode immediately after the U.S. release. HBO also entered into a highly lucrative partnership with Sky Television in the United Kingdom, with Sky creating an entirely new premium channel, Sky Atlantic, to show HBO's content, and entered similar deals with other companies around the world, such as Foxtel in Australia.

The Sky deal at first appeared unnecessary, since HBO's top priority is direct income from U.S. subscribers. However, HBO had realized that in the internet age, it was no longer good enough to have a long gap between U.S. and global transmission. Delaying international transmission meant that early-adopting pirates would download and watch the American broadcast, meaning lost revenue for international broadcasters and less incentive for them to license HBO's content. HBO's move to ensure that everyone could watch *Game of Thrones* as soon after the original U.S. broadcast as possible was far-reaching and effective. It also allowed the creation of a "watercooler" culture with people discussing each episode not just with their colleagues at work, but also online right across the globe.

The effects of this strategy were dramatic. *Game of Thrones* was still heavily downloaded, several times setting new records for being the most pirated television show in history (Hooten 2017), but also generated buzz and revenue like few shows before it. Sky Atlantic's deal with HBO (renewed in 2014) was for $500 million, meaning that this single relationship with one international broadcaster alone netted HBO almost five times the budget of a single *Game of Thrones* season (Robinson 2010; Sweney 2014). Combined with the many other international deals, the massive bump in American subscriptions driven by the series in the United States, legal downloads and DVD and Blu-Ray sales (*Game of Thrones* set several records for being one of the fastest-selling box set of all time in physical media Furness [2015]), it is clear that the profits HBO has made from *Game of Thrones* are remarkable.

These moves have allowed HBO to retain its position as the preeminent American cable service—despite vigorous opposition from basic cable provider AMC with *The Walking Dead*, *Mad Men*, and *Breaking Bad*—and remain relevant in the streaming era. Starting in 2013, the Netflix streaming service entered the original content market with the political drama *House of Cards*. Netflix spent huge amounts of money on its initial slate of original programming in the 2013–2015 period, airing big-budget dramas such as *Sense8* and *Marco Polo* and critically acclaimed shows such as prison drama *Orange Is the New Black*. Netflix even joined forces with Marvel to release a series of interlinked superhero dramas starting with *Daredevil*. With the exception of *Marco Polo*, all of these dramas were successful enough to last for more than two seasons (although *Sense8* will conclude after two seasons plus a TV movie) but arguably none generated the constant "watercooler" discussion that *Game of Thrones* has engendered week in, week out for its entire run. This is despite the fact that Netflix has a simultaneous, worldwide distribution platform and can be viewed on everything from a giant TV to a mobile phone, while HBO's distribution is more fragmented. Netflix would not get its own *Game of Thrones*–rivaling, buzz-generating megahit until 2016, when it launched the 1980s supernatural drama series *Stranger Things* to immense acclaim.

HBO also used *Game of Thrones* to drive its own digital platform, HBO Go. Although HBO Go had been launched in 2010, it had been relatively unsuccessful until the mobile app version was launched, timed to be released alongside *Game of Thrones*'s first season. Despite technical and financial limitations (such as being initially limited to U.S. viewers and existing television subscribers only), the appeal of *Game of Thrones* drove subscribers to the new platform and allowed HBO to remain relevant even as its premium cable business model was starting to look a little tired compared to the convenience and usability of Netflix, Amazon Prime, Apple TV, and Hulu. *Game of Thrones*, its planned spin-off series, and the newer HBO Now service will play a key role in how HBO and its parent company, Time Warner, address this challenge.

Both the streaming giants and HBO's traditional rivals—cable networks AMC, Starz, and Showtime–have responded to the success of *Game of Thrones* with their own big-budget fantasy and period projects. AMC developed *Preacher*, a supernatural drama based on a famous comic book series (and which had previously been in development at HBO), while Starz began production of *Outlander*, a lavish, big-budget costume drama with a time-travel storyline, also based on a series of best-selling novels. Showtime has picked up the rights to *The Kingkiller Chronicle*, the biggest-selling debut fantasy novel series this century, while Netflix is developing *The Witcher*, based on a series of Polish novels and highly successful videogames. The biggest move, however, has been from Amazon. Keen to get their own *Game of Thrones*, in late 2017 they entered into an unprecedented agreement with Warner Brothers to produce a *Lord of the Rings* prequel television series, spending over $200 million just to license the rights and promising a minimum budget of $100–150 million per season. This will comfortably make the series the most expensive in history, and is a sign of how keen Amazon is to leverage the current fantasy craze for their own benefit.

The real impact of *Thrones'* increasing budgets may be its rewriting of the television rulebook on what now constitutes a low-budget, medium-budget, and high-budget show. Television budgets have remained largely static for almost 20 years. In the late 1990s, American network television reached an average budget threshold of around $2 million per hour for dramas and that remained the norm. There were occasional outliers such as ABC's *Lost*, whose budget reached $5 million per episode due to the expense of constant location filming in Hawai'i, and long-running shows which eventually accumulated massive cast salaries (most famously *Friends* in its last couple of seasons) but this was the standard for many years. Premium cable meant that budgets could go higher, most notably (and as previously discussed) with HBO, but otherwise budgets remained relatively low. This was due to the amount of content demanded by the networks. Network TV shows ran for between 22 and 26 episodes per season, so a low budget of $2 million per episode still meant that a full season cost over $44 million. Cable producers such as HBO began experimenting with shorter seasons, with only 12 or 13 (or less) episodes per season for shows like *The Sopranos* and *Sex and the City*. Audiences seemed to respond to this, as this reduction in episodes not only meant more money per episode, but also more preparation and production time, more time for postproduction and effects, and overall higher production quality. Actors also seemed to respond positively to the move, as it freed them up to do other projects or films while their TV show was off the air.

The producers of ABC's *Lost* saw the benefits of this model and successfully convinced ABC to reduce the episode count of the show from 25 episodes for the first three seasons to 16 for the last two. This resulted in tighter storytelling and greater focus, as well as a less arduous production process. Network television has responded in general by being more flexible on shorter episode runs—the old model requiring 100 episodes to be made before national syndication was possible being no longer relevant—but for many of their biggest shows they remain in favor of long runs for advertising revenue, which is also irrelevant for the streaming and premium cable model focused on direct subscriptions.

For *Game of Thrones*, HBO initially considered their normal 12–13 episode season order but soon realized that the complexities involved in writing, preproduction, and shooting would make this difficult. They settled on 10 episodes per season and the producers found even this arduous, due to the decision to film in a large number of countries and the need for elaborate effects, costumes, and sets. Delivering 10 episodes per year at this level of production quality proved so daunting that for the last two seasons, the producers negotiated more time, with a 15-month wait for the seventh season and approximately 18 months for the final season (Otterson 2018).

In this area *Game of Thrones* was trailing the pack rather than leading it. Netflix had already made it the norm to give its big-budget productions

18 months between seasons, allowing the writers and producers to take more time to make the series. *Game of Thrones'* own sister show on HBO, *Westworld*, had an 18-month schedule from the start. In this sense, TV series are now following in the footsteps of films, which at one time allowed only a year for preproduction, shooting, and postproduction, but now typically (for big effects movies) allow three years.

As a result of *Thrones'* success, TV budgets are now increasing dramatically. Netflix has spent $7 million per episode on their new, big-budget cyberpunk series, *Altered Carbon* (2018). They spent a rumored $12 million per episode on their period drama, *The Crown* (2016). Netflix is prepared to even go further. David Wells, chief finance officer at Netflix, told a Goldman Sachs audience: "Is $20 million-an-hour television possible? Certainly. If you have the numbers of people watching it, we certainly can support that level of quality in terms of TV" (Spangler 2017).

However, as critic Maureen Ryan of *Variety* has pointed out (2017), these may be the wrong lessons to learn from *Game of Thrones*. Thanks to the 2008 Writer's Guild of America strike, *Game of Thrones* had an unusually long gestation period. Benioff and Weiss pitched the show to HBO in 2006, it was optioned in 2007, a pilot was shot in 2009, and full production did not start until 2010, with the first season not airing until 2011. This half-decade of development before the show hit the air was unusual and allowed Benioff and Weiss to adapt to working in television, which was a new experience for them both. It also allowed careful consideration of production requirements and a very long preproduction phase that allowed for rewrites and a lot of work to be put into the sets, costumes, music, and effects. Today networks and streaming companies are hurling monster budgets at relatively inexperienced showrunners to get projects on the air as fast as possible, often without going through the pilot process—ordering a drama "straight to series" without the pilot stage used to be highly unusual but now it's becoming the norm.

The fear is that either the TV bubble will burst, with significant losses to the industry, or TV may go in the direction of film and videogames, where there are a small number of high-budget, high-profile productions and a large number of very low-budget indie fare, and not much in between. The amount of scripted drama on American televisions has almost doubled since *Game of Thrones* debuted: 266 shows on air in 2011 to 487 in 2017 (Lynch 2018). This is set to increase in future years, but may be unsustainable in the medium term, as consumers prove less willing to pay for multiple TV and entertainment platforms at a time when income in much of the Western world is stagnant.

This situation may be analogous to the difference in approach between Marvel and DC in their superhero movies: Marvel planning a long, slow burn over many years of building up individual characters and films before bringing the pieces together in a massive climax with the two-part *Avengers: Infinity War* saga, as compared to DC trying to rush the setup to cash in on the same phenomenon (moving straight from one set-up movie, *Man of Steel*, to the *Justice League* team-up), and encountering difficulties along the way. HBO took their time with *Game of Thrones* and built up the show over many years of pre-production before shooting even started. The series and distributors they have inspired are trying to skip to the same level of success without a comparable set-up.

Another key area where *Game of Thrones* has been influential is in the development of long-form serialized storytelling in television. This shift began in earnest in the 1980s, when TV shows such as *Hill Street Blues* and *Dallas* began to challenge the idea that television series should consist of standalone episodes that could be aired in any order. With long-term character development and storylines continuing from week to week, these series became immensely successful. This format continued to become more popular in the 1990s, with *Twin Peaks* and *Babylon 5* in particular being crucial for the development of "arc television." HBO embraced the concept in full with *The Sopranos* and *Carnvàle*, the latter of which was envisaged as a single story unfolding over six seasons, divided into three two-season acts (in the event only the first act was completed, as HBO cancelled the series after its second year). This format continued to be embraced at HBO, which in 2008 adapted it with the inspiration of a long-running series of novels (providing years of ready-made storylines) to create the supernatural drama *True Blood*.

Game of Thrones' massive success as a story adapted from the page to the screen (following on from that of *The Walking Dead*, *True Blood*, *Harry Potter*, and *The Lord of the Rings* beforehand), has inspired Hollywood to look even harder to novels and comics for inspiration. Since *Thrones* hit the small screen, dozens and dozens of books and graphic novels have followed with varying degrees of success. Indeed, television is now the preferred medium for such literary adaptations. Even projects which previously failed in film—such as Philip Pullman's *His Dark Materials* trilogy—have been taken back and redeveloped as television series, and there is already talk that Stephen King's *Dark Tower* series may be reconceived for television following the failure of the 2017 movie version. *The Handmaid's Tale*, based on Margaret Atwood's novel, was only a minor success as a film, but the TV series has been a huge success for Hulu, winning multiple awards and setting up a multi-season run. As previously discussed, Amazon is also developing a five-season *Lord of the Rings* prequel television series, showing the appeal of both long-form series and using pre-existing books (or, in that case, inspiration from a book).

There are possible negative consequences to all of this, however. TV critic Alan Sepinwall has noted that the Amazon *Lord of the Rings* deal was far too expensive, repetitive, and risked backfiring creatively, since the Middle-earth well had already been thoroughly explored through six long movies (Sepinwall 2017). Producer Bryan Fuller also seems to have taken the view that post–*Game of Thrones*, strict budget limitations are optional and took the first season of his series *American Gods* more than $30 million over budget and then demanded more for the second season, to Starz's evident displeasure (as it resulted in his departure from the project; Goldberg [2018]).

After the Storm

When *Game of Thrones* leaves our television screens in 2019, it will leave the field in a very different state than when it started. The show has pushed the envelope for special effects and visual splendor in television. It tapped into the idea of television as a global, unifying medium, with people from Seattle to Sydney being able to discuss each episode of the show immediately after airing. It has championed the idea of mining the best of literature for material to sustain multiple seasons of television drama. It has renewed interest in the fantasy genre, with a whole slew of books now optioned for television. It has also rewritten the book on what is realistic or possible with regards to TV budgets, location filming, and effects requirements. Its impact on television is already visible. Some of these consequences could ultimately be negative, especially if the "Golden Age of Television" bubble bursts in the next few years, but *GoT* will always be seen as a transformative moment in the history of the medium.

NOTES

1. Season Six of *Game of Thrones* cost $10 million per episode (Cuccinello [2016]). The same budget was used for Season Seven despite three fewer episodes, meaning a much higher budget on a per-episode basis ($14.28 million) (McCreesh 2017). Season Eight promises to cost even more—to $16.6 million, although some sources say it'll be about $15 million (Ryan and Littleton 2017).

2. Pre-selling the show means making money on the series before a frame of footage is shot. Both *GoT* Season One and some other recent shows like the new *Star Trek* actually made more money in pre-sales than their first seasons cost, creating profits before they were even made.

REFERENCES

Beaumont-Thomas, Ben. 2014. "Game of Thrones Becomes the Most Popular HBO Show Ever." *The Guardian*, 6 June. Accessed 11 March 2018. https://www.theguardian.com/tv-and-radio/2014/jun/06/game-of-thrones-most-popular-hbo-show-sopranos.

Cuccinello, Hayley. 2016. "'Game of Thrones' Season 6 Costs $10 Million Per Episode, Has Biggest Battle Scene Ever." *Forbes*, 22 April. Accessed 11 March 2018. https://www.forbes.com/sites/hayleycuccinello/2016/04/22/game-of-thrones-season-6-costs-10-million-per-episode-has-biggest-battle-scene-ever/#273b2e141bb.

Furness, Hannah. 2015. "Game of Thrones Becomes Fastest-Selling Box Set in a Decade." *The Telegraph*, 22 February. Accessed 11 March 2018. http://www.telegraph.co.uk/culture/tvandradio/game-of-thrones/11428163/Game-of-Thrones-becomes-fastest-selling-box-set-in-a-decade.html.

Goldberg, Leslie. 2018. "'American Gods' Hires New Showrunner for Season 2 (Exclusive)." *Hollywood Reporter*, 2 February. Accessed 11 March. https://www.hollywoodreporter.com/live-feed/american-gods-hires-new-showrunner-season-2–1080813.

Hibberd, James. 2014. "Could HBO's 'Rome' Rise Again?" *Entertainment Weekly*, 17 February. Accessed 11 March 2018. http://ew.com/article/2014/02/17/rome-hbo/.

Hooten, Christopher. 2017. "Game of Thrones Is Most Torrented TV Show Six Years Running." *The Independent*, 29 December. Accessed 11 March 2018. http://www.independent.co.uk/arts-entertainment/tv/news/game-of-thrones-torrents-streaming-2017-watch-online-hbo-season-7-a8133036.html.

Kachka, Boris. 2008. "Dungeon Master: David Benioff." *New York: Books*, 18 May. Accessed 11 March 2018. http://nymag.com/arts/books/features/47040/.

Lynch, Jason. 2018. "There's No Stopping Peak TV, as 487 Scripted Series Aired in 2017." *Ad Week*, 5 January. Accessed 11 March 2018. http://www.adweek.com/tv-video/theres-no-stopping-peak-tv-as-487-scripted-series-aired-in-2017/.

McCreesh, Louise. 2017. "Game of Thrones Is Going "Epic" in Season 7—with a Bigger Budget per Episode Than Before." *Digital Spy*, 5 June. Accessed 11 March 2018. http://www.digitalspy.com/tv/game-of-thrones/news/a829979/game-of-thrones-season-7-cost-per-episode-bigger-budget/.

Otterson, Joe. 2018. "'Game of Thrones' Season 8 Set to Air in 2019." *Variety*, 4 January. Accessed 11 March 2018. http://variety.com/2018/tv/news/game-of-thrones-season-8-premiere-date-1202653371/.

Robinson, James. 2010. "BSkyB Buys Complete HBO TV Catalogue." *The Guardian*, 28 July. Accessed 11 March 2018. https://www.theguardian.com/media/2010/jul/29/bskyb-buys-hbo-tv-catalogue.

Ryan, Maureen, and Cynthia Littleton. 2017. "TV Series Budgets Hit the Breaking Point as Costs Skyrocket in Peak TV Era." *Variety*, 26 September. Accessed 11 March 2018. http://variety.com/2017/tv/news/tv-series-budgets-costs-rising-peak-tv-1202570158/.

Sepinwall, Alan. 2017. "Ask Alan: Can Amazon Really Make 'Lord of the Rings' the Next 'Game of Thrones'?" *Uproxx*, 1 December. Accessed 11 March 2018. http://uproxx.com/sepinwall/ask-alan-amazon-lord-of-the-rings-game-of-thrones-breaking-bad-101/.

Spangler, Todd. 2017. "Could Netflix Spend $20 Million per Hour on a Series? CFO Says It's Conceivable." *Variety*, 12 September. Accessed 11 March 2018. http://variety.com/2017/digital/news/netflix-20-million-per-hour-series-cfo-1202555399/.

Sweney, Mark. 2014. "BSkyB Signs New Five-Year Deal for Exclusive Rights to HBO TV Catalogue." *The Guardian*, 29 January. Accessed 11 March 2018. https://www.theguardian.com/media/2014/jan/30/bskyb-five-year-deal-exclusive-rights-hbo-tv-catalogue.

Episode List

	Episode Title	Director	Writer	Air Date
1x1	"Winter Is Coming	Tim Van Patten	David Benioff & D.B. Weiss	17 Apr 2011
1x2	"The Kingsroad"	Tim Van Patten	David Benioff & D.B. Weiss	24 Apr 2011
1x3	"Lord Snow"	Brian Kirk	David Benioff & D.B. Weiss	1 May 2011
1x4	"Cipples, Bastards, and Broken Things"	Brian Kirk	Bryan Cogman	8 May 2011
1x5	"The Wolf and the Lion"	Brian Kirk	David Benioff & D.B. Weiss	15 May 2011
1x6	"A Golden Crown"	Daniel Minahan	David Benioff, D.B. Weiss, and Jane Espenson	22 May 2011
1x7	"You Win or You Die"	Daniel Minahan	David Benioff & D.B. Weiss	28 May 2011
1x8	"The Pointy End"	Daniel Minahan	George R.R. Martin	5 Jun 2011
1x9	"Baelor"	Alan Taylor	David Benioff & D.B. Weiss	12 Jun 2011
1x10	"Fire and Blood"	Alan Taylor	David Benioff & D.B. Weiss	19 Jun 2011
2x1	"The North Remembers"	Alan Taylor	David Benioff & D.B. Weiss	1 Apr 2012
2x2	"The Night Lands"	Alan Taylor	David Benioff & D.B. Weiss	8 Apr 2012
2x3	"What Is Dead My Never Die"	Alik Sakharov	Byan Cogman	15 Apr 2012
2x4	"Garden of Bones"	David Petrarca	Vanessa Taylor	22 Apr 2012
2x5	"The Ghost of Harrenhal"	David Petrarca	David Benioff & D.B. Weiss	29 Apr 2012
2x6	"The Old Gods and the New"	David Nutter	Vanessa Taylor	6 May 2012
2x7	"A Man Without Honor"	David Nutter	David Benioff & D.B. Weiss	13 May 2012

	Episode Title	Director	Writer	Air Date
2x8	"The Prince of Winterfell"	Alan Taylor	David Benioff & D.B. Weiss	20 May 2012
2x9	"Blackwater"	Neil Marshall	George R.R. Martin	27 May 2012
2x10	"Valar Morghulis"	Alan Taylor	David Benioff & D.B. Weiss	3 Jun 2012
3x1	"Valar Dohaeris"	Daniel Minahan	David Benioff & D.B. Weiss	31 Mar 2013
3x2	"Dark Wings, Dark Words"	Daniel Minahan	Vanessa Taylor	7 Apr 2013
3x3	"Walk of Punishment"	David Benioff	David Benioff & D.B. Weiss	14 Apr 2013
3x4	"And Now His Watch Is Ended"	Alex Graves	David Benioff & D.B. Weiss	31 Apr 2013
3x5	"Kissed by Fire"	Alex Graves	Bryan Cogman	28 Apr 2013
3x6	"The Climb"	Alik Sakharov	David Benioff & D.B. Weiss	4 May 2013
3x7	"The Bear and the Maiden Fair"	Michelle MacLaren	George R.R. Martin	12 May 2013
3x8	"Second Sons"	Michelle MacLaren	David Benioff & D.B. Weiss	19 May 2013
3x9	"The Rains of Castamere"	David Nutter	David Benioff & D.B. Weiss	2 Jun 2013
3x10	"Mhysa"	Daniel Minahan	David Benioff & D.B. Weiss	9 Jun 2013
4x1	"Two Swords"	D.B. Weiss	David Benioff & D.B. Weiss	6 Apr 2014
4x2	"The Lion and the Rose"	Alex Graves	George R.R. Martin	13 Apr 2014
4x3	"Breaker of Chains"	Alex Graves	David Benioff & D.B. Weiss	20 Apr 2014
4x4	"Oathkeeper"	Michelle MacLaren	Bryan Cogman	27 Apr 2014
4x5	"First of His Name"	Michelle MacLaren	David Benioff & D.B. Weiss	4 May 201
4x6	"The Laws of Gods and Men"	Alik Sakharov	Bryan Cogman	11 May 2014
4x7	"Mockingbird"	Alik Sakharov	David Benioff & D.B. Weiss	18 May 2014
4x8	"The Mountain and the Viper"	Alex Graves	David Benioff & D.B. Weiss	1 Jun 2014
4x9	"The Watchers on the Wall"	Neil Marshall	David Benioff & D.B. Weiss	8 Jun 2014
4x10	"The Children"	Alex Graves	David Benioff & D.B. Weiss	15 Jun 2015
5x1	"The Wars to Come"	Michael Slovis	David Benioff & D.B. Weiss	12 Apr 2015

	Episode Title	Director	Writer	Air Date
5x2	"The House of Black and White"	Michael Slovis	David Benioff & D.B. Weiss	19 Apr 2015
5x3	"High Sparrow"	Mark Mylod	David Benioff & D.B. Weiss	26 Apr 2015
5x4	"Sons of the Harpy"	Mark Mylod	Dave Hill	3 May 2015
5x5	"Kill the Boy"	Jeremy Podeswa	Bryan Cogman	10 May 2015
5x6	"Unbowed, Unbent, Unbroken"	Jeremy Podeswa	Bryan Cogman	17 May 2015
5x7	"The Gift"	Miguel Sapochnik	David Benioff & D.B. Weiss	24 May 2015
5x8	"Hardhome"	Miguel Sapochnik	David Benioff & D.B. Weiss	31 May 2015
5x9	"The Dance of Dragons"	David Nutter	David Benioff & D.B. Weiss	7 Jun 2015
5x10	"Mother's Mercy"	David Nutter	David Benioff & D.B. Weiss	14 Jun 2015
6x1	"The Red Woman"	Jeremy Podeswa	David Benioff & D.B. Weiss	24 Apr 2016
6x2	"Home"	Jeremy Podeswa	Dave Hill	1 May 2016
6x3	"Oathbreaker"	Daniel Sackheim	David Benioff & D.B. Weiss	8 May 2016
6x4	"Book of the Stranger"	Daniel Sackheim	David Benioff & D.B. Weiss	15 May 2016
6x5	"The Door"	Jack Bender	David Benioff & D.B. Weiss	22 May 2016
6x6	"Blood of My Blood"	Jack Bender	Bryan Cogman	29 May 2016
6x7	"The Broken Man"	Mark Mylod	Bryan Cogman	5 Jun 2016
6x8	"No One"	Mark Mylod	David Benioff & D.B. Weiss	12 Jun 2016
6x9	"Battle of the Bastards"	Miguel Sapochnik	David Benioff & D.B. Weiss	19 Jun 2016
6x10	"Winds of Winter"	Miguel Sapochnik	David Benioff & D.B. Weiss	26 Jun 2016
7x1	"Dragonstone"	Jeremy Podeswa	David Benioff & D.B. Weiss	16 Jul 2017
7x2	"Stormborn"	Mark Mylod	Bryan Cogman	23 Jul 2017
7x3	"The Queen's Justice"	Mark Mylod	David Benioff & D.B. Weiss	30 Jul 2017
7x4	"The Spoils of War"	Matt Shakman	David Benioff & D.B. Weiss	6 Aug 2017
7x5	"Eastwatch"	Matt Shakman	Dave Hill	13 Aug 2017
7x6	"Beyond the Wall"	Alan Taylor	David Benioff & D.B. Weiss	20 Aug 2017
7x7	"The Dragon and the Wolf"	Jeremy Podeswa	David Benioff & D.B. Weiss	27 Aug 2017

About the Contributors

Matteo **Barbagello** is a doctoral student and president of the Martin Studies International Network, the first scholarly association dedicated to the study of the works of George R.R. Martin. His research focuses on a comparison between *A Song of Ice and Fire* and literary works of other linguistic backgrounds.

Benjamin **Bartu** is a creative writing and political science double major at Linfield College. His poetry has appeared in *The Albion Review* and *The Mekong Review*. He is at work on two theses and plans to attend graduate school.

Sarah **Beck** is a playwright and an associate lecturer at Goldsmiths, University of London. Writing credits include *This Much Is True* (Theatre 503), *The Kratos Effect* (The Bike Shed Theatre) and the short film *Spoons* (Pangaea Films). She has contributed to *Performing Ethos*, the *International Journal of Scottish Theatre and Screen*, and *Performance in a Militarized Culture*.

Sara **Brady** is an associate professor at Bronx Community College of the City University of New York. She is also managing editor for *TDR: The Drama Review*. She is the author of *Performance, Politics, and the War on Terror* and coeditor with Lindsey Mantoan of *Performance in a Militarized Culture*.

Rose **Butler** is a doctoral student and associate lecturer in film and television studies at Sheffield Hallam University, where she is researching masked murderers in genre cinema. She is co-organizer of Fear 2000, a conference series dedicated to contemporary horror media, and has published on the slasher film, *Stranger Things* and *Game of Thrones*.

Mat **Hardy** is a senior lecturer in Middle East studies at Deakin University, Australia. He spent his youth immersed in fantasy literature and gaming, and he splits his research efforts between exploring the use of roleplay in teaching political science and unpacking how fantasy authors depict Middle Eastern cultures.

Aaron K.H. **Ho** completed his doctorate in English and a doctoral certificate in film studies from the Graduate Center, City University of New York. His articles have been published in *Genders*, *Oscholars*, and *Queer Singapore*. His work focuses on queer studies and the clash between cultures.

Andrew **Howe** is a professor of history at La Sierra University, where he teaches courses in American history and film/television studies. His scholarship includes essays on fan identification and cultural artifacts associated with *Game of Thrones* and the role of cemeteries and burial rites in the western genre.

Carol Parrish **Jamison** is a professor of English at Georgia Southern University, Armstrong campus. She specializes in medieval literature, medievalism, and linguistics. She is the author of *Chivalry in Westeros*. She has published articles on medievalism in *Studies in Medievalism* and *Studies in Medieval and Renaissance Teaching*.

Lindsey **Mantoan** is an assistant professor of theatre at Linfield College. She is the author of *War as Performance: Conflicts in Iraq and Political Theatricality* and coeditor with Sara Brady of *Performance in a Militarized Culture*.

Audrey **Moyce** completed her master's degree in theatre and performance studies at Stanford University. Her performance criticism has appeared on Theatre Is Easy and Broadway World, and she is a regular contributor at Culturebot. In addition to writing on media and performance, she writes educational materials.

Catherine **Pugh** is a writer and independent scholar. She has contributed to *At Home in the Whedonverse* and *The Politics of Race, Gender, and Sexuality in The Walking Dead*. Working with horror and science fiction in all their forms, she is particularly fascinated by the transformative properties of monstrosity and madness.

Ian **Ross** is a scholar of fan studies, pop culture, and masculinity within digital spaces. His work includes early social criticism of the GamerGate movement and game design as semiotic pedagogy. His research involves fan communities and fan production.

Dan **Venning** is an assistant professor of theatre and English at Union College. He has previously taught at NYU, Wagner College, and Baruch and Hunter Colleges, CUNY.

Dan **Ward** is a lecturer in media and cultural studies at the University of Sunderland, where he leads courses on television studies and contemporary cinema. His research interests revolve around masculinity, contemporary stardom and combat sports.

Adam **Whitehead** is a science fiction and fantasy critic and blogger. He has covered the SF&F genre via his genre blog, The Wertzone, since 2006 and has been a moderator on the Westeros.org forum since 2005. In 2010 he founded the Game of Thrones Wiki and the Atlas of Ice and Fire in 2016.

Rachel M.E. **Wolfe** is a scholar of adaptation, theatre history, and gender in the classical tradition. Her previous work has appeared in *Women's Studies* and the *Journal of Adaptation in Film and Performance*.

Michail **Zontos** is a Ph.D. candidate at Utrecht University. His research examines perceptions of Europe in the work of American historians Frederick Jackson Turner and Charles A. Beard. He has contributed essays to *Mastering the Game of Thrones* (McFarland, 2015) and *Approaching Twin Peaks* (McFarland, 2017).

Index